THE MUSIC

AND

MUSICAL INSTRUMENTS

OF

Southern India and the Deccan

THE MUSIC

AND

MUSICAL INSTRUMENTS

OF

Southern India and the Deccan

BY

C. R. DAY

A. J. HIPKINS (INTRODUCTION)

GYAN

Published by

Gyan Publishing House
5, Ansari Road
Daryaganj, New Delhi-110002
Phone: 011-47034999, 9811692060
E-mail: books@gyanbooks.com

Distribution Network
gyanbooks.com
India, USA, Canada, UK, Australia, France

ISBN: 978-93-6280-089-3 (PB)

First Published, 1891

2nd Impression 2023

Printed at: Gyan Press, Delhi.

THE MUSIC AND MUSICAL INSTRUMENTS OF SOUTHERN INDIA AND THE DECCAN

Author: C. R. DAY, A. J. HIPKINS (INTRODUCTION)

The Music

and

Musical Instruments

of

Southern India and The Deccan.

THE MUSIC

AND

MUSICAL INSTRUMENTS

OF

Southern India and The Deccan

BY

C. R. DAY

CAPTAIN, OXFORDSHIRE LIGHT INFANTRY

WITH AN INTRODUCTION BY

A. J. HIPKINS, F.S.A.

THE PLATES DRAWN BY WILLIAM GIBB.

LONDON & NEW YORK: NOVELLO, EWER & CO.

and

ADAM & CHARLES BLACK, LONDON.

MDCCCXCI.

DEDICATED BY PERMISSION

TO

LIEUTENANT-GENERAL HIS ROYAL HIGHNESS

The Duke of Connaught and Strathearn

K.G., K.T., K.P.

CONTENTS.

CONTENTS

LIST OF ILLUSTRATIONS.

INTRODUCTION.

WHETHER music as an attribute of man is as old as speech or not, we cannot say; for present consideration it is sufficient that both can be intensified into poetic expression with a common power in affecting the emotions, notwithstanding that there is a vast and unbridgable distance between the precision of articulate language and the vague suggestion and glamour of musical sound. There is a quality in recited poetry not inaptly described as musical, since it has a special charm due to the choice and rhythm of words, assisted by the personal note of the reciter. But this rhythmic euphony is only allied to the musician's art, it cannot correctly be said to be comprehended in it, owing to the absence of defined musical intervals. From whatever point of view we overlook the human race, its history and development, we can nearly always trace music as having some connection, however slender, with the particular form of culture, or it may even be the absence of culture, under notice. Let us for the moment turn aside from the modern European musician's standpoint, as for him Harmony, although of comparatively recent origin, is indispensable, and we shall find melody in the succession of notes and their rhythmic movement possessing a beauty and exerting a charm which have endured for ages and comprehend the whole art of Music in the older civilisations. In Egypt; in Babylonia, Persia, and Arabia; in Asia Minor, Greece, and Rome—and in India, modern as well as ancient, for here simple melody still reigns supreme. With the exception of the Drone, apparently of Indian origin, which is literally preserved in the Bagpipe and Hurdy Gurdy, and is a characteristic feature in our modern harmonic music—conspicuous as the Pedal point—the traces of any combination of musical intervals, out of Europe, are unimportant and need not be considered in a comparison of our Western music, with its elaborate system of harmony, and that of the rest of the world, whether ancient or modern, where harmony has no place.

Among the heterogeneous populations of India much material may be found that bears upon the history of melody. There is an Aryan strain probably as old as the Vedic Sanskrit, and a Persian which has in these latter days, and especially in Northern India, considerably modified the true Hindu. There are also echoes of an indigenous music which prevails among the hill tribes, remaining in the Indian music of to-day; but yet not so clearly heard that we can say we identify here or there a refrain of an original or pre-historic music, although we may unconsciously be very near it. In the present state of our knowledge it is impossible to affirm that a pentatonic, or system of five notes in the octave, is of greater antiquity than a heptatonic or seven-note system; or that a chromatic or half-tone scale preceded an enharmonic composed of quarter-tones. All these varieties occur in our historic records, and if we argue from the analogies of speech, or consider the measurement of vibrating strings, it is no less plausible to decide for primitive narrow intervals than for primitive wide ones. In every province, go where we will, may be found some melodic or rhythmic habit or turn which it is possible to reckon as proper to it, having its peculiar scales or modes, its figures, rhythms, graces to mark its authenticity, but we may yet be far away from its origin, even as to locality. In the native music of Africa, so far as is known, there is much that may be traced to Asiatic sources.

The oldest civilisation that offers us any substantial information is Egypt. It begins in the earliest historic monuments with a graphic sign representing a fingerboard instrument of the tamboura or guitar kind, which already marks a summit level in instrumental construction and musical conception. We are not likely to learn from civilisations which may have preceded Egypt, as from the non-existence of any form of graphic art they cannot now divulge their secrets.

Another question that has arisen is that of the priority of instrumental or vocal music. There are many difficulties attending a vocal origin of what we understand in varied pitch and recurring rhythm by melody. The poets' music already touched upon, depending upon very small vocal inflections, can no more be measured and retained than the notes of many song birds which yet give us infinite pleasure. Very small musical intervals in traditional use which delight Indian and other Eastern people are clearly of instrumental origin, and to be attributed generally to facilities afforded by strings. This tradition may be of very great antiquity, and such old forms of music that occur to us, it may be Vedic chants or Hebrew psalms, are, in comparison, conceivably modern. A striking instance of a purely instrumental small interval is that of the Hindu musical unit, the s'ruti. The consideration of the value of this interval and of a combination of s'rutis to form an octave scale will be found in Captain Day's lucid exposition, and is as interesting as it is important. There can be no doubt about the origin of the s'ruti in the measurement of a stretched string.

The object of this introduction will be gained if we, for a little while, allow ourselves to forget the glory and splendour of our modern harmony, in favour of those melodic systems which once satisfied the great nations of classical antiquity, and still content those hoary civilisations of the East which preserve so much that is really ancient in their present daily life. Captain Day shows us interesting resemblances between the leading modes of old Greece and Asia Minor and certain favourite modes of the Hindus. There is no sure evidence of an intimate musical connection between those countries and India, a few scattered references in classical writers excepted; but the relationship of sister Aryan languages may have been paralleled by a relationship of musical types sufficient to justify a theory of descent instead of one of imitation.

The greater freedom in musical intervals melodic systems allow must be reckoned as compensating in some measure for the want of those harmonic combinations of which our European music has such inexhaustible wealth. What we lose in the possession of this rich estate is that we are effectually barred from the use and enjoyment of a more pliant melody, free from the fetters imposed by consonant chords, a melody which has a great privilege in easily touching the emotions. Recent scale theories, claiming to have their foundation in natural laws, are insufficient to account for the material which allows the pliability of Eastern melody. But they are insufficient even to account for our common diatonic scale, the structure of which rests upon three harmonic triads, and with chromatic and enharmonic systems are utterly irreconcilable. Under Captain Day's guidance we find that in India an ancient quarter-tone system has become in modern times a half-tone one—substantially our equal temperament, but permitting an expressive or ornamental use of smaller intervals than the half-tone, according to the player's feeling or fancy. Whether this ideally half-tone system is due to a natural transformation tending to simplicity—as we find the rich Sanskrit reduced in modern vernacular dialects—or to an adaptation more suitable for practical use than a fine-spun theory of ancient music teachers, must, like nearly all the questions that have here been propounded, remain open or be regarded as beyond the possibility of answer.

It must not be overlooked that the Persian and Arab musicians have also their enharmonic systems, and if these may be referred back to an older Babylonian, the delight felt in such melodic freedom may have been widespread in a remote antiquity. We would not, however, resign our harmony for this freedom, although we admit its great power to incite a poetic impression when we are in certain moods. What Indian music offers to mood will be found in Captain Day's pages, and, studied from this point of view, the information he offers cannot but be of the highest value. He shows us the existence of a really intimate expressive melodic music, capable of the greatest refinement of treatment, and altogether outside the experience of the Western musician. What we learn from such inquiries is that the debated opinions of musical theorists, the cherished beliefs of those who devote themselves to the practice of the art, the deductions we evolve from historic studies—all have to be submitted to larger conceptions, based upon a recognition of humanity as evolved from the teachings of ethnology. We must forget what is merely European, national, or conventional, and submit the whole of the phenomena to a philosophical as well as a sympathetic consideration, such as, in this century, is conceded to language, but has not yet found its way to music.

A. J. HIPKINS.

PREFACE.

OF late years so many works of importance, dealing with the subject of National music, have appeared that for the publication of this book the author feels that some apology is necessary.

The subject of Indian music, presenting, as it does, ideas so fresh and a musical system so distinct from what we in Europe are accustomed to, necessarily offers an ever-widening field for research and study. It is curious to note that while so many works upon the arts or industries of India have, in recent times, appeared, the subject of Indian music has been generally thought devoid of all science and unworthy, therefore, of any serious consideration.

Sir William Jones, at the end of the last century, endeavoured to dispel ideas of this nature, and his learned essay upon *The Musical Modes of the Hindus* has formed the basis of almost all Indian musical research. Some forty years later Captain Augustus Willard, who at that time commanded the troops in the service of H.H. the Nawab of Banda, published an interesting little *Treatise upon the Music of Hindustan*, a book which is now so scarce as to be almost unobtainable. Notwithstanding the real interest of both these works they are, unfortunately, of comparatively small practical use to the ordinary musical enquirer, unless, indeed, he is fortunate enough to possess a considerable previous knowledge of the subject.

The work which is now published has been the result of much study and research during a term of foreign service while the author's regiment was in India. And it is hoped that the information here offered for the first time may prove of interest, and may assist in some small degree in supplying a want hitherto felt among musicians and students of National musical literature. To render the book of greater value, and to assist those who may make further research, a catalogue of various works dealing with the subject has been added, together with a carefully prepared list of various Sanskrit authorities. Notice has been taken of the legendary origin of music among the Aryans, and of its principles as understood in Modern India; the peculiar scales and rhythms employed have been described in detail; and examples of various airs are given in notation. In order to show the principles of form upon which the Indian musicians construct their melodies an analysis of some of the examples has been attempted.

The subject of Temperament, concerning which so many theories have been propounded, has been treated of. The thanks of the author are due to the late Dr. A. J. Ellis, F.R.S., for his great kindness in working out many special experiments concerning the temperament of the Indian scale, and for his permission to publish them here; also for his exhaustive account of the S'ruti vina, given in the Appendix.

The author takes this opportunity of acknowledging his thanks to his friend, Mr. A. J. Hipkins, F.S.A., both for his great help and sympathy, without which this work would never have been published; also for his learned Introduction. The author begs also to thank Mr. Cecil Bendall, of the British Museum, and Professor T. W. Rhys Davids, for much valuable help and information.

The Illustrations have been confided to the hands of Mr. William Gibb, and form seventeen plates, all of them admirable representations of Indian musical instruments. The author is indebted to the kindness of Miss Edith Hipkins for her very beautiful drawings, which are reproduced in Plates II., III., and IV.

Many thanks are due to H.H. the late Maharajah of Travancore and to H.H. the Maharajah of Mysore for their kindness in affording facilities for enquiry, and for allowing access to valuable manuscripts; and to the Râjah Sir Sourendro Mohun Tagore for permission to quote from his various works. Acknowledgment is also due to Messrs. Balwant Trimback Sahasrabadhe, and T. M. Venkatasesha S'astri, of the Poona Gayana Samaj; M. Narasimhayya, of the London Mission High School, Bangalore; Maula Bux of Baroda; and to many other native gentlemen too numerous, unfortunately, to mention by name.

ARMY AND NAVY CLUB,
April, 1891.

A Sitar Player.

(From a Marathi Instruction Book.)

CHAPTER I.

Indian music—How changed in the course of years—Its decline under Mahomedan rule—Hindu ideas of music—How encouraged in the South of India—Connection with religion—Influence of religion upon music—Legends—Difficulty of deciphering the ancient treatises—How differing from European music—Most noticeable peculiarities.

AMONG the many arts and industries of India gradually decaying from want of patronage, but which, since the accession of the British Government, have again been fostered and encouraged, that of music has hitherto found no place. To Europeans it is certainly the least known of all Indian arts. Almost every traveller in India comes away with the idea that the music of the country consists of mere noise and nasal drawling of the most repulsive kind, often accompanied by contortions and gestures of the most ludicrous description. Perhaps the traveller may have fancied that he has seen a nautch—he has possibly been asked to some such entertainment at the house of a wealthy native; or, more likely, he has possessed a treasure of a "boy," who has been able to make the necessary arrangements with the "nautchnees" for a performance of the kind. But in certainly two-thirds of such cases the singing and dancing witnessed has been of the commonest, and the performers of the most abandoned and depraved of the city—and the traveller has therefore received a false impression, which may abide through life, or impede the progress of a more correct appreciation of the real value of Indian music. But it is hardly fair that an art so little really understood, even among the natives of India themselves, should be judged by such a criterion and then put aside as worthless because solitary individuals have been deceived by parties of outcast charlatans whose object is mere gain. For that Indian music is an art, and a very intricate and difficult one too, can hardly be denied. But to appreciate it one must first put away all thought of European music, and then judge of it by an Indian standard, and impartially upon its own merits—of the ingenuity of the performer—the peculiar rhythm of the music—the extraordinary scales used—the recitatives—the amount of imitation—the wonderful execution and memory of the performer—and his skill in employing small intervals as grace. Then when we hear old "Slokes" and "Ghuzals," songs written hundreds of years ago, sung with the same sweet dreamy cadences, the same wild melody, to the same soft beats of little hands, and the same soft tinkle of the silver cymbals, we shall perhaps begin to feel that music of this kind can be as welcome and tasteful to ears accustomed to it as the music of the West, with its exaggerated sonorousness, is to us; and so our contempt will gradually give way to wonder, and, upon acquaintance, possibly to love. For this music, let us remember, daily gives pleasure to as many thousands as its more cultivated European sister gives to hundreds. There is hardly any festivity in India in which some part is not assigned to music—and for religious ceremonies its use is universal. Since the Vedic times it has been cultivated as an art. The hymns of the Rig and Yagur Vedas were set and sung to music ages ago. The Vedic chant, composed in the simple Sanskrit spoken three thousand years ago, and handed down from generation to generation for more than thirty centuries, has a thrilling effect upon a cultivated Hindu mind. The Vedic chant is to Hindus what plain song is to us. For this ancient chant—like plain song—is bound up with the sacred ceremonials, and is wedded to language alike sonorous and dignified. And the place where it is heard, for it is only heard in the temple, is considered so holy, and the strain itself is so simple and devotional, that all who hear it cannot fail to be impressed.[1]

Indian music, like its sister art in Europe, seems to have undergone many changes before reaching its present stage. In remote ages the art seems to have been highly cultivated, and musicians were held in great esteem; but under the Mussalman dynasty, and owing to the almost perpetual strife between petty princes, music, like other arts, through want of encouragement, fell almost into abeyance. There is, therefore, little information to be had concerning the music of those times.

From early periods, however, many learned and elaborate treatises (mostly in MSS.) upon the art yet remain. The later of these show that even then music had passed through several stages of transition. Since the Sangíta Pârijâta, which is believed to be one of the latest of these Sanskrit

[1] An interesting explanation of these chants is given by Mr. A. C. Burnell, Ph.D., in his "Arsheyabrahmana" [Mangalore, 1876], and reprinted in Tagore's "Hindu Music from Various Sources." This explanation will enable anyone to note the Sâma Vedic chant, as printed in the Bibliotheca Indica edition, in ordinary notation.

works, had been written by Ahobala, two separate schools or systems of music have arisen and are now known by the names of Hindustani and Karnâtik. The Karnâtik appears to have been elaborated as a distinct system subsequent to the advent of the Aryans to the South of India. The two systems, although sprung from the same origin, have since undergone independently considerable changes, and are now totally distinct from each other.

Of Hindu music in Southern India, since the fall of the Hindu Empire of Vijayanagur, Tanjore has been the only school, and from it those of Travancore and other places have doubtless been founded. Unfortunately, there is no record remaining of what had been done in former times in Tanjore; but within the last few centuries the people there, as in Europe, have been aroused to a great state of musical activity, and there had sprung up a school of musicians, ending with Tiâgyarâj, destined to effect great changes and improvements in the art. There are still papers in the library of the Tanjore Palace which show that various attempts have been made to improve the existing notation, such as it is, of Indian music. With the cession of the Tanjore territory to the British, at the close of the last century, there came a time when arts and sciences were cultivated in peace; under encouragement of the noble and wealthy, music, so long neglected, once more sprang up with vigour to strike out for itself a new path and to enjoy a fresh existence. History in parallel instances shows that such has always been the case when arts long neglected are revived and become rapidly popular. The earlier music of the Sanskrit period bears a close resemblance, as far as we can judge, to that of the ancient Greeks, going far to prove that music has been derived from the same Aryan source, which seems probable, and has been discussed freely by different writers.

The most flourishing age of Indian music was during the period of native princes, a little before the Mahomedan conquest; and with the advent of the Mahomedans its decline commenced; indeed, it is wonderful that it survived at all.

The Emperor Aurangzib abolished the court musicians. Mr. Blochmann, in his translation of the "Ain-i-akbari,"[2] quotes a curious story from the historian Khan Khan as to what occurred when this order was given. The court musicians brought a bier in front of the window where the Emperor used to show himself daily to the people, and wailed so loud as to attract

---

[2] "Ain-i-akbari, or Institutes of the Emperor Akbar." Translated from the original Persian by H. Blochmann. Vol. V.

Aurangzib's attention. He came to the window and asked what it meant. They replied that melody was dead, and that they were taking him to the graveyard. The Emperor replied, "Very well, make the grave deep, so that neither voice nor echo may issue from it."

"The more severe of the Mussalman doctors," writes Captain Willard, one of the few Englishmen who have studied the subject, "like the Puritans, even now prohibit the use of music as irreligious and profane, while others are somewhat indulgent and permit it with certain restrictions. A few, convinced of its excellence, but dreading the censure of casuists, have prudently preferred silence. Some have considered it as exhilarating the spirits, and others, perhaps with more reason, declare it to be an incentive to the bent of the inclination, and, consequently, possessing the property of producing both good and evil."[3]

Opinions of the kind just quoted, held by the educated and influential, naturally enough have tended to lower the standing of a musician, and the art itself has suffered in consequence. Hence, though there are many Mahomedan professors who are skilled executants, they are rarely men of any social position or educational attainments, and their knowledge of the theory of their art is but slight. Of course to this there are exceptions—men such as Maula Bux of Baroda, or Bhande Ali of Indore, might be mentioned who have studied much and who love their art for its own sake. But such are few and far between. Still, Mahomedan music, taken as a whole, has little to recommend itself even at the present day. The ideas professed by Hindus offer a curious contrast. For music, from a Hindu standpoint, is associated with all that is bright and sweet in life; its origin, ascribed directly to Divine providence, causes it to be regarded as surrounded by a halo of sanctity. Almost all the religious literature of the Hindus breathes music. The ancient writings on Hindu music are known as the Gandhârva Veda. The Gíta Govinda, the Indian Song of Songs,[4] is music itself from beginning to end. It is difficult to imagine imagery more vivid, or to picture scenes more charming than those in which Krishna, with his fair Gopi companions, on the banks of the Yamna, played and sang those witching strains that, like those of Orpheus, held all creation spellbound. And so music with Hindus is a resource to which they always fly in joy or grief, for prayer or praise.

But still the old idea that music as a profession is a degraded employment, fit only for the stroller or the dancing girl, to some extent lingers on, so strong is

---

[3] "A Treatise on the Music of Hindustan." Capt. N. Willard. Calcutta, 1834.

[4] Sir Edwin Arnold's charming paraphrase of this beautiful poem should be read by all earnest students of Oriental Music.

the influence caused by the long ordeal of Mahomedan conquest. And Mahomedans even now, though liking and enjoying music, often prefer to engage singers and instrumentalists rather than learn the art themselves; indeed, it is not difficult to find Hindus who do the same, and hold very similar prejudices.

Happily, in Southern India, ideas of this kind cannot be said to prevail generally; proofs to the contrary may be found in the many living musicians who are men of education and poets in their way. Music has almost without interruption flourished there from very remote ages.[5] This can be accounted for by the country having been more under Hindu rule than other parts of India, and having suffered perhaps less from internal commotions. From the study of Sanskrit, which has been maintained amongst the musicians of the courts of Mysore, Tanjore, and Travancore, music has not been left, as in other parts, almost entirely in the hands of ignorant dancing girls and their attendants.

It is a common idea among the Hindus that the greatest musicians should live like hermits, far removed from all people. This seems to have been the practice of some of the ancients, and as similar legends are found in the mythologies of other nations, there is reason to believe they are based upon facts.

The higher branches of the musical profession were formerly confined to either Brahmins (Bhagavatas) or to men of very high caste. Music being of Divine origin was regarded as sacred, and it was considered impious for any but men of the sacred caste to wish to acquire any knowledge of its principles. It was and still is called the fifth Veda. Hence the ancient Brahmins of the country would have excommunicated any of their number who would have so far presumed as to betray the sacred writings to any but the elect, whose mouths only were esteemed sufficiently holy to utter words so sacred. Indeed, it was the knowledge of which they were possessed that was the chief cause of the reverence and adoration paid to the Brahmins of old, and which gave them the power and influence they prized so much. It was thus that the ancient musicians sang their own compositions. In later years music became a distinct trade, especially under Mussalman rulers, and passed into the hands of the lower orders and the unlearned, and to this cause operating through a long succession of years the differences between the Hindustani and Karnâtik systems must be in a great measure attributed.

---

[5] Colonel Meadows Taylor, remarking upon this, says: "Mahomedan historians of the period relate that when the Deccan was invaded by Allah-ood-deen Togluk in A.D. 1294, and the conquest of Southern India completed by the Mogul General Mullikkafoor several years afterwards, the profession of music was found to be in a condition so far in advance of the North that singers, male and female, and their Brahmin instructors, were taken with the royal armies and settled in the North."—"Proceedings, Royal Irish Academy." Vol. IX., Part i.

Religion, bound up as it is with almost everything in India, naturally exercises a most powerful influence upon all the arts, and upon music especially. The earliest use of music was doubtless for religious purposes. Hindu music can hardly be said to have ever shaken itself free from being in some way or other connected with the religion of the country, traces of which are everywhere apparent. Almost all the books, especially the most ancient, relating to the art contain constant references to mythological traditions. The language used is at times so figurative that in many cases no one but a finished scholar can decipher its real purport. More importance is paid to such trifling details as the proper attributes—colour, caste, or wives—of each deified melody type (râga) or mode (thât) than to the arrangements of notes which compose it and to the practical directions for its performance. Each note, scale, râga, and measure is canonized, and long chapters are devoted to the description of the habitations, wives, raiment, &c., of these demigods and nymphs. Much valuable information can of course be gleaned from these books, but many of them contain a good deal of what is quite useless to the musician, though most interesting from an antiquarian point of view. Besides these Sanskrit works, there are few books upon the art existing.

Most of the vernacular works upon music have been written by Pandits, who have endeavoured to adapt the principles contained in the ancient works to their own ideas. Many of these books consist but of a string of quotations—often contradictory—taken at random from Sanskrit works of all dates, and interlarded with comments rather worse than useless, unless it be to mystify the reader. The writers of such books rarely know anything of the modern practice of music. They still try to fetter it by hard and fast rules learnt from books. Rules of the sort, of course, were made at a time when music as an art was comparatively in its infancy, but were never intended to apply to modern Indian music. It would be just as absurd to suppose that treatises on the music of the eighth and ninth centuries, where progressions by chords of $\begin{Bmatrix}8\\5\\1\end{Bmatrix}$ were not only allowed but admired,[6] would apply to the elaborate harmony of to-day.

Other works in the vernaculars have been written by practical musicians who really do possess the knowledge they try to impart, but will not do so without mixing it with the absurdities of these so-called Pandits. The fear of criticism

---

[6] Organum was the name given to this rude harmony. An instrument called Organistrum, in use in the ninth century, enabled these chords to be played in succession. And the organ itself appears to have been so constructed, the origin in fact of the modern mixture stops.—See Gerbert, "De cantu et musicâ sacra," St. Blaise, 1774.

or ridicule is one cause of this; but it is also due to the great dislike all native musicians have to imparting instruction to any but a favoured few; indeed, they rather prefer that the general public should continue in ignorance. This has, naturally enough, tended to hinder the growth of a popular taste for music until quite within the past few years. Societies, such as the Gayan Samaj of Poona and Madras, have recently sprung up and are doing much to encourage popular music; with the advance of general education there has been a growing feeling in favour of teaching singing in the schools, and in future years it is to be hoped that all such idle prejudices will have been rooted out completely, and that the study of the national music of the country will occupy, as it should, a foremost place in all Indian schools.

At the present day, however, it is absolutely impossible for anyone to gather an accurate knowledge of the principles of Hindu music without the aid of learned natives, a *practical acquaintance* with the capabilities of their instruments, and without consulting the best living performers—things that few persons have opportunity or leisure to attempt.

Of the astonishing power which music is believed by the ancients to have had, not only over men and passions, but also over animals and inanimate things, Hindu legends, like those of most ancient nations, are redolent.

"I have been assured by a credible eye-witness," says Sir William Jones, "that two wild antelopes used often to come to the woods to the place where a mere savage beast, Siraj ud Doulah, entertained himself with concerts, and that they listened to the strain with an appearance of pleasure till the monster, in whose soul there was no music, shot one of them to display his archery; secondly, a learned native of this country told me that he had frequently seen the most venomous and indignant snakes leave their holes upon hearing tunes on a flute, which he supposed gave them peculiar delight; and thirdly, an intelligent Persian, who repeated his story again and again and permitted me to write it down from his lips, told me that he had more than once been present when a celebrated lutenist, Mirza Mahomed, surnamed Bulbul, was playing to a large company in a grove near Shiraz, that he distinctly saw the nightingales trying to vie with the musician—sometimes warbling on the trees, sometimes fluttering from branch to branch, as if they wished to approach the instrument whence the melody proceeded, and at length dropping on the ground in a kind of timid ecstasy, from which they were soon raised, he assured me, by a change of the mode."[7]

---

[7] "On the Musical Modes of the Hindus."—See "Asiatic Researches." Vol. III. Calcutta, 1792.

Musicians in the South of India believe that powers such as these are associated with the performance of the melody types or râgas called Sâranga and Kaliâni. Some legends of the influence of certain râgas over nature, that are handed down and still believed by many, are very curious, and remind us of the legends of Orpheus and Apollo.

Sir William Ouseley relates how Mir Tansên, a wonderful musician in the time of the Emperor Akbar, sang one of the night râgas at mid-day. The powers of his music were such that it instantly became night, and the darkness extended in a circle round the palace as far as the sound of his voice could be heard.

The râgas Nâgavarâli and Punâgatódi are believed to have the power to attract serpents and to make them leave their hiding places and come where they hear the music. There is a story of a certain Mysore prince who wished to test the truth of this, so, in company with one of the Court musicians, he ascended a neighbouring hill known as the abode of numerous poisonous snakes. The musicians then began to play their strains. From all sides the serpents came and formed a ring around the two, erecting their heads and swaying to and fro, fascinated by the music. As soon as the strains ceased they glided rapidly away without attempting to injure the players.

Colonel Meadows Taylor relates a somewhat similar circumstance: "One very large cobra which frequented my garden at Ellichpur, and of which everyone was in dread, was caught by some professional snake charmers in my own presence by means of the 'pungi.'[8] It was played at first very softly before the aloe bush underneath which the snake lived in a hole, and gradually the performer increased the tone and time of his playing, and, as the snake showed his head, he retreated gently till it was fairly outside and erected itself in a defiant manner. At that moment another man stepped dexterously behind and, while the snake's attention was absorbed by the player before, threw a heavy blanket upon it, seizing it by the head under the jaws. The head was then pinned down by a forked stick, and the fangs and teeth extracted by strong pincers; the snake was then turned loose, completely cowed and exhausted. There was no doubt about the identity of the reptile, for a portion of its tail had been shot off in an attempt to destroy it."[9]

It is considered extremely unlucky for anyone to impart or receive instruction in the Varâli râga. When an unwelcome pupil presents himself, a master will

---

[8] The native name for the snake-charmer's pipe.

[9] "Proceedings, Royal Irish Academy." Vol. IX., Part i.

therefore decline to teach him anything else but this râga, knowing that to be a sure way of ridding himself of the intruder.

The Megharángini (or Megh-mallâr, as it is elsewhere called), when played incessantly, was said to be productive of immediate rain. Stories of how skilful musicians have averted famine by drawing down rain with the strains of this râga are common all through the country.

Of the fiery power attributed to the râga Dîpaka there are many legends. One states that long ago the sacred lamps in the shrine of some temple in Mysore, said to have been lighted ages ago by some Divine agency, had been extinguished through the carelessness of the ministering priest, who neglected to supply them with fresh oil. The soothsayers foretold some great disaster to the surrounding country should they be rekindled by mortal hands. A famous musician, hearing of this, offered his services to the authorities, and, at the request of the Râjah, hastened to the temple. Sitting down in the "S'ri-Kovil" —the most holy place of all—before the shrine, he played this râga, while the priest made solemn supplication that success might attend his efforts. Presently the darkness of the shrine was broken—for a moment a faint glimmering was apparent, and the lamps became mysteriously lighted. Thus confidence was restored to the country round and dire calamities averted.

Another favourite story is that the Emperor Akbar ordered Nayuk Gopâl, a celebrated musician, to sing this râga. "He endeavoured to excuse himself, but in vain—the Emperor insisted on obedience. He therefore requested permission to go home and bid farewell to his family and friends. It was winter when he returned, after an absence of six months. Before he began to sing he placed himself in the waters of the Jumna till they reached his neck. As soon as he had performed a strain or two the river gradually became hot—at length began to boil—and the agonies of the unhappy musician were nearly insupportable. Suspending for a moment the melody thus cruelly extorted, he sued for mercy from the monarch, but sued in vain—Akbar wished to prove more strongly the power of the râga. Nayuk Gopâl renewed the fatal song. Flames burst with violence from his body, and though immersed in the waters of the Jumna he was consumed to ashes."[10]

The râga Gúndakrýa is so called from its having been first performed by the god Hanumân, who was called upon to decide a dispute between the celestial musicians Nârada and Tumburu. Each was jealous of the other's

---

[10] "An Essay on the Music of Hindustan," by Sir W. Ouseley.—See "Oriental Collections, illustrating the History, Antiquities, and Literature, &c., of Asia." London, 1797-1800. Vol. I.

powers, and claimed to be most skilled. They appealed to Hanumân to settle their differences and award the palm to the best performer. He heard them both and was unable to decide, so taking the vina himself, he sat down, and resting the instrument against the rock, began to play. So ravishing was the strain that the very rock melted into tears, and the vina, dropping from the hands of the god, sank into the lake thus formed. The music ceasing, the rock once more assumed its natural form. Then the god, turning to the two who stood by amazed, said : "The palm is his who plays this strain." Each essayed the feat, but failed. Hanumân then decided that the skill of both was equal, and thus settled their differences amicably. This râga, then played for the first time, was called "Gúndakrýa," or "that which melts rocks."

Hanumân after this became exceedingly proud of his musical abilities, and used to boast of his skill continually. The demigod Râma, hearing of this, devised a plan to humble the god, and accomplished it in the following manner :—There lived in a forest near Ayódhya (Râma's capital) a certain Ríshi or bard, who had devoted himself to music all his life with such success that he had caused the Septasvâras, or seven notes, to become embodied in the form of seven daughters. To this forest Râma took Hanumân as if upon a hunting excursion, and halting within hearing of the Ríshi's dwelling, whose existence was unknown to the other, asked for some music. Hanumân accordingly took up his vina and began to accompany himself. Constant practice and self-confidence had made him careless, and it chanced that as the seven nymphs passed on their way to draw water for their father's house he sang a note falsely. No sooner had the nymph to whom this note belonged heard it than she swooned and died. Her sisters made piteous lamentations, and ran to tell their father. The Ríshi came, and seeing Hanumân engrossed in his art and still singing, at once guessed the cause of his daughter's death. After listening for a while he heard the same note sung constantly out of tune. Then going up to the god he upbraided his want of care, and taking the vina from him played the râga truly, when the dead nymph revived and merrily joined her sisters.

The râga Kadâra is seldom heard, there being a superstition that trouble of various kinds always follows in the footsteps of those who sing this strain.

It is said that those who play the râga Ahiri shall go without food for the rest of the day. Many have essayed to do so, but have for some unaccountable reason always failed. Years ago—such is the story—there was a musician who was determined to discover whether or not there was any truth in the power attributed to this râga. After packing some food in a basket, he took his instrument and set out upon his travels. Very soon he came to a large tank, with a cool and shady grove of bamboos by its side; there he thought he would rest during the heat of the day. Accordingly he hung up his basket on one of the overhanging bamboos and began to sing. When he had sung for some hours he began to feel hungry, and so looked about for a place to cook his mid-day meal; but to his great chagrin he found that as the sun rose higher the bamboo upon which his basket was hung had bent upwards out of his reach. This solution of his difficulty did not however satisfy him, as he thought it due to his own neglect rather than to Divine interference. Continuing his journey, in the evening he arrived at a large town, the Râjah of which had built a "Chattram," or rest house, for the free accommodation of all poor travellers. The musician was hospitably received there, and food was laid before him. The Râni herself used to serve the guests with ghi, or clarified butter, before they commenced to eat. As she served the musician he was unable to restrain his glee, and exclaimed, "At last have I overcome thee, Ahiri!" Unfortunately for him, the name of the Râni happened to be Ahiri, and she naturally fancied that he intended some impertinence. He was promptly arrested and condemned to be impaled. As he was led to execution he implored the Râjah to grant him a hearing; his request was complied with, and he told the whole story. The Râjah then commanded that he should be set at liberty, and dismissed him with a present, bidding him at the same time refrain from tempting the gods farther, as it had already so nearly cost him his life.

Many other such legends may be found in the works of poets and writers upon religious subjects, and others have been handed down orally by musicians and would well merit collection.

The ancient theory of Indian music has been comparatively little studied, except by learned Pandits, many really good performers being ignorant of anything but the modern custom. This is probably because many of the ancient treatises that remain were purposely worded so that only Brahmins skilled in sacred lore could decipher their meaning. And now the improvements and alterations introduced from time to time by musicians of the day have come to be looked upon as authentic, a fact that in some degree tends to account for the differences that apparently exist between the ancient and modern systems.

The theoretical part of Hindu music when compared to that of Europe is naturally very simple, as it treats entirely of simple melody and measure. The most noticeable points are the extraordinary importance which the Hindus, like all the ancient nations, have from the first attached to mode--the transposition of the natural scales; the peculiar rhythmical measures, frequently irregular; the noisy methods of beating time; and the almost entire absence of harmony. The only harmony, if it can be called so, is a continuation as a pedal of the tonic or dominant, as was done in old "pastorales," and which is still found in Scotch or Irish bagpipe music. The use of all kinds of grace is common. The rules laid down for the composition of pieces in what are called râgas are curious, and should be noticed; certain progressions of melody being forbidden, while others are lawful. Whether the ancient Greeks made any employment of râga is not known, but it seems extremely probable, since they attributed the greater part of their science of music to India,[11] and that most Eastern nations still employ either râga or its equivalent.[12]

Roman music was brought to perfection by Greek musicians and their pupils, and Greek modes were introduced by them. The early ecclesiastical modes appear to have been derived from those of the Greeks. Many of the older contrapuntal rules as to the employment of intervals had their origin in the imperfect scales in which the ecclesiastical modes were composed. All this goes far to show the possibility of the elaborate counterpoint of the present day having had its prototype in the old Sanskrit râga system.

Of the two systems practised in Southern India at the present time, the Hindustani is somewhat akin to that of Northern India and Bengal. It is practised mostly by Mussalman musicians, while the Karnâtik is confined more to those of the Southern races. The latter, which may be called the national music of the South, is far more scientific and refined than the Hindustani, and its professors are, as a rule, men of much better education; a fact that is not without influence upon their music, and seems apparent in all their melodies, but particularly in the renderings they give of them.

---

[11] Strabo X. iii.

[12] The Greek practice of Melopœia appears very similar to that of râga.—*Vide* Mr. Chappell's "History of Music." London, 1874. See also Plutarch, περὶ Μουσικῆς. Cap. xviii., xix.

CHAPTER II.

Preservation of music in Southern India—Modern Karnâtik system believed to be closely akin to the ancient—Sanskrit treatises—Definition of s'ruti—System of twenty-two—Formation of scales (grâma)—Relation of major and minor modes—Deviation of intervals of system of twenty-two from those of just intonation—Comparison of ancient scale with European diatonic—Results of recent observation—System of twelve hinted at in Sanskrit—Murchanas—Râga—How differing from mode—Tâla or rhythm—Time, how estimated—Ancient varieties of rhythm—Ancient notation.

THE theory, modes, and notation in present use throughout the whole of India are derived from that taught originally by the earlier Sanskrit musicians; but owing to the South of India having been less disturbed by internal commotions, and having been more subject to Hindu rule than either the Deccan or Northern provinces, the science of music would seem to have been maintained and cultivated long after the original art had been lost in the North.

Hence Southern Indian music, or, as it is more usually called, Karnâtik, bears, as far as we can judge, a very close resemblance to what the Sanskrit must have been, and in many cases we can clearly trace the development and refinements introduced from time to time upon the original râgas.

One of the principal Sanskrit works upon the theory of music is the Sangíta Ratnâkera, or "Ocean of Music," written by Sârnga Deva at a very early date, probably about A.D. 200. This book, with the exception of Bhârata S'astra, noticed hereafter, is considered to be the oldest reliable musical work extant, and is quoted in many subsequent treatises. The Sangíta Dâmódara is also a well known and very ancient work.

Later than this we have the Sangíta Naráyana, by Naráyanadéva, in which the Dâmódara is frequently quoted.

There are also the Râganâva,[1] or "Sea of Passions"; the Sangíta

[1] This work, together with the Sábha Vinóda and Râga Darpana, is quoted by Mirza Khan, but there seems to be no copy known at present.

Ratnâvali; the Sábha Vinóda,[2] or "Delight of Assemblies"; and the Sangíta Darpana, or "Mirror of Music," written by Dâmódara Misra—all works of more or less value in the elucidation of the music of the ancients.

The Râga Vívodha, or "Doctrine of Musical Modes," by Somanath, or Soma Raj, is one of the most valuable of the ancient treatises that have been handed down to us. This book was evidently written at a much later date than the Ratnâkera, which it quotes from several times; but it is doubtless a very ancient composition. The first, third, and fourth chapters explain the doctrine of musical sounds—their division and succession, the variation of scales by temperament, and the enumeration of modes. The second chapter contains a minute description of different vinas, with rules for playing upon them.[3] The last chapter contains strains noted in letters. The whole work is singularly clear from mythological references.

The Persian writer, Mirza Khan, under the patronage of Aazim Shah, wrote a work entitled "Tohfuht-ul-Hind," which contains a chapter upon music, the information for which was extracted, with the assistance of Pandits, from various Sanskrit works. Mirza Khan describes four principal systems of music—viz., those of Isvara; of Bhârata; of Hanumân, or Pavân; and of Callanath. All four are mentioned also in the Râga Vívodha.

The main principles contained in most of these ancient works are very similar. The differences consist mostly in the names and the constitution of the different modes and râgas.

Written at a still later date than any of the former, to judge by all appearances, is the Sangíta Pârijâta,[4] or "Flower of Music," by the Pandit Ahobala.

The system of music described in the Pârijâta differs from that of the Ratnâkera, in that it admits of greater intervals than a tone or four s'rutis, and of less intervals than a semitone or two s'rutis, being, therefore, capable of forming numerous enharmonic scales. All the notes, except the first and fifth, are occasionally shifted above or below, and the fourth is never omitted in the scale.[5]

This work contains the key to the present Karnâtik system, and many of the râgas contained in it are practically the same as those now in use in Southern India.

---

[2] This work is mentioned by Sir William Jones. As far as I have been able to ascertain, there is at present no known copy in existence, unless, indeed, this work is identical with one called Sangíta Vinóda, a copy of which is in the library of H.H. the Maharajah of Bikanîr.

[3] Sir W. Jones.

[4] According to the Mahabhârata, Pârijâta is the name of the celestial tree in Indraloka.

[5] See Preface to edition of Sangíta Pârijâta, edited by Kálivára Védantabágísa. Calcutta, 1879. See also the list of modern Karnâtik scales given upon pages 32—35.

The ancients divided their octave into twenty-two intervals, called s'rutis.

The names of these s'rutis are differently given by the various authors, but the following list, taken from the Sangíta Ratnâkera, is the one which, at the present day, is best known:—

S'ruti	Note	S'ruti	Note	S'ruti	Note
1. Tivra	Shadja or Sa.	10. Vajrikâ	Madhyama or Ma.	18. Madanti	Dhaivata or Dha.
2. Kumadvati		11. Prasârini		19. Rôhini	
3. Mandâ		12. Prití		20. Ramyâ	
4. Chandōvati		13. Mâjaní		21. Vugrâ	Nishâda or Ni.[6]
5. Dayâvati	Rishaba or Ri.	14. Kshiti	Panchama or Pa.	22. Kshôbini	
6. Ranjanî		15. Raktâ			
7. Raktikâ		16. Sandîpa			
8. Rudri	Gandhâra or Ga.	17. Alâpi			
9. Krodhâ					

The exact definition of what constituted a s'ruti is difficult to determine, but it is thus vaguely given by the Sangíta Ratnâvali:—"A s'ruti is formed by the smallest intervals of sound, and is perceivable by the ear; it is of twenty-two kinds" (*i.e.*, as shown above); also "every distinct audible sound is a s'ruti; it is a s'ruti because it is to be heard by the ear."

The scales are formed from the s'rutis, four s'rutis being allotted to a major tone, three to a minor (which would appear to have been of a pitch somewhat flatter than the tone and sharper than the semitone; doubts, however, exist as to whether the intervals of the s'rutis were equal or not), and two to a semitone.

The s'rutis are differently arranged in grâmas, or scales, three in number—viz., Shadja-grâma, Madhyama-grâma, and Gandhâra-grâma.

The literal meaning of grâma signifies "a stopping place" or "village." Hence the word came to be used for scale, since the s'rutis are arranged in a scale as mankind in villages.

The Shadja-grâma consists of two tetrachords similar to each other, and separated by a major tone—nearly our diatonic major scale.

The Madhyama-grâma is formed from the preceding by a transposition of the major tone, between Pa and Dha, and of a minor tone between Dha and Ni—precisely our diatonic major scale.

---

[6] "In the arrangement of the s'rutis, modern usage is diametrically opposite to the classical one: the latter placing them before the note to which they respectively belong, while the former gives their position after the notes. It is difficult to determine when or by whom the alteration was effected. The arrangement of the frets of the vina and other stringed instruments accords with the modern acceptation of the principle. According to the rule laid down in the classical treatises, the disposition of the notes is reversed in the case of Daravi (*lit.*, wooden—*i.e.*, stringed) instruments, and out of this reversed arrangement, perhaps, the modern theory about the arrangement of the position of the s'rutis has been worked."—"The Musical Scales of the Hindus." S. M. Tagore. Calcutta, 1884.

Hence the two grâmas stand in the following relation :—

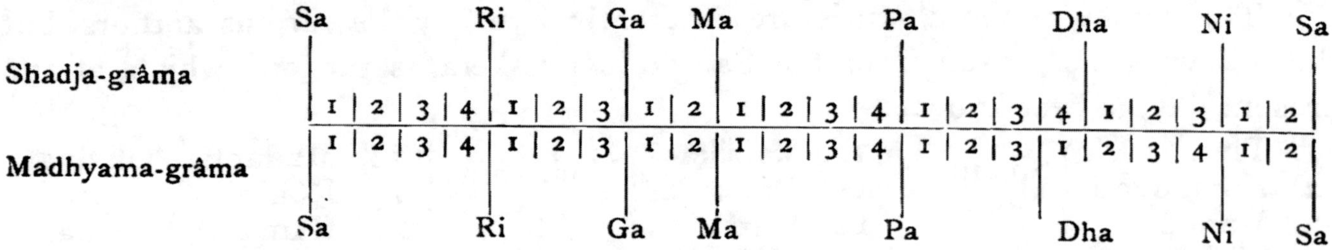

The third grâma is called the Gandhâra-grâma. Its construction is not clearly laid down, and if it ever existed in practice its use has long been discontinued. According to the Dâmódara its construction is only known in Indraloka, the mythical heaven of the god Indra, thus dispensing with the difficulty conveniently.

The Sangíta Pârijâta mentions that it merely differs from the other grâmas in that the note Ni will have four s'rutis, and that Sa will consequently have only three.[7]

The Sangíta Darpana points out *three* changes in the scales in forming the Gandhâra-grâma from the Madhyama-grâma.

Upon this Mr. Paterson[8] makes the following remarks :—

1st. Gandhâra takes one s'ruti from Rishaba and becomes of three—*i.e.*, by rendering the note Ga flat, the interval between Ri and Ga is reduced a semitone, and that between Ga and Ma becomes a minor tone.

2nd. Panchama loses one s'ruti to Gandhâra. I am at a loss to know how this can take place. I rather suspect an error in the text, and would propose to substitute Dha, the sixth note, instead of Gandhâra. The three s'rutis of Panchama make the interval between the fifth and sixth; by losing one, it is reduced to a semitone; but it cannot lose this one to Gandhâra, which is the third note. There are but two methods of reducing this interval to a semitone—one by raising the fifth note, the other by rendering the sixth flat. But here the interval between the fourth and fifth remains unaltered. It must in this case be done by making Dha, the sixth note, flat; or, in the language of Hindu music, by giving one of Panchama's s'rutis to Dhaivata.

3rd. Suddhasvâra gives one s'ruti to Nishâda. Here Nishâda is rendered one s'ruti flat. Suddhasvâra is not the name of a note, but is explained to me to be a term applied to a note possessing its full complement of s'rutis. It may, therefore, in this case be applied to Dhaivata; for although it may give one s'ruti to Nishâda, yet it gains one from Panchama, and still retains four complete s'rutis. If these conjectures are admitted, and we compare it with the Madhyama-grâma, to which these changes evidently refer, it will stand thus—

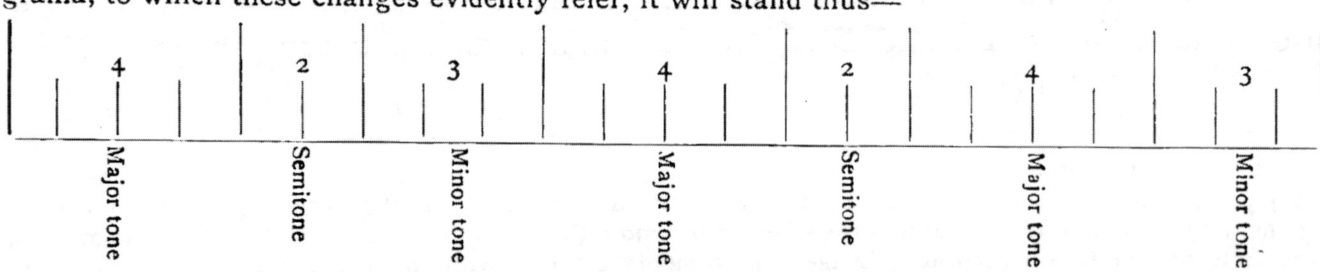

[7] The disposition of the s'rutis in this case would be preceding their respective notes, otherwise Sa would be shifted one s'ruti, and this is not so, as has been already remarked when mentioning the Pârijâta first.

[8] " On the Grâmas or Musical Scales of the Hindus."—" Asiatic Researches." Vol. IX. Calcutta, 1807.

That the Hindus probably by this division of the octave meant nothing more than what I have before supposed may appear from the following table, in which the intervals between each note and the note above it are taken from Mr. Malcolm's series of the octave in the two modes (as given by Mr. Chambers under the article "Scale"). This I have done in order to compare these intervals with the s'ruti of the Hindus, and to show the differences—

Malcolm's Series of the Octave.	Malcolm's Series of the Octave.
$\frac{8}{9}$ $\frac{4}{5}$ $\frac{3}{4}$ $\frac{2}{3}$ $\frac{3}{5}$ $\frac{8}{15}$ $\frac{1}{2}$	$\frac{8}{9}$ $\frac{5}{6}$ $\frac{3}{4}$ $\frac{2}{3}$ $\frac{5}{8}$ $\frac{5}{9}$ $\frac{1}{2}$
Major mode, or Madhyama-grâma.	Minor mode, or Gandhâra-grâma.

The difference between	Proportion of the intervals between each note and the note above it.	What they ought to be if the scale was divided into 22 parts, or the whole string into 44.	What they are as stated by the Hindus.	The difference between	Proportion of the intervals between each note and the note above it.	What they ought to be if the scale was divided into 22 parts, or the whole string into 44.	What they are as stated by the Hindus.
1 & $\frac{8}{9}$	$\frac{1}{9}$	$4\frac{8}{9}$	4	1 & $\frac{8}{9}$	$\frac{1}{9}$	$4\frac{8}{9}$	4
$\frac{8}{9}$ & $\frac{4}{5}$	$\frac{4}{45}$	$3\frac{41}{45}$	3	$\frac{8}{9}$ & $\frac{5}{6}$	$\frac{1}{18}$	$2\frac{4}{9}$	2
$\frac{4}{5}$ & $\frac{3}{4}$	$\frac{1}{20}$	$2\frac{1}{5}$	2	$\frac{5}{6}$ & $\frac{3}{4}$	$\frac{1}{12}$	$3\frac{2}{3}$	3
$\frac{3}{4}$ & $\frac{2}{3}$	$\frac{1}{12}$	$3\frac{2}{3}$	4	$\frac{3}{4}$ & $\frac{2}{3}$	$\frac{1}{12}$	$3\frac{2}{3}$	4
$\frac{2}{3}$ & $\frac{3}{5}$	$\frac{1}{15}$	$2\frac{14}{15}$	3	$\frac{2}{3}$ & $\frac{5}{8}$	$\frac{1}{24}$	$1\frac{5}{6}$	2
$\frac{3}{5}$ & $\frac{8}{15}$	$\frac{5}{75}$	$2\frac{14}{15}$	4	$\frac{5}{8}$ & $\frac{5}{9}$	$\frac{5}{72}$	$3\frac{1}{18}$	4
$\frac{8}{15}$ & $\frac{1}{2}$	$\frac{1}{30}$	$1\frac{7}{15}$	2	$\frac{5}{9}$ & $\frac{1}{2}$	$\frac{1}{18}$	$2\frac{4}{9}$	3

In a paper read to the Royal Society,[9] in 1877, upon the Hindu division of the octave, Mr. Bosanquet shows that the fifths and thirds produced by dividing the octave into twenty-two equal intervals do not deviate very widely from the exact intervals which are the foundation of the diatonic scale, the fifth being only

[9] "Proceedings of Royal Society." Vol. XXVI., page 372.

·07 or very nearly $\frac{1}{3}$ of a comma[10] sharp, and the major third ·045 or nearly $\frac{1}{5}$ of a comma flat.

He also gives the following table in order to show the deviation of the other intervals of the scale from those of just intonation:—

SYSTEM OF TWENTY-TWO.

Interval.	Difference of	Units.	Interval.	Exact Interval.
Fourth	Fifth and Octave	9	4·9091	4·9805
Major Tone ...	Fourth and Fifth	4	2·1818	2·0391
Minor Tone ...	Third and Major Tone	3	1·6363	1·8240
Major Semitone	Third and Fourth	2	1·0909	1·1174
Minor Third ...	Fifth and Third	6	3·2727	3·1564
Minor Semitone	Major Tone and Minor Third	1	·5454	·7067

"In regarding these numbers," he observes, "we must remember that as far as European musicians are concerned, the deviation from equal temperament is the most important thing in a melodic point of view.

"Intervals which deviate widely from equal temperament sound out of tune to the European ear, and as harmony is not employed, the justification which derivation from perfect concords is felt to give in harmony has no opportunity of asserting itself."

This calculation of Mr. Bosanquet's was made on the assumption that all the s'rutis were equal. That such could not have been in reality the case, or that the employment of the system of twenty-two never entered *practically* into Indian music, would seem to be from all evidence almost certain.[11]

This will be more evident by a reference to the following comparative diagram of the primitive Sanskrit Shadja-grâma and the European diatonic scale, as drawn for the Râjah Sir S. M. Tagore, and published in his work

---

[10] Comma of $\frac{81}{80}$ = ·21506.

[11] See also "The Twenty-two Musical S'rutis of the Hindus." S. M. Tagore. Calcutta, 1886.

upon the "Musical Scales of the Hindus," from data supplied by the ancient treatises, the measurements being those of a string 90 inches long :—

PRIMITIVE SANSKRIT SHADJA-GRÂMA.

90 inches.

20	16	9	15	$13\frac{1}{3}$	$10\frac{2}{3}$	6
20	16	9	15	12	12	6

EUROPEAN DIATONIC SCALE.

The only difference, it will be seen, is in the fact that the sixth is in the European diatonic scale flatter than in the ancient one ; so that the ancient Sanskrit sixth had apparently the same ratio, theoretically, as the Pythagorean sixth of the Greeks.

This seems probable, for the historian Strabo says that among the Greeks those who regard all Asia *as far as India* as a country sacred to Dionysius, "attribute to that country the invention of nearly all the science of music."[12]

But as concerns string measurements by the monochord, the late Mr. A. J. Ellis, F.R.S., in a most exhaustive paper read before the Society of Arts,[13] notices the above table of the Râjah's and remarks : "These divisions are made on the supposition that the vibrations are inversely as the length of the strings, which all my observations and experiments show is not the case on any practical instrument."

Mr. T. M. Venkatas'esha S'astri, a well-known authority upon theoretical music in Southern India, in a letter to the author, says that the word "s'ruti" appears to have undergone a great change in its meaning, and he inclines to the belief—but on what grounds it is difficult to say—that the suddha septa svâras, as understood at present in Southern India, meaning, as already explained, the seven notes of the scale containing their full number of s'rutis, are as follows :—

This tends to account in some measure for the preference given to the scale Mâyamâlavagaula, described in another chapter.

Mr. A. J. Ellis has given a table in the above-mentioned paper[14] of the

[12] Strabo, book X., iii.

[13] On "The Musical Scales of Various Nations," by A. J. Ellis, F.R.S., F.S.A., &c.—See "Journal of Society of Arts." 27th March, 1885, No. 1,688, Vol. XXXIII.

[14] See previous note.

comparative differences in the chromatic scales formed by the division of a string into parts, according to both the ancient directions and to what the Râjah Sir S. M. Tagore states[15] to be the modern Bengali use. The figures are in cents—that is to say, the hundredth parts of an equal semitone. He says:—

I give the number of degrees (s'rutis) and the calculation of their value on both plans, *old* and *new*, with the names of the nineteen Indian notes, assuming that the pitch varies inversely as the length of the string, as shown by the position of F and the octave, and that any errors thus arising have been corrected by ear.

INDIAN CHROMATIC SCALES.

Degrees	1	2	3	4	5	6	7	8	9	10	11
Notes	C	D♭♭	D♭	—	D	E♭♭	E♭	E	E♯	F	—
Old	0	51	102	153	204	264⅔	325⅓	386	442	498	549
New	0	49	99	151	204	259	316	374	435	498	543

Degrees	12	13	14	15	16	17	18	19	20	21	22
Notes	F♯	F♯♯	G	A♭♭	A♭	—	A	B♭♭	B♭	B	B♯
Old	600	651	702	753	804	855	906	966⅔	1027⅓	1088	1144
New	589	637	685	736	787	841	896	952	1011	1070	1135

The only values agreeing in each are C, D, F, while new E♭ is the just minor third—a mere accident. The nine degrees from C to F vary from 49 to 63 cents, and then there is a sudden break, after which the thirteen degrees from F to the octave vary from 45 to 65 cents. This is the first intelligible presentment of the Indian scale which I have been able to effect. It will be seen that C, D♭, D, E♭, E, F, F♯, G, A♭, A, B♭, B are represented pretty well by our equally tempered notes; but that the seven intermediate notes—D♭♭, E♭♭, E♯, F♯♯, A♭♭, B♭♭, B♯—could only be tempered in the quarter-tone system used in Syria. Hence in the usual transcription these seven notes are identified with some of the others. . . . These comparisons necessarily injure the original character of the music and give it a harmonisable appearance which is entirely foreign to Indian music.

Mr. Ellis also examined a vina from Southern India, now in the South Kensington Museum, with the following result:—

Cents	0	97	195	312	397	515	596	692	782	883	997	1092	1207
Notes	G	A♭	A	B♭	B	c	d♭	d	e♭♭	e	f	f♯	g

He remarks: "This is very close indeed to our scale of twelve semitones, and may be taken for it"; thus proving scientifically what has been found by experiment to be invariably the case with vinas used by Karnâtik musicians (*vide* page 31—footnote).

In a communication received from Mr. A. J. Hipkins, it is not acknowledged that there is any connection between the old Indian grâmas of 22 quarter-tones, or s'rutis, and the modern European scales, which, with major and minor tones

[15] "The Musical Scales of the Hindus." Calcutta, 1884.

and semitones, are founded upon the knowledge and practice of harmony. The Indian scale intervals ought to be understood as they are explained by native writers—namely, as a tone,[16] a $\frac{3}{4}$-tone, and a $\frac{1}{2}$-tone, composed of 4, 3, and 2 s'rutis respectively. With this conception of intervals, and it must be borne in mind the $\frac{3}{4}$-tone is still approved of in the East, a division of the octave into 24 equal quarter-tones becomes impossible. For as it was essential to secure an approximately perfect fourth with 9 s'rutis, and a fifth with 13, the division of the octave by 22 was the only one available. The error in the fourth of 9 equal s'rutis of a 22 division is no more than $\frac{1}{3}$-comma, in melody scarcely noticeable, but the error in a 21 or in a 23 division could not have been easily tolerated. The s'rutis thus being a little wider than exactly equal quarter-tones, $54\frac{6}{11}$ cents instead of 50, the Indian grâmas in most intervals come near to those of our just intonation scales, but this resemblance is accidental, as the foundation is different. It must, however, not be forgotten that this scale of probably equal s'rutis was theoretical, and has long since been superseded by another and more practical system, and that equal measurements of a string will not represent accurately this old Hindu conception.

The comparison of the 22 s'ruti scale with the European one of just intonation is as follows. The figures are equal semitones to two places of decimals (or the late Mr. A. J. Ellis's cents).

Indian	2·18	3·82	4·91	7·09	9·27	10·91	12·00
European	2·04	3·86	4·98	7·02	8·84 (or 9·06, with comma added to make 5th to D.)	10·88	12·00

The following table, kindly sent me by the late Mr. Ellis, shows the results obtained from a most minute and careful examination made by him and by Mr. A. J. Hipkins of a beautiful old vina, in perfect condition, now in my possession. This instrument is between two and three hundred years old, and is from the collection in the Tanjore Palace. The results, as will be seen, tend to prove that the frets were purposely arranged for something like equal temperament. We see, therefore, that in India much the same results have been independently arrived at by native musicians as have been attained by subsequent science in Europe.

---

[16] Mr. Hipkins states: "The Pythagorean tone—*i.e.*, the distance by which a perfect fifth overlaps a perfect fourth—which is here meant, is 2·04 equal semitones, and the greater tone that from the harmonic seventh completes the octave is 2·31. The four s'rutis amount to 2·18."

1	2	3	4	5	6	7	8
Frets.	Millimetres from nut.	Sounding lengths of string.	Pitch or numbers of double vibrations. Nov. 18, 1887.	Cents in the interval from the lowest note.	Intervals in cents from note to note.	Intervals in cents calculated from column 3.	Cents in the interval from the lowest note from column 3.
Nut	0	555	210·7	0	0	0	0
1	31	524	222·8	97	97	99	99
2	59	496	236·6	201	104	96	195
3	85	470	246·2	270	69	93	288
4	110	445	260·9	370	100	94	382
5	134	421	275·0	461	91	96	478
6	156	399	289·2	548	87	93	571
7	179	376	310·5	671	123	104	675
8	200	355	325·3	752	81	99	774
9	219	336	346·3	860	108	95	869
10	236	319	365·6	954	94	90	959
11	253	302	385·8	1047	93	95	1054
12	269	286	421·5	1200	153	94	1148
13	286	269	447·2	1303	103	106	1254
14	301	254	472·5	1398	95	99	1353
15	314	241	494·1	1476	77	91	1444
16	327	228	523·6	1576	100	99	1548
17	341	214	553·3	1672	96	107	1650
18	352	203	583·4	1763	91	91	1741
19	363	192				97	1838
20	373	182				102	1990
21	383	172				98	3028
22	392	163				93	2121
23	401	154				99	2220
24	410	145				104	2324
bridge	553	0					
100 times these numbers give the cents in equal temperament.	to the beginning of the bridge, but the real sounding length is as 555 millimetres.	From these lengths are calculated columns 7 and 8 on the hypothesis that pitch varies inversely as the sounding lengths	The rest of the notes were too high for my forks. The height of the string above the frets varied from 1 to 5 millimetres. A cent is the hundredth part of an equal semitone.	(see Auxiliary Table below)	The great uncertainty in these intervals renders any hypothesis as to the intended nature of the scale impossible. But col. 7, in conjunction with the auxiliary table in col. 5, shows that the mechanical rule of making the successive lengths as 18 : 19, or 17 : 18, or 16 : 17 was applied, and hence that the maker intended the frets to be arranged for equal temperament.		Compared with column 5, this shows the erroneous nature of the hypothesis that pitch varies as the sounding length on fretted instruments.

Auxiliary Table.

Cents.	Intervals.
92	128 : 135 or larger limma
94	18 : 19
99	17 : 18
100	84 : 89
105	16 : 17
112	15 : 16
151	11 : 12
155	32 : 35

Applied in column 7.

The system by which the octave is divided into twelve semitones is clearly hinted at in the Sangíta Darpana, which states that there are seven pure tones (Suddha or Prakrita), which appear to refer to the intervals composing the diatonic major scale; and twelve impure tones (Vikrita), by which we may conclude that the chromatic scale is implied.[17]

[17] For other information about Prakrita and Vikrita notes, see "The Musical Scales of the Hindus." S. M. Tagore. Calcutta, 1884.

The s'rutis are arranged in their different svâras, or intervals of the scale, according to the "murchanas." Of what these murchanas really consisted is very doubtful.

Sir William Jones states that the murchanas, of which there are seven in each grâma, appear to be no more than "seven pieces of diapason multiplied by three, according to the difference of pitch in the compass of the three octaves."

This view seems to be that taken by Kóhala, an ancient musician, from whose pen fragments of a treatise in Sanskrit are still remaining.[18]

Mr. Paterson, on the other hand, conjectures that they are the intervals of each grâma, and arranges them in the following classification :—

Shadja-grâma	Sa	to	Ri	1st	2nd	1st Tetrachord.
	,,	,,	Ga	,,	3rd	
	,,	,,	Ma	,,	4th	
	Pa	,,	Dha	,,	2nd	2nd Tetrachord.
	,,	,,	Ni	,,	3rd	
	,,	,,	Sa	,,	4th	
	Sa	,,	Sa	,,	Octave	
Madhyama-grâma	Sa	,,	Ri	2nd		
	,,	,,	Ga	Greater third		
	,,	,,	Ma	4th		
	,,	,,	Pa	5th		
	,,	,,	Dha	Greater sixth		
	,,	,,	Ni	7th		
	,,	,,	Sa	Octave		
Gandhâra-grâma	Sa	to	Ri	2nd		
	,,	,,	Ga	Minor third		
	,,	,,	Ma	4th		
	,,	,,	Pa	5th		
	,,	,,	Dha	Minor sixth		
	,,	,,	Ni	7th[19]		
	,,	,,	Sa	8th		

The seven intervals of each scale are arranged in what are called râgas.

Sir W. Jones employs the term râga as synonymous with mode.

Mode and râga are, however, perfectly distinct from each other—Mode

---

[18] The Sangíta Darpana gives a totally different meaning to murchana, describing the murchanas as the permutations produced by a method somewhat like change ringing; the number of murchanas being the continued product of the number of notes employed. Hence, from a grâma of seven tones we get 5,040 different murchanas. The method of producing these permutations is called "Kundameru" by native musicians.

[19] Whether major or minor is not stated by Mr. Paterson.

being termed *thât*, and not râga or râgini. Now *thât* consists in determining the relative intervals between several sounds, which constitute an octave with respect to each other. A râga is formed from these, in its composition employing the whole or less number of the intervals of the *thât*, and with a peculiar melodic style of its own; in fact, a melody type formed upon a mode. This, however, is more fully explained in another chapter.

In no two Sanskrit works do we find that the râgas agree either as to their names or their notation; the modes or scales of these different râgas are not given, and, in most cases, it is therefore only a matter of conjecture as to how they were performed. In almost all these works a somewhat similar classification of the râgs and râginis has been adopted. There are six principal râgas personified as demigods, each of which has a certain number of râginis (personified as the wives of the râgas)—sometimes five and sometimes six—appended to it.

The following classification is that of Hanumân[20]:—

I.—Bhairavâ ....Dha, ni, sa, ga, ma, dha.
Madhyamadi ....Ma, pa, dha, ni, sa, ri, ga, ma.
Bháiravi ....(1.) Ma, pa, dha, ni, sa, ri, ga, ma. (1.) Ascending.
(2.) Dha, ni, sa, ga, ma, pa. (2.) Descending.
Vangâli ....Sa, ga, ma, pa, ni, sa,
Ma, pa, dha, ni, sa, ri, ga, ma.
Varâti ....Sa, ri, ga, ma, pa, dha, ni, sa.
Syindavi ....Sa, ri, ga, ma, pa, dha, ni, sa,
Sa, ga, ma, pa, dha, ni, sa.

II.—Mâlavakúsika.....Sa, ri, ga, ma, pa, dha, ni, sa.
Tódi ....Ma, pa, dha, ni, sa, ri, ga, ma.
Sa, ri, ga, ma, pa, dha, ni, sa.
Kambâvati ....Dha, ni, sa, ri, ga, ma, dha.
Gauri ....Sa, ga, ma, dha, ni, sa.
Gunâkeri ....Dha, ni, sa, ga, ma, pa, ni.
Sa, ga, ma, pa, ni, sa.
Kakobhâ ....Dha, ni, sa, ri, na, ma, pa, dha.

III.—Hindola ....Sa, ga, ma, pa, ni, sa, ni, pa, ma, ga, sa.
Velâveli ....Dha, ni, sa, ri, ga, ma, pa, dha.
Râmakeri............Sa, ri, ga, ma, pa, dha, ni, sa.
Sa, ni, dha, ma, ga, ri, sa.
Déshaks'ya ....Ga, ma, pa, dha, ni, sa, ga.
Palamángeri ....Pa, dha, ni, sa, ri, ga, ma, pa.

---

[20] See "Sangíta Sâra Sángrahâ," a collection of various Sanskrit authorities, edited by S. M. Tagore. Calcutta, 1875.

	Lalíta	Sa, ri, ga, ma, pa, dha, ni, sa, sa. Dha, ni, sa, ga, ma, dha, dha.
IV.—	Dîpaka	Sa, ri, ga, ma, pa, dha, ni, sa.
	Kadâra	Ni, sa, ga, ma, pa, ni, ni.
	Kanada	Ni, sa, ri, ga, ma, pa, dha, ni, ni.
	Deshi	Ri, ga, ma, dha, ni, sa, ri.
	Kaumodi	Dha, ni, sa, ri, ga, ma, pa, dha.
	Nâtika	Sa, ri, ga, ma, pa, dha, ni, sa.
V.—	S'ri-Râga	Ni, ga, ma, pa, dha, ni, sa, ri.
	Vasantha	Sa, ri, ga, ma, pa, dha, ni, sa.
	Mâlava	Ni, sa, ga, ma, dha, ni.
	Mâlava-s'ri	Sa, ri, ga, ma, pa, dha, ni, sa.
	Dunâsri	Sa, ga, ma, pa, dha, ni, sa.
	Asâveri	Dha, ni, sa, ma, pa, dha. Ma, dha, ni, sa, ri, ga, ma.
VI.—	Mégharâga	Dha, ni, sa, ri, ga, ma, pa, dha.
	Gauri	Dha, ni, ri, ga, ma, dha.
	Déshakâri	Sa, ri, ga, ma, pa, dha, ni, sa.
	Bhupâli	Sa, ri, ga, ma, pa, dha, ni, sa. Sa, ga, ma, pa, ni, sa.
	Gaurjeri	Ri, ga, ma, pa, dha, ni, sa, ri.
	Dakhâ	Sa, ri, ga, ma, pa, dha, ni, sa, sa.

The Sangíta Naráyana shows that thirty-six "modes" or râgas are in general use, and the rest very rarely applied to practice. These modes are shown by Sir William Jones in his essay on the musical modes of the Hindus, and will be found in many respects similar to those described in the Sangíta Darpana, and shown above. Thirty-six modes from the Râga Vívodha, and thirty-six from the work of Mirza Khan, have also been described by the same eminent scholar, and need not, therefore, be reproduced here.

The rhythm of the early music seems to have been very complicated, and the most exact directions as to the value of notes and the division into "tâlas" or rhythmical periods are given. These, again, vary in different authors.

For example, in order to estimate the relative time value of successive notes, the sage Anginayya gives the following poetical directions :—

Take one hundred petals of the lotus flower, place them then one upon the other; and when pierced with a needle, the time in which the point passes through a single petal is called one second; eight such seconds are called one lavâ; eight lavâs one koshtâ; eight koshtâs one nimishâ; eight nimishâs one kalâ; four kalâs one anudruthâ; two anudruthâs one druthâ; two druthâs one lâgu; two lâgus one guru; three lâgus one plutha; four lâgus one kakupathâ.

Of these, later on in his work, he employs the following, calling druthâ a half matra, and this he takes as the limit.

Hence we can deduce the following table :—

Written	Name	Value
o	Druthâ	·5 Matras
ı	Lâgu	1 Matra
ξ	Guru	2 Matras
ξ'	Plutha	3 Matras
C	Biramâ (or rest)	Not stated

The common and triple time here implied is striking, and in some measure tends to prove that the employment of triple time is not of such comparatively recent introduction as some writers endeavour to show.

Formed upon the above basis, several hundreds of different tâlas or measures—many of them extremely complicated—are given.[21]

The rhythm of some of these ancient tâlas is still employed in practice, although the complicated system of signature is no longer in use. The following table, taken from the work of Anginayya, comprises some of these ancient tâlas, together with their value in modern notation.

The sign of C or rest, although its value is not definitely stated by Anginayya, can be—judging from the performances of modern Mridang or Tabla players—correctly taken to be of the same value as the note immediately preceding; or else it may be employed as a "dot," when placed after a note, to lengthen its value by one-half.

Captain Willard, in his "Treatise upon the Music of Hindustan," has given another and very complete list of these ancient tâlas, differing in many ways from the following; but, unfortunately, he does not state from what authority he gathered them.

To judge by the very complicated nature of many of these tâlas, and the fact that they vary widely in almost all the authorities, it seems hardly likely that they were ever in very common use; but they are, nevertheless, interesting as showing the great variety of rhythm that can be produced by such simple means as beating the two hands together—the earliest kind of rhythmical accompaniment; and some slight idea of the peculiarities of modern Indian drum playing can also be gleaned from this table :—

[21] Extracts from Anginayya's work have been given by the Râjah Sir S. M. Tagore, in "Sangíta Sâra Sángrahâ," which see for further information upon this subject, p. 207 and following pages.

No.	Name of Tâla.	Originally written.
1	Âdi	|
2	Dviteya	o o | |
3	Tríteya	o | °.
4	Chaturúshra	| o
5	Panchãma	o o
6	Nis'ankalíla	§c §c § § |
7	Durpana	o o §c
8	Simhâvikramâ	§ § § | §c | § §c
9	Ratilíla	| | § §
10	Simhalíla	| o o o
11	Kanderpâ	o o §c § |
12	Vírevíkruma	| o o §
13	Rangahâ	o o o o §
14	S'ri-Rangahâ	| | § | §c
15	Cháchari	{o o' | o o' | o o' | o o' | o o' | o o' | o o' | o o' |}
16	Prátiangâ	§ § § | |
17	Yétilagnâ	o o |
18	Gájalíla	| | | |c
19	Hámsalíla	| |'
20	Vérnabhína	o o | §
21	Tribhinhâ	| § §c
22	Râga-chudâmanni	o o | | | o o | §
23	Rangadíotahâ	§ § § | §c
24	Rangapradîpaka	§ § § | § §c
25	Râjah-châsraha	| | o o | |
26	Mitravérnahâ	§c § o o | § §
27	Simhavikrídita	| | §c | § §c | §c § §c §c
28	Savahâ	| | § | | o o
29	Vanumâli.	| o o o o §
30	Hâmsanâda	| §c o o §c
31	S'ìmhanâda	| § § | §
32	Kúrdúkahâ	o o | |
33	Turangalíla	o o' o o
34	S'arabhalíla	| | o o o o | |
35	Chaturásrahâ	§ | o o §
36	Simhânandanâ	§ § | §c | § o o § § | §c | §c §
37	Tribhángihi	| | § §
38	Rángabhirnahâ	§ § | | §c
39	Mángikahâ	| | § | | | |'
40	Májahâ	§ | | o' o'
41	Mádritâ-mángahâ	§ | | | | | |'
42	Vâmangahâ	§ | | o' o'

Value in English Notation.

There exist, as will be explained later on, at present in Karnâtik music seventy-two modes or scales, all formed from seven of the twelve semitones in the octave differently disposed upon a tonic of equal pitch. If we are to understand that the râgas described by Sir W. Jones were simply such scales or modes, the only way in which it is possible to reconcile the theory to the present system is to imagine that for ascending the scale they employed a perfect fourth (or, as a Karnâtik musician would say, for Arohâna Suddha-madhyama), and for descending the augmented fourth (Práti-madhyama), or possibly the reverse, like the Chinese practice at the present day.

From the earliest time the râgas seem to have been appointed to be sung at certain hours of the day or night, and no musician, unless specially ordered, would deviate from custom so far as to sing a râga out of its appointed season.

The râgas are, however, differently distributed in the different works, and the modern custom differs widely from the directions of the Sanskrit.

The notation given in all the ancient treatises is very similar to that at present in use, letters only being employed to express the notes. The following, a *fac-simile* of the most ancient form of notation, is from the work of Sóma, and has been thus rendered into the European notation by Sir William Jones, who remarks :—

> I have noted Sóma's air in the major mode[22] of A, or Sa, which, from its gaiety and brilliancy, well expresses the general hilarity of the song; but the sentiment, often under pain even in a season of delights, from the remembrance of pleasures no longer attainable, would require in our music a change to the minor mode; and the air might be disposed of in the form of a rondo ending with the second line, or even with the third, where the sense is equally full, if it should be thought proper to express by another modulation that *imitativc melody* which the poet has manifestly attempted: the measure is very rapid, and the air should be gay or even quick in exact proportion to it :—

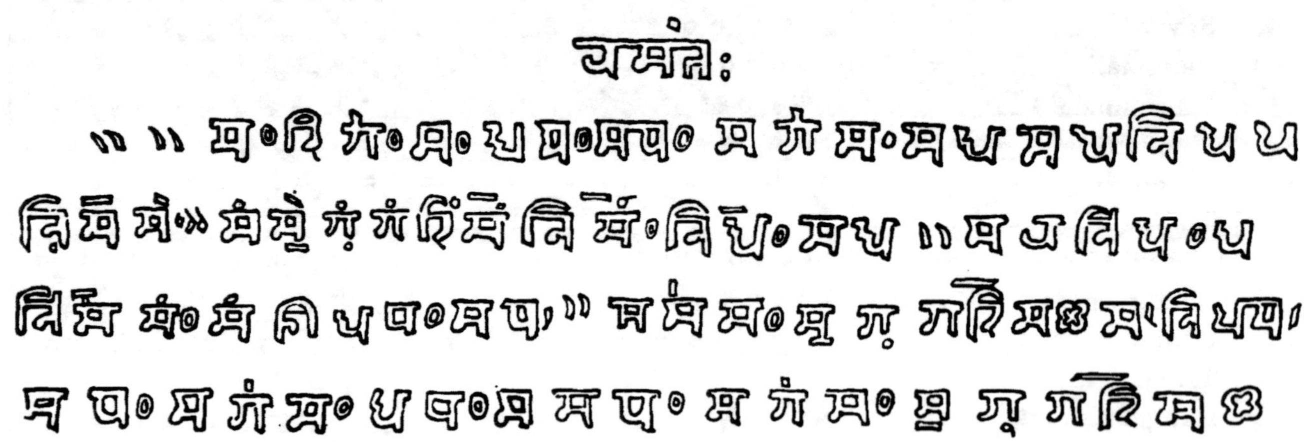

[22] It is rather difficult to understand why Sir William Jones employs this key instead of that of C, which seems to have been the most natural that would have suggested itself.

TRANSLATION OF THE ABOVE.[23]

[23] This translation must, of course, be more or less hypothetical; and as it is so entirely different in character and style to all modern Indian music, and airs heard now in India which are said to be very ancient, its correctness appears to be very doubtful. A comparison with the examples quoted later will show how widely it differs.

CHAPTER III.

Modern theory—How differing from ancient—Notation—Arrangement of gamut—Scales—Time, how signified—Application of measure to music.

THE modern theory of Indian music differs widely from that described in the ancient Sanskrit treatises, having, as has been said, passed through many changes in the course of time before assuming its present form.

The peculiar division of the octave into twenty-two parts or s'rutis exists no longer in practice, and the employment of s'rutis or intervals less than semitones is *limited to grace.*

The râgas in present use in most respects differ from those previously mentioned, and, in fact, the whole system has undergone a complete change and gradual refinement, until between the ancient and modern music there exists a difference as clearly marked and perceivable, to even the most casual observer, as between the modern Anglican chant and the ancient Gregorian tones.

The notes employed in Indian music are expressed by the following characters[1] (termed, when sounded, svâras). These characters are repeated as often as is necessary, should more notes be required to complete a passage. No stave, as in the European system, is necessary, the characters being written in one line only.

Name	How sung	Signified	Corresponding to European
Shadja	Sa	స	Do
Rishaba	Ri	ర	Re
Gandhâra	Ga	గ	Mi
Madhyama	Ma	మ	Fa
Panchãma	Pa	ప	Sol
Dhaivata	Dha	ధ	La
Nishâda	Ni	ని	Si

[1] The characters here represented are Telegu, that being the most musical language of Southern India. The corresponding letters of Tamil, Mahrathi, Sanskrit, &c., are frequently employed in the same way.

These seven notes correspond to those of the European diatonic major scale, unless the intervals are modified to those of some special scale.

The Hindu octave, like the European, is divided into twelve semitones.[2]

From these twelve semitones, seventy-two scales or modes, each consisting of seven notes, are formed upon a tonic of the same pitch.

As the intervals of every scale or mode are signified by the above letters, it will be seen that there exists no method by which accidentals can be noted.

The following table shows the arrangement of the twelve semitones under their respective significations.

The note Pa (ప), as will be seen, is invariably the fifth of the scale.

The keynote Sa (స) may be of any pitch as may best suit the requirements of the performer.

Relation.	Sa. స	Ri. ర	Ga. గ	Ma. మ	Pa. ప	Dha. ద	Ni. న	Sa. స
C								—
B							Kakeli[3]	
A♯						Shat-s'ruti	Kaisika[3]	
A						Chatur-s'ruti	Suddha	
G♯						Suddha		
G					—			
F♯				Prati				
F				Suddha				
E			Sadharama[3]					
D♯		Shat-s'ruti	Antara[3]					
D		Chatur-s'ruti	Suddha					
C♯		Suddha						
C	—							

[2] This view is supported by both Sir W. Jones and Mr. Fowke ("Asiatic Researches"). Sir W. Jones remarks: "I tried in vain to discover in practice any difference between the Indian scale and that of our own; but knowing my ear to be very insufficiently exercised, I requested a German professor of music to accompany on his violin a Hindu lutenist, who sang by note some popular airs on the loves of Krishna and Radha, and he assured me that the scales were the same; and Mr. Shore afterwards informed me that when the voice of a native singer was in tune with his harpsichord, he found the Hindu series of seven notes to

[3] M. Grosset gives an interesting explanation of these terms, as used by Bhârata, in his *Contribution à l'étude de la musique Hindoue.* Paris, 1888. The terms are used in a slightly different sense, but the explanation should be read by those who wish to make further research.

From the above table it may be easily understood that although every scale is sung to the syllables "Sa, Ri, Ga, Ma, Pa, Dha, Ni," the intervals implied by these syllables vary in the different scales.

For instance, Ri may be employed to denote either D♭, D♮, or D♯, as the case may be; assuming, of course, that Sa corresponds with C. When the names of the notes vary it has been noticed in the column under each respective head. These names should be prefixed to those of the notes, as Suddha-gandhâra, Antara-gandhâra.

The scales formed upon these intervals are seventy-two in number, and are divided into two divisions of thirty-six in each.

Those of the first division are styled "Suddha-madhyama," from the fact that in their construction they employ that note, or the perfect fourth, throughout. Those of the second, for a similar reason, are styled "Prati-madhyama," and employ the augmented or tritone fourth. In theoretical works the scales are classified in sets or "chacrams" of six; the construction of each chacram, as will be noticed, being very similar.

The following is a list of all the scales,[4] with their names and reference numbers, arranged by "chacrams" or sets of six *precisely* as given in treatises in the vernacular, the only difference being that European notation has been substituted for the Indian :—

SUDDHA-MADHYAMA.

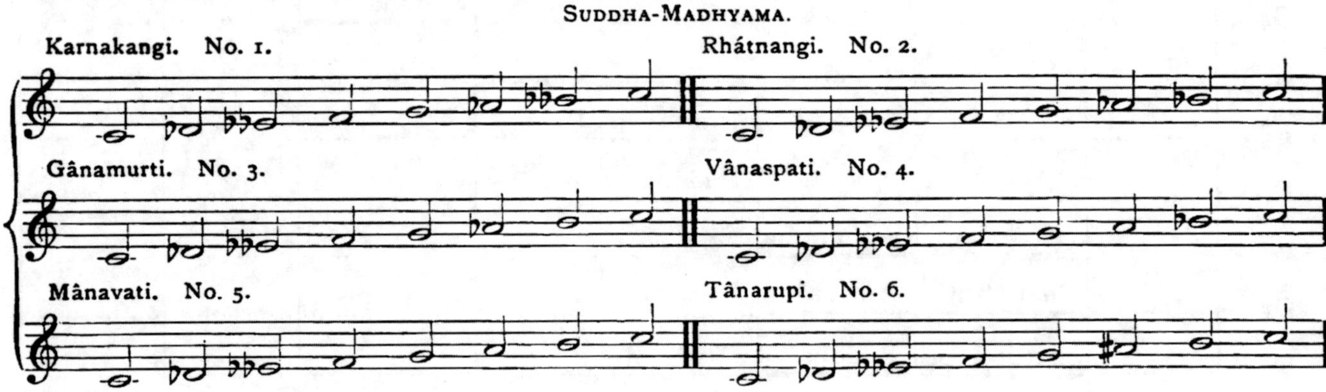

---

ascend like ours—by a sharp third." From many experiments I am led to believe that a wrong idea as to the temperament of the Indian scale—as practically employed—has hitherto been held. I played over all the various scales shown later upon a pianoforte—tuned to equal temperament—in the presence of several well-known Hindustani and Karnâtik musicians, all of whom assured me that they corresponded exactly to those of the vina. Upon comparing the two instruments this was found to be the case—as far as could be judged by the ear alone—in every instance. Native airs are played by the private band of H.H. the Maharajah of Mysore; and as far as *melody* is concerned they are acknowledged to be perfectly in tune, according to Indian ideas, by all. Native airs are also played by the band of H.H. the Gaeckwar of Baroda, the chief musician at whose court—"Professor" Maula Bux—a man of considerable attainments, took pains to explain to me that the tempering of the *modern* Indian scales differed in no whit from the European. In fact, in practice, as among the ancient Greeks, the old enharmonic genus would seem to have given place to the chromatic.

[4] The scales here shown are those of the Karnâtik system. Those used in the Hindustani system are fewer in number and are differently named. They will be found upon page 91.

Sânapati. No. 7.
Hanumatódi. No. 8.
Dânuka. No. 9.
Nâtakaprýa. No. 10.
Kókilaprýa. No. 11.
Rúpavati. No. 12.

Gáiakaprýa. No. 13.
Vakhulabhárna. No. 14.
Máyamâlavagaula. No. 15.
Cháckravaka. No. 16.
Suryakánta. No. 17.
Hatakambâri. No. 18.

S'ankâradvâni. No. 19.
Nâtabhairavi No. 20.
Kyravâni. No. 21.
Kârahâraprýa. No. 22.
Gaurimanohâri. No. 23.
Vârunaprýa. No. 24.

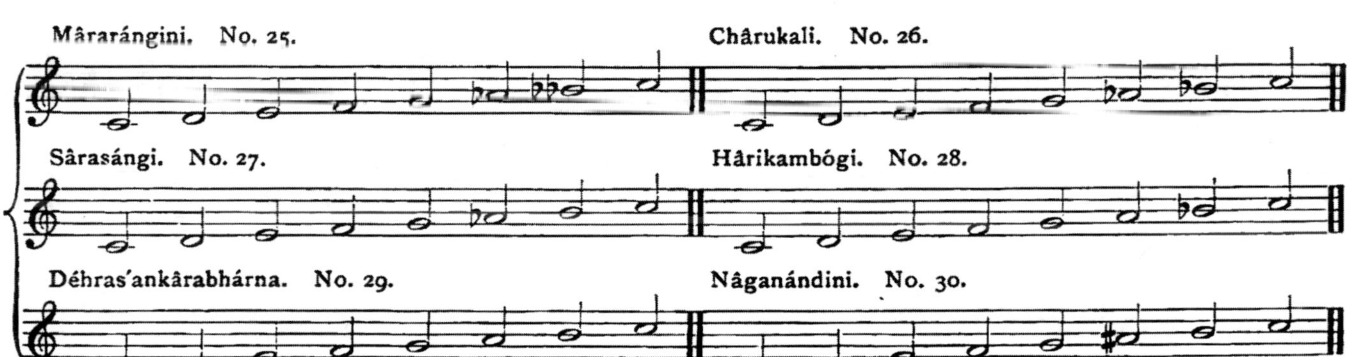
Mâraràngini. No. 25.
Chârukali. No. 26.
Sârasángi. No. 27.
Hârikambógi. No. 28.
Déhras'ankârabhárna. No. 29.
Nâganándini. No. 30.

PRATI-MADHYAMA.

In Hindu music usually three octaves only, termed Sthâyis, are taken into consideration.

Instruments such as the vina, &c., have, however, a compass of nearly four octaves. In order to signify the octave in which a note is to be played, a dot or dots are usually placed above or below it. There is no definite rule for this; each musician or writer upon music apparently advocates some method of his own.

Music is not, as with us, divided by bars of equal duration. Divisions styled Gitalu are in use, and are signified thus | or —; they can be placed anywhere, at the composer's discretion, and denote parts or phrases so to speak.

They are frequently marked thus || or =, when they denote the repetition of a part, or the conclusion of a strain.

The sign of the lotus flower is used by some writers for the same purpose.

Time, by which is implied the relative values of a succession of notes, cannot be expressed with any degree of accuracy without indeed so complicated an arrangement of signs as to be almost unintelligible. The method is described fully in the Sanskrit works, but from this reason it has fallen into disuse. The value of the note is invariably taught orally by a master, and the ear is thereby cultivated to a very high degree.

The following signs (or their equivalents if the character is Devanâgari) are, however, made use of in order to convey—approximately only—whether notes are to be of long or short duration :—

Dirgha : This sign, used in conjunction with the musical characters, signifies that they represent "long notes"—

సా రీ గా మా పా దా నీ

Votu : This sign in the same way represents "short notes"—

స్స ర్రి గ్గ మ్మ ప్ప ద్ద న్ని

The different degrees of time are termed Tâlas, of which there are seven, each being sub-divided into five "jâtis," or kinds ; so that there are in use no less than thirty-five distinct measures.

By the annexed table the various tâlas and their respective jâtis will be understood at a glance, the figures signifying the number of beats of equal duration made in a bar.

Name of Tâla.	Name of Jâti. Chaturúshra.	Tishra.	Mishra.	Cúndha.	Sankirna.
Dhruva	4, 2, 4, 4[5]	3, 2, 3, 3	7, 2, 7, 7	5, 2, 5, 5	9, 2, 9, 9
Mátsya	4, 2, 4	3, 2, 3	7, 2, 7	5, 2, 5	9, 2, 9
Rûpaka	4, 2	3, 2	7, 2	5, 2	9, 2
Jhampa	4, 1, 2	3, 1, 2	7, 1, 2	5, 1, 2	9, 1, 2
Triputa	4, 2, 2	3, 2, 2	7, 2, 2	5, 2, 2	9, 2, 2
Atatâla	4, 4, 2, 2	3, 3, 2, 2	7, 7, 2, 2	5, 5, 2, 2	9, 9, 2, 2
Ekatâla	4	3	7	5	6

[5] Sometimes in practice this is played 6, 4, 4, although theoretically wrong.

Tâlas can be denoted by the following signatures:—

Anudruthâ	ᴗ	denoting	1	unit of	time.
Druthâ	*o*	,,	2	,,	,,
Lâgu	*ı*	,,	4	,,	,,
Guru	8	,,	8	,,	,,
Pluthâ	3	,,	12	,,	,,
Kakupathâ	+	,,	16	,,	,,

The jâti of the tâla is usually appended to the signature in words. Should nothing be appended, then the Chaturúshra is generally understood.

In order to employ these signs they should be substituted for the figures in the table: thus *ı o ı ı* will denote the Chaturúshra jâti of Druvatâla. Hence, when written in European notation, there is often a constant rotation corresponding to the tâla of bars of different time signatures.

Each tâla can be played in any order—*i.e.*, 4244 can be played 2444, 4424, or 4442.

The application of the tâlas to an air is called Grahâ, and is of four kinds, viz.:—

(1.) Sâma[6]—When the first beat of the tâla falls upon the first note of the air.

(2.) Anagatâ—When the air commences after the first beat of the tâla which therefore falls upon a rest.

(3.) Atiyita—When the tâla continues after the air is finished, the last beat therefore falling upon a rest.

(4.) Vichâma—Comprises any irregularity not included in the above three, such as the beat of a tâla falling upon the first note of a bar tied to the last note of the bar preceding, &c.

The Chaturúshra jâti of Triputa Tâla is also known by the name of Âditâla, and is a very common time for javadis, and other love songs.

There being practically no harmony in Hindu music, clefs, as in the European system, are not employed. The keynote is always Sa, and, as already stated, is taken of any pitch to suit the requirements of the performer or the nature of the instrument.

---

[6] This term is also used to signify the strong accent.

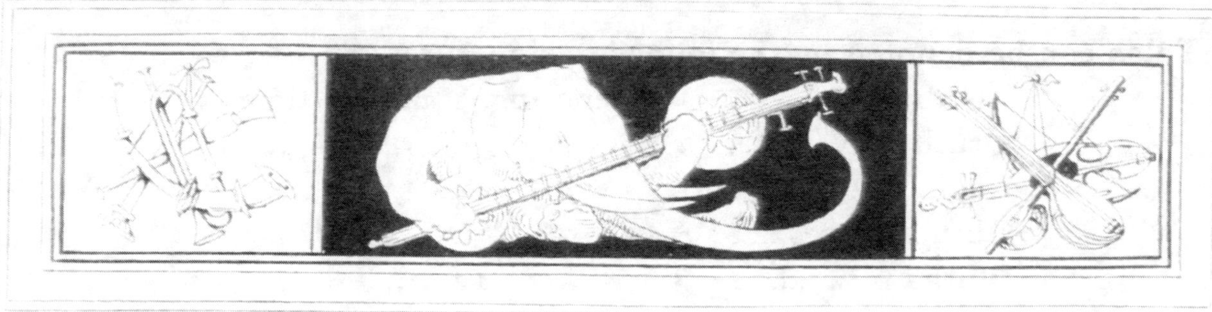

CHAPTER IV.

Râga—How defined—Notes essential to composition of—Vâdi and Samvâdi notes—Modern meaning of Murchana—Examples of Murchana applied—Ancient and modern methods of performance of râga—How differing—Alâpa—Madhyamakâla—Gamakas—Classification of râgas—Popular scales for—Allied to certain passions—Peculiarities—How apportioned to seasons and hours—"Kattika," or list of modern râgas.

AS râga constitutes what may be called the very foundation of Indian music, it merits a chapter to itself. The term râga may be best explained as "melody type," since it is a melodic extension of certain notes of a particular scale or mode (thât), according to certain fixed rules called the murchana.[1]

The literal meaning of the word râga is "that which creates passion," and hence, according to the Hindu idea, a râga signifies a succession of notes so arranged, according to prescribed rules, as to awaken a certain feeling of the mind and an effect differing, it may be, in the minutest particulars from that derivable from another râga.

These notes can be played in any degree or movement of time without destroying the inherent character of the râga, though the mode or thât must remain the same throughout.

The notes essential to the composition of a râga are of four kinds—viz., vâdi, samvâdi, anuvâdi, and vivâdi.

By the vâdi is meant any note which, by reason of its continual recurrence,

[1] The word Râga does not appear to have been used in its present technical sense until a date later than has been generally supposed. It is worthy of note that in the oldest Indian musical treatise, the Bhârata Natya S'astra, the word Râga appears hardly at all; and no special ādhyaya is devoted to it, as is invariably the case in all subsequent Sanskrit treatises. The employment of râga as understood in the Sangíta Ratnâkera and subsequently was evidently unknown at the time when Bhârata wrote. But in its place there was a system of what are called by Bhârata *jâtis*. This word, meaning literally genus, would seem to be of kindred meaning to the old Greek musical term *γένος*. Some centuries later, when the Sangíta Ratnâkera was written, the term râga appears to have been substituted for jâti.

or by its being specially accentuated or dwelt upon, shows to the best advantage the characteristics of the râga. Hence the vâdi is called the "Râjah" (king), and by Hindustani musicians the "Jân" or life and soul of the râga.

The samvâdi is usually either the fourth or fifth, the vâdi being taken as the tonic, or both fourth and fifth when both are admissible in the râga.

The samvâdis are commonly arranged as follows :—

Vâdi.	Samvâdi.
Shadja	Madhyama and Panchāma
Rishaba	Dhaivata
Gandhâra	Nishâda
Madhyama... ...	Nishâda and Shadja
Panchāma	Shadja
Dhaivata	Rishaba
Nishâda	Gandhâra and Madhyama

A list of these notes has been given because in many of the Sanskrit treatises directions are given to employ samvâdi alternating or otherwise in conjunction with the vâdi notes in the performance of certain râgas. In the text these samvâdi notes are not shown; but they are known from their respective vâdis, in much the same way that an accompanying harmony to an air used to be, in European music, often merely figured.

In modern dispositions Panchāma is admitted as a samvâdi to Rishaba and *vice versâ*. According to the authorities, Nishâda cannot be samvâdi to any other note than Gandhâra, and *vice versâ*. Madhyama therefore can have only one samvâdi, which will be Shadja; though, according to the calculations, it is shown to have Nishâda too for its samvâdi; Nishâda will have Gandhâra only for its samvâdi.

By the vivâdi, or enemy, is meant a note which, being inadmissible, would therefore destroy the special characteristics of any râga.

All other notes not comprised among the foregoing are styled Anuvâdi.

The rules for determining the succession and style of the notes composing a râga are called the murchana of that râga.

By the murchana is meant not only the style, but also the time; it gives the relative values assigned to the different notes, the accentuation, and any peculiarity of expression or tempo essential to the correct execution of the râga, such as can only be learned by actually hearing it performed.

In a musician's kattika, or scale book, the ascending and descending modes alone of a râga are given, no directions as to the value of the notes, &c., being assigned; indeed, often the scale itself is not given.

All this is implied in the murchana, and without understanding the murchana it is therefore impossible to play any râga.

The murchana is never written, but is invariably taught orally; often by means of songs, &c., in the same râga.

For example, in the kattika, the text of the râga "S'ri" is given thus:—

Ascending mode—Sa, ri, ma, pa, ri, sa.

Descending mode—Sa, ri, pa, dha, ni, pa, ma, ri, ga, ri, sa.

These notes must follow each other in proper succession; for instance, when the melody is ascending, the note Ma must follow Ri; in descending, a similar method of progression must be adhered to. Hence from these notes, without breaking the rules, many melodies can be formed.

But yet there is a certain style peculiar to each râga: certain notes must be dwelt upon, some played staccato; others with a peculiar expression, grace or tremor.

If the notes of one of these melodies were written as No. 1 below, no two persons could play them alike; each would naturally put his own interpretation upon them. The interpretation, therefore, is supplied by the murchana, when the melody appears as No. 2:—

No. 1. S'ri Raga.

No. 2.[2]

When a composition is said to be in a certain râga, it means that it employs

[2] The grace here implied is more the "Bebung," or *vibrato*, than anything else, and cannot therefore be executed upon a pianoforte. In the clavichord it consists in giving to the key a certain trembling pressure producing a pulsation of sound without any interval of silence. In stringed instruments the effect is obtained by a rocking movement of the finger without raising it from the string. This peculiar grace must be remembered as applying *specially* to all Indian melodies. It should be borne in mind that Indian stringed instruments, owing to the great length of their strings in proportion to the thickness, are far less confined in their intonation than are European instruments, consequently they are capable of producing an infinity of delicate grace by modification of pitch that cannot be expressed in our notation.

the same scale, melody-type and notes; and, in fact, illustrates the character and style of that râga in every way.

How widely the characters of the various râgas differ can be told by a glance at the following short melodies, all of which show as much as possible the full murchanas of their respective râgas :—

Since the early days of Indian music the essential conditions under which the râgas were composed and performed have altered greatly. Formerly, we learn, the râgas in performance were divided into four parts or movements, called respectively the Sthâyi, (2) the Antâra, (3) the Sanchari, (4) the Abhoga. The precise meaning attached to these terms, when applied thus,[3] seems to have been lost in obscurity. At the present time, however, it matters little, for the modern theory teaches that in the performance of râga as a solo, two movements only are taken into consideration. These movements are known as the Alâpa and the Madhyamakâla, and answer approximately to the Adagio (perhaps rhapsody would convey a nearer meaning) and Scherzo of a sonata.

To convey in writing an adequate idea of what an alâpa consists is somewhat difficult; it is not exactly a song, the music not being set to any particular words; neither is it an air, for it is not confined in its rhythm. An alâpa may be said to be rather a kind of rhapsody, which abounds with grace and embellishments of all kinds, and is formed by an extension, according to the murchana, of the notes of the râga, in such a way that all the characteristics of

[3] For the modern interpretation of these terms, see page 86.

that râga are prominently shown, and scope is given to the performer's power of improvising.

The phrases vary in length, some being slow, with quick modulations succeeding, and others *vice versâ*, the beats upon the accompanying strings marking the time being given at the performer's fancy.

As a rule the voice is not employed in the performance of an alâpa; but if used at all it is either in unison with the instrument or else accompanied by a simple running accompaniment upon the open strings. Occasionally the voice is relieved by the instruments taking up the melody, varied with soft imitations in the same râga. In fact, so much is left to the taste and fancy of the musician, that it is impossible to lay down any definite rules for the constitution of an alâpa; hence, as may be imagined, in movements of this sort, there is a kind of wild charm which seems to carry with it a plaintive refrain that lingers on in the mind of the listener long after the music has ceased. Perhaps the only composer who appears to have caught the entire spirit of these peculiar improvisations is Chopin; though, as far as we know, his acquaintance with Oriental music must have been limited.

Following the alâpa is the madhyamakâla, or second movement. This, as has been said before, can be compared to the Scherzo of a sonata—the music being very lively and catchy, while the tempo is quick and regular throughout.

Like the alâpa, the madhyamakâla consists of an extension according to the proper rules of the râga; in fact, a development of thânas, explained elsewhere, reduced to a definite measure. The periods are usually shorter, and the rhythm regular throughout. The original subject is imitated and varied, as the performer's fancy may dictate, in the same râga. The whole construction of this movement is symmetrical.

The madhyamakâla consists usually of two parts, the second only differing from the first in that the tempo is more rapid.

In the performance of a râga there is usually a short pause between the two movements; also between the two parts of the madhyamakâla; but it is entirely optional to the player.

The methods by which the different notes are varied, or follow each other, are styled by the Sanskrit treatises "Gámakas," and are arranged as follows:—

1. Arohâna—ascending.
2. Avarohâna—descending.
3. Dhâlu—alternating with any given note.
4. Sphurita—repeated; ascending.
5. Kampitâ—trembling.

6. Ahatâ—slurred.
7. Prátya-ahatâ—repeated; descending.
8. Tripastyâ—the first and second notes thrice repeated, the third twice, thus: ∪∪∪ | ∪∪∪ | —∪ | or ∪∪∪ | ∪∪∪ | ∪∪ |
9. Andhóla—the two first notes and the fourth of short duration; the third long, thus: ∪∪—∪

Râgas are generally classified as follows:—

(i.) Sampúrna—in which all seven notes of the gamut are employed.
(ii.) Shârava—in which six notes only are employed.
(iii.) Oravâ—in which five notes only are employed.

These three classes are again sub-divided into three, viz:—

Suddha, or pure, which show the characteristic of one râga only.
Salanka, or mixed, showing the characteristics of two râgas.
Sankírna, or mixed, showing the characteristics of more than two râgas.

The six original râgas are the only instances of the Suddha class; but opinions differ so widely as to the present names of these six râgas, and as to how the modern râgas have assumed their present form, that it would be nearly impossible to make any classification. The nomenclature of all the râgas differs in various parts of India; and so many and subtle are the distinctions between the different râgas, each of which has a character of its own, exclusive, if a mixed râga, of that of the râgas from which it may be derived, that to give more than a few examples would be an almost endless, if not impossible, task.

Râgas in the following scales seem to be the most popular[4]:—

Máyamâlavagaula	Hârikambógi	Kâmavârdini
Nâta-Bhairavi	Déhra-S'ankârabhárna	Mátsyakaliâni
Kârahâraprya	Chalanâta	Jâlavarâli
Hanumatódi		

Some râgas are commonly supposed to create particular passions. Those more usually met with are the following:—

Bhupâli—beauty	Nâta—valour
Mángari—kindness	Mâlava—fear
Bhairavi—anger	S'ri—grandeur

Bhángala—wonder

Râgas derived from any of the above are said to possess the same inherent qualities.

[4] It may be interesting to notice that the Greek chromatic genus is represented by the scale Máyamâlavagaula, and the Greek diatonic modes thus: Dorian, Hanumatódi; Phrygian, Kârahâraprya; Lydian, Déhra-S'ankârabhárna; Hypolydian, Mátsyakaliâni; Ionic, Hârikambógi; and Æolic, Nâta-Bhairavi.

The following râgas resemble each other so closely that they are very difficult to distinguish apart, and are frequently used as tests of skill by musicians of repute :—

Móhanna and Régupti	Durbar and Nayuki
Lálita and Vasantha	Bilahâri and Déshackshi
Bhaúli and Bhupâli	Pántovarâli and Kârmavirdini
Tôdi and Deshyatôdi	Purvi-Kaliâni and Gamanâsrama
Ârabi and Dévagândâri	Sâranga and Bhúpa-Kaliâni
Mângi and Huséni	Mohanna-Kaliâni and Kaliâni-Késeri

In the performance of certain râgas it is usual to employ accidentals in place of some of the notes shown in the text. The reason for this is not evident, but it seems to be an almost universal custom among Hindu musicians. This might be accounted for as being in imitation of Northern Indian music, in which a pure râga is seldom played, but usually a melody composed of three or four râgas. It seems far more likely, however, that the use of accidentals has been employed from the undeniable beauty that they add to a melody, much as when a change of keys is made in modulation. Examples of melodies in mixed râgas will be found upon pages 88, 89.

The most important of these râgas are the following :—

Râga.	Mode.	Note marked.	Note played.
Kómbodi	Hârikambógi	Kaisika Ni, B♭ ...	Kakeli Ni, B♮
Biâg	,, ...	Suddha Ma, F♮ ...	Prati Ma, F♯
Athâna...	,, ...	Sadharama Ga, E♮	Antara Ga, D♯
Nâtakurângi ...	,, ...	———	Pa, G♮
Bhairavi	Nâta-Bhairavi	Suddha Dha, A♭..	Chatusruti Dha, A♮
Anánda-Bhairavi..	,, ...	Kaisika Ni, A♭ ...	Kakeli Ni, B♮
Tódi	Hanumatódi	Anta Ga, D♯ ...	Suddha Ga, D♮
Kâfi	Kârahâraprya	Kaisika Ni, B♭ ...	Kakeli Ni, B♮
Biâgada	Dèhra-S'ankârabharna	Kakeli Ni, B♮ ...	Kaisika Ni, A♯
Bilahâri	Mâtsya-Kaliâni ...	Kakeli Ni, B♮ ...	,, ,,
Severi	Máyamâlavagaula ...	Antara Ga, E ... Kakeli Ni, B ...	Sadharama Ga, D♯ Kaisika Ni, A♯
Anánda-Bhairavi..	Nâta-Bhairavi	Suddha Dha, A♭... Sadharama Ga, E♭	Chatusruti Dha, A♮ Antara Ga, E♮ [5]
Khamas	Hârikambógi	Kaisika Ni, B♭ ...	Kakeli Ni, B
Kedara Gaula ...	,, ...	,, ,, ...	,, ,,
Surati	,, ...	,, ,, ...	,, ,,
Janjuti	,, ...	Antara Ga, E ...	Sadharama Ga, D♯

[5] The Anánda-Bhairavi of this kind is very popular in Travancore and the adjacent parts.

In the extension of some râgas a note, either above or below a particular note of the text, may be employed, although itself not an essential part of the râga. If this is done the performer will invariably take the preceding note of the text *again* before he plays that following. For example, the text may show "dha sa" (*i.e.*, "ni" omitted). If "ni" is employed, "dha" is repeated immediately before "sa," as "dha, ni, dha, sa," and not "dha, ni, sa."

The foregoing are some of the more important of the many rules attached to the performance of râgas, and only by the strict observance of them can a piece be correctly executed.

It is perhaps needless to add that in so intricate and scientific a system justice is seldom done except at the hands of very skilful musicians, and they are but rarely met with.

In all the Sanskrit treatises a system seems to have been laid down by which the different râgas are apportioned to certain seasons of the year and hours of the day.

In modern times this system, as far as the hour of the day is concerned, is still carried out, and no musician, unless specially ordered, will sing any râga out of the proper time of day apportioned for it. The reason given for this is, according to Willard, that musicians declare that the times and seasons allotted to each are those at which the divinities are at leisure to attend at the place where their favourite tune is sung, and to inspire the performer with due warmth in his execution. Superstition seems to have given birth to this absurd custom, and it still exercises a strong hold upon all professional musicians, principally from the fact that it has been handed down from time immemorial; therefore it would be considered improper to make any change. Even in educated circles among Hindus it would be thought a display of ignorance to call for a particular râga, unless for some special reason, at an improper season.

The modern custom which lays down this hard and fast law seems to differ widely from that of all the ancient authorities, the names of the râgas now apportioned to the different periods of the day being quite at variance with the directions contained in the Sanskrit; indeed, the writer of each treatise seems to have had a classification of his own distinct from that of other authorities. At the present time musicians divide the twenty-four hours of the day into four periods, each of which is sub-divided into two parts. The following table shows at a glance the hours appointed for the performance of the popular râgas according to the Karnâtik system :—

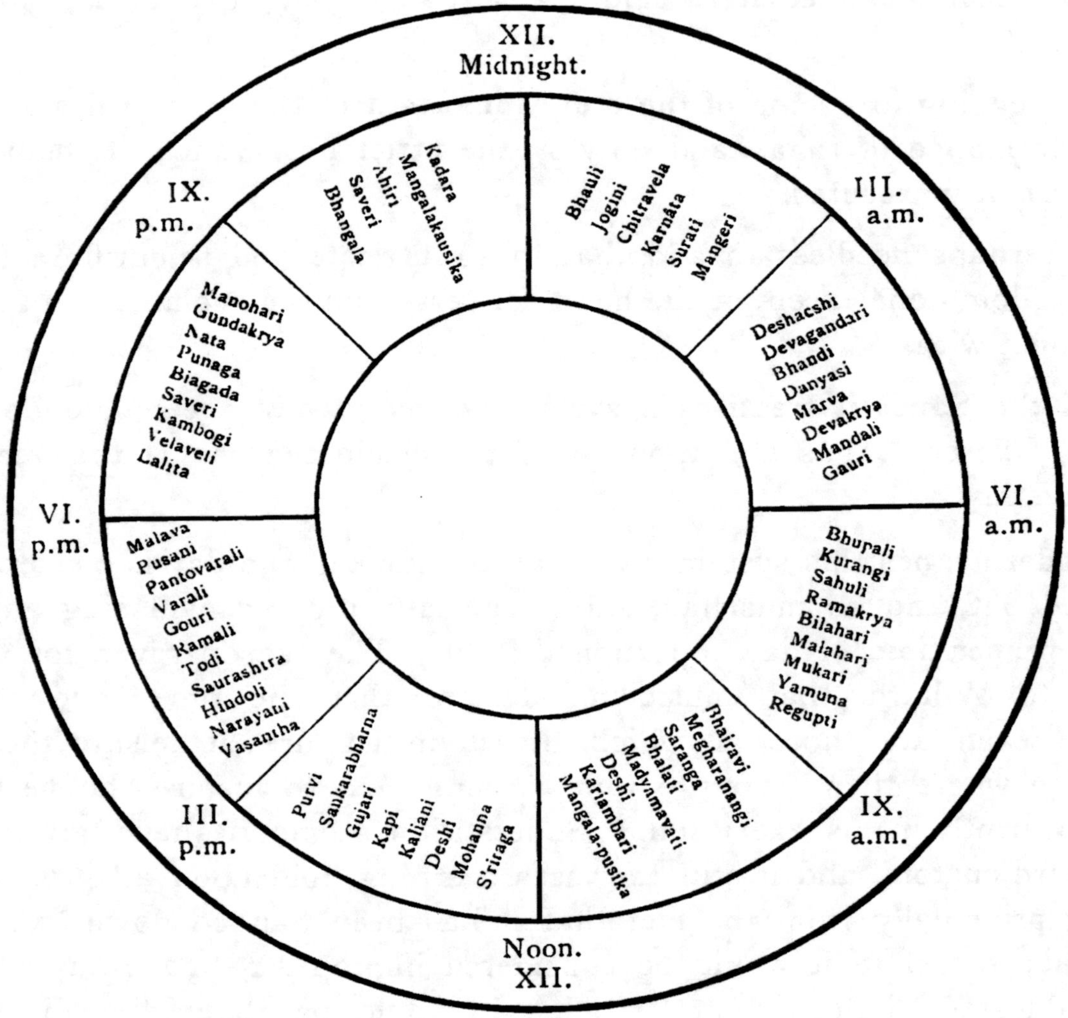

In Northern India, and among Hindustani musicians, a different time classification of the râgas is in use.

The following is a list of all the râgas used in Southern Indian music, together with their modes and text, arranged precisely as in a native musician's Kattika or scale book. Notes that are specially emphasised or continually dwelt upon are underlined :—

SCALE OF MÁYAMÂLAVAGAULA.

Name of Râga.	Ascending Mode.	Descending Mode.
Matsya-Bhauli	C D♭ E G A♭ B C	C B A♭ G F E D♭ C
Malahâri	C D♭ F G A♭ C	C A♭ G F E D♭ C
Bhauli	C D♭ E G A♭ C	C B A♭ G E D♭ C
Sindutha-Rangini	C D♭ E F A♭ B C	C B G A♭ F E D♭ C
Karnâtika-Sarânga	C D♭ E F E G B A♭ F G A♭ B C	C A♭ F G F E D♭ C
Gauri	C D♭ F G B C	C B A♭ G F E D♭ C
Sâranga-Nâta	C D♭ F G A♭ C	C B A♭ G F D♭ F E D♭ C
Mégha-Rangini	C D♭ F G A♭ B C	C A♭ G F E D♭ C
Purvi †	C D♭ E F G A♭ B G C	C B A♭ G F E D♭ C
Kóhkila-vírdani	C F E G A♭ B C	C B A♭ F E D♭ C
Nebo-Rángini	C D♭ E D♭ F G A♭ B C	C B A♭ F E C
Gaula	C D♭ F G B C	C B G F E F D♭ E F D♭ C
Mâruva †	C D♭ F G B C	C B A♭ G F E F D♭ C
Sudda-krýa	C D♭ F G A♭ G B C	C B A♭ G F D♭ E F D♭ C
Jagan-móhini	C E F G B C	C B G F E D♭ C
Gaujari	C D♭ E F G A♭ C	C A♭ G F E D♭ C
Síndhu-râmakrýa	C D♭ F G A♭ B A♭ C	C B G F D♭ E D♭ C
Gúndakrýa †	C D♭ E D♭ F G B A♭ B C	C B A♭ G F E D♭ E C
Phírju	C F G A♭ F E D♭ E D♭ E F G A♭ B C	C B A♭ G F E D♭ C
Râmakrýa	C D♭ E F G F A♭ B C	C B A♭ G F E F C
Purna-sadyamâ	C D♭ E F G A♭	G F E D♭ C B A♭ B C
Sârasa-mángala	C E F B A♭ C	C A♭ G F E D♭ C
Râma-Lalíta	C D♭ E F G B G C	C B A♭ F G F E C
Lalíta	C F E A♭ B C	C B A♭ F E D♭ C
Bibâsu	C D♭ E G A♭ C	C A♭ G E D♭ C
Gaulipantu †	C D♭ F G B C	C B A♭ G F A♭ F E D♭ C
Vasántha	C E F A♭ B C	C B A♭ F E D♭ C
Severi	C D♭ F G A♭ C	C B A♭ G F E D♭ C
Bulângi	C E D♭ E F G A♭ G C	C B A♭ G F E D♭ C
Bógi	C D♭ F G A♭ C	C A♭ B A♭ G F D♭ F E D♭ C
Nâda-nâmakrýa	C D♭ F E F G A♭ C	C B A♭ G F E D♭ C
Désya-gaula	C D♭ C G A♭ B C	C B A♭ G D♭ C

SCALE OF NÂTA-BHAIRAVI.

Name of Râga.	Ascending Mode.	Descending Mode.
Sudda-Deshi	C D F G A♭ B♭ C	C B♭ A♭ G F E♭ D C
Bhairavi	C E♭ D E♭ F G A♭ B♭ C	C B♭ A♭ F G F E♭ D C
Riti-gaula	C E♭ D E♭ F B♭ A♭ B♭ C	C B♭ A♭ F E♭ F G F E♭ D C
Anánda-Bhairavi †	C E♭ D E♭ F G C	C B♭ A♭ G F E♭ D C
Nâta-Mangala	C E♭ E♭ F G A♭ B♭ C	C B♭ A♭ G F D E♭ D C
Súddha-Danyâshi	C E♭ F G B♭ C	C B♭ G F E♭ C
Hindóla-Vasánthan	C D F G A♭ B♭ A♭ C	C B♭ A♭ G F A♭ F E♭ D C
Amruta-vâhini	C E♭ F G A♭ B♭ C	C B♭ A♭ F E♭ D C
Jankâravani	C D D E♭ F G B♭ C	C B♭ A♭ G F D C
Abheri	C E♭ D E♭ F B♭ C	C B♭ A♭ G F E♭ D C
Abhógi	C D E♭ F A♭ C	C A♭ F E♭ D C
Kânaka-Vasántha	C D F G B♭ C	C B♭ G F E♭ D F E♭ C
Karyâmati	C D E♭ G A♭ C	C B♭ A♭ G A♭ F E♭ D C
Yoga-Bhairavi	C D E♭ F G A♭ C	C B♭ A♭ G D C
Adi-Bhairavi	C E♭ D E♭ F G A♭ C	C A♭ G F G E♭ D C
Mangi	C D E♭ F G B♭ A♭ B♭ G A♭ B♭ C	C B♭ A♭ G F E♭ F G E♭ D C
Chalana-Varâli	C D E♭ F A♭ B♭ A♭ C	C B♭ A♭ F E♭ D C

NOTE.—Râgas marked † have two readings, the other readings are given at the end of this chapter.

Name of Râga.	Ascending Mode.	Descending Mode.
	SCALE OF NÂTA-BHAIRAVI—*continued.*	
Nava-Manohari	C D F A♭ B♭ C	C B♭ G F D C
Vasantha-Varâli	C E♭ F G A♭ B♭	C A♭ G E♭ D C
Woodya-chandrika †	C D E♭ F G A♭ B♭ C	C A♭ G F D C
Kanara-gaula	C E♭ D E♭ F G A♭ B♭ C	C B♭ A♭ G F E♭ D C
Mâra-Rangini	C D E♭ F G A♭ B♭ C	C A♭ G E♭ D C
Rudraganthara	C D E♭ D F G F A♭ B♭ G C	C B♭ A♭ F E♭ C
Mukâri	C D F G B♭ A♭ C	C B♭ A♭ G F E♭ D C
Hamakrya	C D E♭ F G A♭ B♭ C	C A♭ G F D E♭ F D C
Chandrika-Bhairavi	C E♭ D E♭ F A♭ B♭ C	C B♭ A♭ F E♭ D C
	SCALE OF HANUMATÓDI.	
Nâga-Varâli	C B♭ C♭ D♭ F G A♭	G F E♭ D♭ C B♭ C
Punaga-Tódi	B♭ A♭ B♭ C D♭ E♭ F G A♭ B♭	A♭ G F E♭ D♭ C B♭ A♭ B♭ C
Danyâs'i	C E♭ F G B♭ C	C B♭ A♭ G F E♭ D♭ C
Tódi	C D♭ E♭ F A♭ B♭ C	C B♭ A♭ F E♭ D♭ C
Des'ya-Tódi	C D♭ E♭ F G A♭ B♭ C	C B♭ A♭ B♭ A♭ G F E♭ D♭ C
Ghambhira-Vasantha	C F E♭ F D♭ E♭ F G B♭ A♭ B♭ G C	C A♭ G F D♭ C
Hima-virdini	C D♭ F G B♭ C	C B♭ A♭ G F A♭ F E♭ D♭ C
Suddha-samantha	C D♭ E♭ F G B♭ A♭ C	C A♭ B♭ G A♭ F E♭ D♭ C
Shadola-rava	C D♭ F G A♭ C	C B♭ A♭ B♭ G F E♭ D♭ C
	SCALE OF CHACRAVAKA.	
Vaga-vahini	C D♭ E F G A B♭ A C	C B♭ A G F E D♭ C
Kalavati	C D♭ E F G A B♭ G C	C B♭ A B♭ G F E D♭ C
Bhalati	C D♭ E F G A B♭ C	C B♭ G F D♭ E
Rudra-Panchama	C E F B♭ A C	C B♭ A F E D♭ C
Vasantha-lila	C D♭ F G A B♭ C	C B♭ A G E D♭ C
Bhujangha	C D♭ C F E F B♭ A B♭ C	C B♭ A F E D♭ C
	SCALE OF SÚRYAKÁNTA.	
Saurâshtra	C D♭ F E F G A B C	C A G F E C
Ahiri †	C F E F G A B C	C B A G F E D♭ C
Sâhuli	C E F G B C	C B A G E D♭ C
Síndhu	C E D♭ F G A B C	C A G F E D♭ E C
Râgamâlini	C D♭ E F G A C	C A D♭ A G F E F D♭ C
Suddha-gandirvi	C D♭ E F G A B C	C A G F D♭ C
	SCALE OF KÂRAHÂRAPRÝA.	
Manirángu	C D F G B♭ C	C B♭ G F E♭ D C
S'irâga	C D F G B♭ C	C B♭ G A B♭ G F D E♭ D C
Madyamâvati	C D F G B♭ C	C B♭ G F D C
Sindhu-Danyâsi	C D E♭ F G B♭ A C	C B♭ A G F E♭ D C
Thâno-Vasantha	C E♭ F G B♭ C	C B♭ A G F E♭ D C
Karnâka-Varâli	C D F G B♭ C	C B♭ A B♭ G F E♭ D C
Panchama	C D A G B♭ C	C B♭ A G F E♭ D C

NOTE.—Râgas marked † have two readings, the other readings are given at the end of this chapter.

SCALE OF KÂRAHÂRAPRÝA—*continued.*

Name of Râga.	Ascending Mode.	Descending Mode.
Deva-krýa	C E♭ D E♭ F G A B♭ A C	C B♭ A G F E♭ D C
Syindavi	B♭ A B♭ C D E♭ F G A B♭	B♭ A G F E♭ D C B♭ A B♭ C
Manohâri	C E♭ D E♭ F G A C	C A G F E♭ D E♭ C
Suddha-Bhangala	C D F G A C	C B♭ A G F E♭ D C
Suddha-Bhairavi	C E♭ D F G B♭ A B♭ C	C B♭ A G F D E♭ F D C
Kâpi †	C D E♭ F G A B♭ C	C A G F D E♭ F D C
Palâ-Mangeri †	C E♭ F A C	C B♭ A G F E♭ D C
Jey-Manohari	C D E♭ F A C	C B♭ G F E♭ D C
Nayuki	C D F G A B♭ G C	C B♭ A G F E♭ D C
Vasâni	C D E♭ F G B♭ A B♭ C	C B♭ A F G F E♭ D C
Mangeri	C D E♭ F G B♭ C	C B♭ A F E♭ D C
Nâdatha-Rangini	C D F G A G B♭ C	C A B♭ G A F E♭ D E♭ C
Bhoga-Kanara	C D E♭ F A B♭ C	C B♭ A F E♭ D C
Brundavâna-Saranga	C D F G B♭ C	C B♭ G F D E♭ F D C
Aruna-chandrika	C E♭ F G B♭ C	C B♭ G A G F E♭ C
Deva-Mukâri	C D E♭ F G A B♭ C	C B♭ A F G F D E♭ F D C
Sama-Mukâri	C D E♭ F G A B♭ C	C A B♭ A F G F E♭ C
Suddhanapâla	C D E♭ F G A C	C B♭ A F E♭ D E♭ C
Durbar †	C D F G A B♭ C	C B♭ A G F G A G E♭ D C
S'arnga Râma	C D F A B♭ G C	C B♭ A E♭ D C
Deva-Manohari	C D F G B♭ A B♭ C	C B♭ A G F E♭ D C

SCALE OF HÂRIKAMBÓGI.

Name of Râga.	Ascending Mode.	Descending Mode.
Kambógi †	C D E F G A C	C B♭ A G F E D C
Kathara-gaula	C D F G B♭ C	C B♭ A G F E D C
Narayani	C D F G A C	C B♭ A G F D C
Purna-Kambógi	C D E F G B♭ C	C A G F E D C
Narayana-gaula	C D F G B♭ A B♭ C	C B♭ A G F E D C
Chaiatha-Rangini	C D E D E F G A B♭ A B♭ C	C B♭ A B♭ F E F D E D C
Balahámsa	C D F G A C	C B♭ A G F D F E C
Prathapa-Varâli	C D F G A B♭ A G A B♭ C	C B♭ A G F E D C
Mathâ-kohkila †	C D G A B♭ C	C A B♭ A G D C
Kohkila-dvâni	C D E F A B♭ A C	C B♭ A B♭ G F E D E F E D C
Sarasvati	C D E F G B♭ A B♭ C	C B♭ G A F G D E C
Sarasvati-Manohari	C D E F A C	C B♭ A B♭ G F E D C
Navarasa-Kanara	C E F G A G C	C B♭ A F E D C
Bhángala	C D E F G C	C B♭ A G F D E D C
Ravi-chandrika	C D E F A B♭ A C	C B♭ A F E D C
Janjúti †	C B♭ A C D E F G A B♭	A G F E D C B♭ A G A C
Kánthala-Varâli	C F G A B♭ A C	C B♭ A G F C
Yedukúla-Kambógi †	C D F G A C	C B♭ A G F E D C
Mohànna	C D E G A C	C A G D E G D C
Súrati	C D F G B♭ C	C B♭ A G F E G F D C
Mâlava	C D E F G B♭ F A B♭ C	C B♭ A B♭ G F E F D C
Nâta-Kurangi	C D E F A B♭ G A B♭ C	C B♭ A F E C
Athâna	C D F G A B♭ C	C B♭ A G F G E D C
Kamâchi	C F E F G A B♭ C	C B♭ A G F E F C
Drijaranti	C D E F G F A G B♭ A B♭ C	C A G A B♭ A G F E F E D C

NOTE.—Râgas marked † have two readings, the other readings are given at the end of this chapter.

SCALE OF HÂRIKAMBÓGI—*continued.*

Name of Râga.	Ascending Mode.	Descending Mode.
Biâg †	C D E F C E F G B♭ A B♭ G A B♭ C	C B♭ G A B♭ A G F E D E F E C
Nâgasvarâvali	C E F G A C	C A G F E C
Sâra-vilambi	C E F G B♭ C	C B♭ A G F E D C
Jeyarama	C D E F G A B♭ C	C B♭ A G F E C
Súrabi-prýa	C D E G B♭ C	C B♭ A G F E D C
Kâlabhárna	C D E F G A B♭ C	C A G E D C
Megha-jeyánti	C D F E G A B♭ C	C G F E D C
S'rangi	C D F G A B♭ C	C G F E D C
Jelashéykera	C D E F G B♭ A B♭ C	C A G F D E D C
Siva-Kambógi	C D E F B♭ C	C B♭ G F E D C
Ratna-joti	C E F G B♭ C	C B♭ A E D C
Jogi-Bhairavi	C D E F G A B♭ C	C B♭ A G F B♭ A F E D F E C
Nilâmberi †	C D E F C A F G B♭ C	C B♭ G A B♭ G F E F D E D F E C
Régupti	C D E G A C	C A G E D C
Deva-Rangini	C D E G A C	C A G F E D C
Arunakantha	C D F G F A B♭ C	C B♭ A G F A F E D C
Ben-Kambógi	C F E D C F G A B♭ C	C B♭ G B♭ F E D C

SCALE OF DÉHRA-S'ANKÂRABHARNA.

Name of Râga.	Ascending Mode.	Descending Mode.
Hari-Nâta	C F E F G A B C	C B G A B G F E C
Kanara	C E F A B C	C A G F E F D C
Kânada	C D E F G F A B C	C B A B G F G E D C
Biâgada	C E D E F G A G C	C B A G F E D C
Jenkarâm	C D E F A D C	C B A F E D C
Suddha-Sâranga	C D E F G A B A C	C A G F D E D C
Vivardini	C F G C	C B A G F E D C
Vedangini	C E F G F A B C	C B A G A F E D C
Navarâju	G A B C D E F G	F E D C B A C
Gaja-virdinam	C E F A B C	C A G F E D C
Kadâram	C F E F G B C	C B G F E D C
Mahóri	C F E F D E F G A B C	C A G F D E F C
Jana-Rangini	C D E F G A G B C	C A G F D C
Kolahallam	C D E F G B A B C	C B G A F E D C
Deshachsi	C D F G A B C	C B A G F E D C
Purnódiam	C D F G A C	C B G F D E D C
Bhinnavikrama	C D E F G A C	C B A G D C
Suddha-Sâveri	C D F G A C	C A G F D C
Purna-chándrika	C D E F G F A B C	C B G A G F E F D C
Gauda-malâri	C D E F G E F G A B C	C B A G F E D C
Parti-rava	C F E F G A B C	C B A G F E F E D C
Arabi	C D F G A C	C B A G F E D C
Puruhútika	C F G A B C	C B A G F C
Nâgadvâni	C E D E F E F G A B A G B A B G A B C	C B A B A G F A G F D E F E D E C
Garudadvâni	C D E F G A B C	C A G E D C
Hamsadvâni	C D E G B C	C B G E D C
Girvana-prýa	C B E F A C	C B A F E D C
S'ankârabharna	C D E F G A B C	C A G F E D C
Kurangi	C B C E D E F G A	G F E D C B C
Kandadruma	C E F A F B C	C B F E D C

NOTE.—Râgas marked † have two readings, the other readings are given at the end of this chapter.

SCALE OF DÉHRA-S'ANKÂRABHARNA—*continued.*		
Name of Râga.	**Ascending Mode.**	**Descending Mode.**
S'ahanna †	C D E F G F A B C	C B A G F E F E D C
Jogi-Vasantha	C D E F G A B C	A B A G F E D C
Druthavirdana	C D E F G A C	C B A G F D E D C
Gamanabhaskera	C D E F G A G B C	C A G F E C
Bilahâri	C D E G A C	C B A G F E D C
Sâmbhu-krýa	C E D F G B F E D F G B C	C B G B F E D C
Girganâmbheri	C D E F G A B C	C B A G F D C
Viraprātâpa	C E F G A B	C B A G F E D C
SCALE OF CHALANÂTA.		
Woodya-ravi-chandrika	C D♯ E F A♯ B C	C B A♯ F E D♯ C
Ghambhirya-Nâta	C E F G B C	C B G F E C
Nâta	C D♯ E F G A♯ B G B C	C B G F D♯ C
Suddha-Nâta	C E F G B A♯ B C	C B A♯ G F D♯ C
Mâravasimánta	C F E F G A♯ G C	C B A♯ G F E D♯ C
SCALE OF KÂNAKÂNGI.		
Kâmakâmbheri	C D♭ E♭♭ F G A♭ C	C B♭♭ A♭ G F E♭♭ D♭ C
Suddha-Mukâri	C E♭♭ D♭ E♭♭ F G B♭♭ A♭ C	C B♭♭ A♭ F E♭♭ D♭ C
SCALE OF RHATNÂNGI.		
Ghantârava	C B♭ C E♭♭ D♭ E♭♭ F G B♭ C	C B♭ A♭ G F E♭♭ D♭ C
Asâveri †	C D♭ F G A♭ C	C B♭ A♭ G F E♭♭ D♭ C
Pénaduti	C D♭ F G A♭ B♭ C	C B♭ A♭ F E♭♭ D♭ C
Sâvakala-Mángeri	C D♭ E♭♭ G A♭ B♭ C	C B♭ A♭ F E♭♭ D♭ C
SCALE OF VÂNASPATI.		
Bhânumati	C D♭ E♭♭ D♭ F G C	C A G F E♭♭ D♭ C
Rasâvali	C D♭ E♭♭ F A B♭ C	C B♭ A G F E♭♭ D♭ C
SCALE OF SANÂPATI.		
Bhógi-chintâmani	C D♭ F G A♭ C	C B♭♭ A♭ G F E♭ D♭ C
Bhógi	C E♭ F G A♭ G A♭ B♭♭ C	C B♭♭ A♭ G F A♭ G F E♭ D♭ C
Mâlini	C D♭ E♭ F G C	C B♭♭ A♭ F E♭ D♭ C
SCALE OF NÂTAKAPRÝA.		
S'oka-Varâli †	C D♭ F E♭ F G F A D C F G A B♭ A C	C B♭ A F E♭ D♭ C
Mâgada-S'rirâga	C D♭ E♭ F G A C	C B♭ G E♭ C

Note—Râgas marked † have two readings, the other readings are given at the end of this chapter.

Name of Râga.	Ascending Mode.	Descending Mode.
SCALE OF KOHKILAPRÝA.		
Kóhkila-râva	C D♭ E♭ F G A C	C B A G F E♭ D♭ C
Rátnamani	C D♭ E♭ F G A B C	C B A G E♭ D♭ C
Chítramani	C D♭ F G A B C	C B A G F E♭ D♭ C
SCALE OF GAIAKAPRÝA.		
Kalakanti	C D♭ E F G B♭♭ A♭ B♭♭ C	C B♭♭ A♭ F E D♭ C
Kalgarda	C D♭ F E D♭ E F G A♭ B♭♭ C	C B♭♭ G A♭ B♭♭ A♭ G F E D♭ C
SCALE OF VAKULABHÁRNA.		
Vasántha-Mukâri	C E D♭ E F G B♭ A♭ B♭ C	C B♭ A♭ G F D♭ C
Kâmala-Mánohâri	C E F G B♭ C	C B♭ A♭ G F E C
SCALE OF KYRAVÂNI.		
Kiranavâli	C D F G A♭ B C	C B A♭ G F E♭ D C
Sangivani	C E♭ D E♭ F G A♭ B C	C B A♭ G F E♭ D C
Kaliâna-Vasantha	C F E♭ F G A♭ B C	C B A♭ G F E♭ D C
Mâdavi †	C D E♭ F A♭ B A♭ F G A♭ B C	C B G E♭ D C
Sârasa-vâhini	C D E♭ D F G A♭ B C	C A♭ G F E♭ D C
Népâla	C D F E♭ F G B C	C B A♭ G F D C
SCALE OF SARASÁNGI.		
Sarasânana	C D E F A♭ B C	C B A♭ F E D C
Râma-Mánohâri	C E F G B C	C B A♭ G F E C
Bhogalila	C D E G A♭ B C	C B A♭ F E D C
SCALE OF YAGAPRÝA.		
Kalahámsa	C D♯ E F G A♭ C	C B♭♭ A♭ G F E D♯ C
SCALE OF GANGAIABHUSÂNI.		
Anándalila	C D♯ E F G B C	C B A♭ G F E D♯ C
SCALE OF SHOLINI.		
Trishuli	C E F G B C	C B A G F D♯ C
SCALE OF JALAVARÂLI.		
Kohkila-Panchami	C D♭ E♭♭ G A♭ B C	C B A♭ G F♯ E♭♭ D♭ C
Kusuma-Rangini	C D♭ F♯ G A♭ B C	C B A♭ B G F♯ E♭♭ D♭ C
Varâli	C E♭♭ D♭ E♭♭ F♯ G A♭ B C	C B A♭ G F♯ E♭♭ D♭ C
Bhopala-Panchami	C E♭♭ D♭ E♭♭ G F♯ A♭ C	C G A♭ F♯ E♭♭ D♭ C
Vijaya-kohkila	C D♭ E♭♭ F♯ G A♭ C	C B A♭ G F♯ E♭♭ D♭ C

NOTE.—Râgas marked † have two readings, the other readings are given at the end of this chapter.

Name of Râga.	Ascending Mode.	Descending Mode.
SCALE OF NÂVANITA.		
Nabōmani	C D♭ E♭♭ D♭ F♯ G C	C B♭ A G F♯ E♭♭ D♭ C
Deviamani	C D♭ E♭♭ F♯ G A G B♭ C	C B♭ A G F♯ E♭♭ D♭ C
SCALE OF PAVÂNI.		
Chandrajotì	C D♭ E♭♭ F♯ G A G B C	C B G A G F♯ E♭♭ D♭ C
SCALE OF REGONPRÝA.		
Ghandarva	G A♯ B G D♭ E♭♭ D♭ C B G	F♯ G A♯ B C B G
Ghomatti	B C D♭ E♭♭ F♯ G A♯ B	G F♯ E♭♭ D♭ C B C
SCALE OF BHAVAPRÝA.		
Kalamurti	C E♭ D♭ E♭ F♯ G C	C B♭ A♭ G F♯ E♭ D♭ C
SCALE OF SÁBHAPÁNTOVARÂLI.		
Panto-Varâli	C D♭ E♭ F♯ G A♭ B C	C B A♭ G F♯ A♭ F♯ E♭ D♭ C
Rudra-mangeri	C D♭ E♭ G B A♭ C	C B A♭ G F♯ E♭ D♭ C
Bhaulamuki	C D♭ E♭ F♯ G B C	C B A♭ G F♯ E♭ D♭ C
Saddaks'eri	C E♭ D♭ E♭ F♯ G A♭ B C	C B A♭ F♯ E♭ D♭ C
Deviakánthala	C D♭ E♭ F♯ G A♭ C	C B A♭ G F♯ E♭ D♭ C
Kâmarángini	C D♭ E♭ D♭ F♯ G A♭ B C	C B A♭ F♯ E♭ D♭ E♭ C
Govirdani	E♭ D♭ E♭ G A♭ C	C B A♭ B F♯ E♭ D♭ C
Nâga-Panchami	C E♭ F♯ G B C	C B A♭ G F♯ E♭ D♭ C
Gârudavírdani	C D♭ E♭ F♯ B A♭ F♯ G A♭ B C	C B G F♯ D♭ C
Latâmati	C D♭ E♭ G F♯ G A♭ G C	C B A♭ G F♯ A♭ F♯ E♭ D♭ C
SCALE OF SUVARANÁNGI.		
Rati	C E♭ D♭ E♭ F♯ G A B C	C B A G F♯ E♭ D♭ C
Vrushabhâ-vâhini	C D♭ F♯ G A B C	C B A F♯ E♭ D♭ C
Mamáchsheri	C D♭ E♭ F♯ G B C	C B A G F♯ E♭ F♯ D♭ C
Ratnâmati	C E♭ F♯ G F♯ A B C	C A G F♯ G E♭ D♭ C
SCALE OF KÂMAVÍRDANI.		
Râmakrýa	C D♭ E F♯ G A♭ B C	C B A♭ G F♯ D♭ F♯ E D♭ C
Dîpaka	C E F♯ G A♭ G C	C B A♭ B C E G F♯ E D♭ C
Dévagiri †	C D♭ F♯ G A♭ C	C B A♭ G F♯ E D♭ C
Vilâmbini	C F♯ E F♯ G B A♭ B C	C B A♭ B G F♯ E C
Rudragandâri	C D♭ E F♯ B C	C B G F♯ D♭ C
Vipramandâra	C D♭ F♯ G A♭ B C	C A♭ G F♯ E D♭ C
Svatâmbodi	C D♭ E F♯ G C	C B A♭ G F♯ E D♭ C
Pankâruham	C F♯ E F♯ G B A♭ B C	C B G F♯ E D♭ C
Viâgranándanam	C D♭ E G A♭ C	C B A♭ B A♭ G F♯ E D♭ C
Manmatâlata	C B C D♭ E F♯ G A♭ B C	C A♭ G F♯ E D♭ C B C
Pushpalalita	C E F♯ A♭ B C	C A♭ G F♯ D♭ C
Kúmudaprâbhâ	C D♭ E A♭ B C	C G F♯ E B C

NOTE.—Râgas marked † have two readings, the other readings are given at the end of this chapter.

SCALE OF GÂMANÂS'RYA.

Name of Râga.	Ascending Mode.	Descending Mode.
Gamakakrŷa	C D♭ E F♯ G B C	C B G F♯ E D♭ C
Purvi-Kaliâni	C D♭ E F♯ G A B G A B G C	C B A G F♯ E D♭ C
Partiravam	C D♭ E F♯ G A B C	C B A B G A G F♯ E F♯ E D♭ F♯ C
Jeya-Mohanna †	C E F♯ G A C	C B A G F♯ E D♭ C
S'ri-Lalita	C D♭ E D♭ F♯ G B A G C	C B A G F♯ E D♭ C
Darpa-Mangeri	C E D♭ E F♯ G B C	C B A G F♯ E C
Maivra-Vasantha	C D♭ E F♯ G A B C	C B G A B A G F♯ D♭ F♯ E D♭ E C

SCALE OF S'RIMHANDRA.

Name of Râga.	Ascending Mode.	Descending Mode.
Siâmala	C E♭ D E♭ F♯ G A♭ B A♭ C	C B A♭ G F♯ E♭ C D
Simanthini	C D E♭ F♯ G A♭ B C	C G F♯ E♭ D C D C
Madhava-Manohari	C E♭ D E♭ F♯ G B A♭ B C	C B A♭ F♯ E♭ F♯ E♭ D C
Suddha-râga †	C D E♭ F♯ G B C	C B G F♯ E♭ C
Mâra-jeyantham	C D F♯ G A♭ B C	C B A♭ G F♯ E♭ D C

SCALE OF HÉMOVASÁNTHA.

Name of Râga.	Ascending Mode.	Descending Mode.
Sinhâravam	C D F♯ G B♭ C	C B♭ G F♯ D E♭ D C
Chandrârekha	C D E♭ F♯ G A C	C B♭ A F♯ E♭ D C
Sankâravam	C E♭ D E♭ F♯ G A B♭ C	C B♭ G F♯ E♭ D C
Yeshâprŷa	C D F♯ G B♭ C	C B♭ A G F♯ E♭ D C
Sinhâdvâni	C D C E♭ F♯ G A B♭ C	C B♭ A G F♯ E♭ C
Chackōradvâni	C D E♭ F♯ G A B♭ C	C B♭ F♯ E♭ D C

SCALE OF DHURMOVATI.

Name of Râga.	Ascending Mode.	Descending Mode.
Rángini	C D E♭ F♯ A C	C B A F♯ E♭ C D C
Dúmyarâga	C D E♭ F♯ G A C	C B A G F♯ E♭ D C
Arunajualita	C D E♭ F♯ A B C	C B A G F♯ E♭ D C

SCALE OF NETTIMATTI.

Name of Râga.	Ascending Mode.	Descending Mode.
Hamsanâda	C D F♯ G A♯ B C	C B A♯ B G F♯ D C
Gaurikrŷa	C E♭ F♯ G A♯ B C	C B A♯ B G F♯ E♭ C

SCALE OF VÁCHASPATI.

Name of Râga.	Ascending Mode.	Descending Mode.
Bhus'âvali	C D E F♯ G A C	C B♭ A G F♯ E D C
Barbara	C E F♯ D E F♯ A B♭ A C	C B♭ A F♯ E D C
Sarasvâti	C E F♯ G A C	C B♭ A G F♯ D C
Vutâri	C E F♯ G A B♭ C	C B♭ A F♯ E C
Sunya-madhyama	C D F♯ G B♭ A C	C B♭ A G F♯ E D C

NOTE.—Râgas marked † have two readings, the other readings are given at the end of this chapter.

SCALE OF MATSYA-KALIÂNI.		
Name of Râga.	**Ascending Mode.**	**Descending Mode.**
Kaliâni	C D E F♯ G A B C	C B A G F♯ E G D C
Sâranga †	C D E F♯ G A B C	C A G F♯ D E F♯ D C
Kumúrdaki	C D E F♯ B C	C B F♯ E D C
Hamîro-Kaliâni	C D E F♯ G A B G A B C	C B A G F♯ E D C
Yamuna-Kaliani	C D E F♯ G A C	C A G F♯ G E D C
Shama-Kaliâni	C D E F♯ G B C	C B G A G F♯ E D C
Mohánna-Kaliâni	C D E G A C	C B A G F♯ E D C
Bhupa-Kaliâni	C D F♯ G A C	C B A G F♯ E D C
Sârasa-Kâliani	C D E F♯ G A B C	C B A G F♯ E F♯ D C
Shrâr-Nâva	C D E F♯ G A C	C B A G F♯ E C
Bhurángini	C D E G A B C	C B A F♯ E D C
Shahradâmati	C D F♯ G A B C	C B G F♯ E D C
Nagavâgi	C D E F♯ G C	C B A G F♯ E D C
Kaliâna-Késeri	C D E G A C	C A — F♯ G F♯ E D C
Râjah-Kaliâni	C E F♯ A B C	C B A F♯ E D C
Shambharântakam	C E F♯ G A C	C B A G F♯ E D C
Dhirgadurshi	C D F♯ G A B A C	C B A G F♯ E F♯ C
Yogajoti	C D F♯ G B A C	C B A G F♯ E D C
Dvimokaprýa	C E D F♯ G B C	C B A F♯ E D C
Deshakaliâni	C D E F♯ G A G B C	C A G F♯ E D C
Chitaduti	C D F♯ G A B C	C B A G F♯ E D C
Mruganândana	C D E A B C	C B A F♯ A E D C
Kryabharna	C D E F♯ G B A C	C B A F♯ E D C

SCALE OF SUCHARITRA.		
Chato-Rangini	C F♯ E F♯ G B♭♭ C	C B♭♭ A♭ B♭♭ G E F♯ D♯ C

SCALE OF DHARTOVARDANI.		
Devarâshtra	C D♯ E F♯ G B C	C B A♭ G F♯ E D♯ C
Dhato-panchami	C D♯ E F♯ G B G C	C B A♭ G F♯ D♯ E F♯ D♯ C

NOTE.—Ragas marked † have two readings, the other readings are given at the end of this chapter.

Some MSS. give the text of the râgas marked ‡ in the following list as here shown.

The authenticity of the others is doubtful, but they are generally accepted by Indian musicians.

SUPPLEMENTARY LIST OF RÂGAS.			
Name of Râga.	**Ascending Mode.**	**Descending Mode.**	**Scale.**
[6] Bhupâli	C D♭ E♭ G A♭ C	C A♭ G E♭ D♭ C	No. 8
‡Ahiri	C F G A♭ G F E♭ D♭ C D♭ C E♭ F G A♭ B♭ C	C B♭ A♭ G F E♭ D♭ C	,, ,,
‡Asâveri	C D♭ F G A♭ G F G A♭ C	C B♭ A♭ G F E♭ D♭ C	,, ,,
‡S'oka-Varâli	C E♭ F B♭ A♭ G F E♭ F G B	G F E♭ D♭ F E♭ D♭ C	,, 9

[6] This râga is sometimes called Bhauli. Another reading will be found under the scale of Máyamâlavagaula.

SUPPLEMENTARY LIST OF RÂGAS—*continued.*

Name of Râga.	Ascending Mode.	Descending Mode.	Scale.
‡Purvi	F G A♭ B C D♭ E F G A♭ B C.	C B A♭ G F E D♭ C	No. 15
‡Mâruva	C E F G A♭ B A♭ G C	C B G F A♭ F G F E D♭ C	„ „
‡Gúndakrýa	C D♭ F G F E D♭ F G B C	C B G A♭ G F E D♭ C	„ „
‡Gaulipantu	C D♭ E D♭ F G A♭ G B C	C B A♭ G F A♭ F E D♭ C	„ „
Chaia-Nâta	C D♭ E F G F G C	C B♭ A B♭ G F D♭ C	„ 16
‡Purna-s'adyama	C E♭ D E♭ F B♭ C	C B♭ G F E♭ D C	„ 20
‡Anánda-Bhairavi	C E♭ D C E♭ F G A♭ G B♭ C	C B♭ A♭ F G F E♭ D C	„ „
‡Woodya-chandrika	C E♭ F G B♭ C G B♭ C	C B♭ G F E♭ C	„ „
‡Mâdavi	C F E♭ F G A♭ B C	C B A♭ G F G F E♭ D C	„ 21
‡Palâ-Mangeri	C E♭ F G F A E♭ F A C	C B♭ A G F E♭ F D C	„ 22
‡Durbar	C D F D G A B♭ C	C B♭ A G F E♭ D C	„ „
‡Kâpi	C D E♭ F G F E♭ D E♭ F G A B♭ C	C B♭ A G F E♭ D C	„ „
Velâvali	C D E♭ F G A C	C B A G F E♭ D C	„ 23
Késeri	C D E F G F A♭ G A♭ C	C A♭ B♭♭ A♭ G F E D C	„ 25
‡Kambógi	F E F G A G A C	B A G F E D C	„ 28
‡Mathâ-kohkila	C D G A B♭	A G D C	„ „
‡Janjúti	C D E F G A B♭	A G F E D C	„ „
‡Yedukúla-Kambógi	C D F G A B♭ A G A C	C B♭ A G F E F E D C	„ „
‡Biâg	C D E F G A B♭ C	C B♭ A B♭ G A G F E D E C	„ „
‡Nilâmberi	C D E F G A B♭ A C	C B♭ A G F E D E C	„ „
‡S'ahanna	G A G F E D C D E F G A B C	C B A G D E F G F E D C	„ 29
Déva-gandâri	C D E F G A B C	C B A G F E D C D E D C	„ „
‡Jeya-Mohanna	C D♭ F♯ G F♯ D♭ F♯ G A♭ B♭ C	C B♭ A♭ B♭ A♭ G F♯ E♭♭ D♭ C	„ 38
Mandâra	C D♭ E F♯ G A♭ G F♯ E F♯ G A B♭ C	C B♭ G F♯ E D♭ C	„ 50
Pratâpa	C E F♯ G A♭ B♭ C	C B♭ A♭ G F♯ E D♭ C	„ „
Nâmadâ	C D♭ E F♯ D♭ E F♯ A♭ B♭ C	C B♭ A♭ F♯ G F♯ E D♭ C	„ „
‡Devâgiri	C D♭ F♯ G F♯ G F♯ E D♭ F♯ G C	C B A♭ G F♯ E D♭ C	„ 51
Râma-Manohari	C D♭ E F♯ G A B♭ A C	C B♭ A G F♯ E D♭ C	„ 52
Gurugád̤a	E♭ F♯ G A♭ B♭	A♭ G F♯ E♭ D	„ 56
Trimúrti	C D E♭ A♭ B♭	C B♭ A♭ G E♭ D C	„ „
‡Suddha râga	C D E♭ D E♭ F♯ G F♯ G B C	C B G B G F♯ E♭ D E♭ C	„ 57
S'ruti-Rangini	C D E F♯ G A♭ G F♯ E F♯ G A♭ B♭♭	C B♭♭ A♭ G E C D C	„ 61
‡Sâranga	C D E F♯ G A G F♯ E F♯ G A B C	C B A G F♯ D C	„ 65
Jotismatti	C D♯ E F♯ G C	C B♭ A♭ F♯ G F♯ C D♯ C	„ 68

CHAPTER V.

Taste of European and Oriental nations: how differing—Reason for non-employment of harmony—Method of singing—Of Indian melodies—Form—Classification of—Rhythm Employment of mixed times—Tonality often doubtful—Resemblance of Indian music to that of other countries—Examples of popular melodies—Hindustani musical system: how differing from Karnâtik—Examples of Hindustani melodies—Scales employed in the Hindustani system.

THE wide divergence of taste in the matter of music between European and Asiatic nations has doubtless arisen from the fact that while Western nations gradually discarded the employment of mode, and clothed the melody with harmony, the Eastern nations in this respect made little or no progress; and now, in India, the employment of authentic modes and melody types (or râgas) is still jealously adhered to.

Speaking of this, Willard remarks: "To expect an endless variety in the melody of Hindustan would be an injudicious hope, as their authentic melody is limited to a certain number, said to have been composed by professors universally acknowledged to have possessed not only real merit, but also the original genius of composition, beyond the precincts of whose authority it would be criminal to trespass. What the more reputed of the moderns have done is that they have adapted them to their own purposes, and found others by the combination of two or more of them. Thus far they are licensed, but they dare not proceed a step farther. Whatever merit an entire modern composition might possess, should it have no resemblance to the established melody of the country, it would be looked upon as spurious. It is implicitly believed that it is impossible to add to the number of these one single melody of equal merit, so tenacious are the natives of Hindustan of the ancient practices."[1]

---

[1] "A Treatise on the Music of Hindustan." Capt. N. A. Willard. Calcutta, 1834.

This continued employment of mode, combined with the almost entire absence of harmony, has prevented Indian music from reaching any higher pitch of development, such as has been attained elsewhere. It stands to reason also that this is the chief cause of the monotony which causes Indian music to be little appreciated by, if not repellent to, European ears.

Since the early periods of Indian history, music would seem to have been cultivated more as a science than an art. More attention seems to have been paid to elaborate and tedious artistic skill than to simple and natural melody. Hence arose technical rules that marred the pristine sweetness of melody—the very life of all real music. To a great extent this must be attributed to the art falling into the hands of illiterate *virtuosi*. Their influence, which caused music to suffer both in purity of style and simplicity, is being felt less and less. The great aim of all music—"Rakti," or the power of affecting the heart—now asserts itself more and more, and is slowly but surely bringing about a return to the early type of sweet, simple melody.

Very little of the good or classical music of India is heard by Europeans. What is usually played to them consists, as Colonel Meadows Taylor very truly remarks, of modern ditties, sung by ill-instructed, screaming, dancing women, at crowded native durbars, marriages, and other ceremonials. And when this is the case, it does not cause much surprise to hear native music often described as abominable, and devoid of all melody. But music of great intrinsic beauty nevertheless exists, and only requires to be heard by an unprejudiced ear to be appreciated. Throughout India music and poetry go hand in hand. Their influence may be seen and felt in almost every phase of native life, from the palace of the râjah to the humble dwelling of the ryot. Music has there been developed to a degree far greater than has been generally recognised in Europe. It is there felt to be a means of passionate expression, such as is apparently unknown amongst nations farther East. And indeed the very soul of all Indian music may be said to be râga—which in its literal sense means *that which creates passion*. And that this has been fully appreciated in Europe would seem to be evident, for a musical reviewer writing in the *Athenæum*, and contrasting the music of India with that of Japan and Siam, recently wrote: "In the Indian Peninsula we are really in another world. We exchange a music in which noise and dry executive skill prevail for one vibrating with sentiment and passion, and that combines a refined execution with the highly nervous organization that makes the poetic artist. Such a one was a Jeypore *been* player (*been*—a kind of vina), who was to be heard, but we fear was not much heard, at a little exhibition called 'India in London,' in 1886. To go from one of the clever Siamese *ranat* players of the Inventions Exhibition the year before to this man, was to quit the atmosphere of a desert for one redolent of sweet air and flower scents. The Hindu chromatic scale, from which the numerous modes and melody types are selected, does not appear to differ from our own. As there is no harmony, slight differences may pass without notice. Very much of Hindu music impresses the European as being in the minor scale; but deflections in the stringed instruments, and possible accommodations in the wind, introduce an enharmonic elaboration that defies notation."[2] And here it might be interesting to quote the opinion of a learned native gentleman:[3] "Many of the Hindus themselves," he writes, "labour under a false impression concerning the difference between Indian and European music, even as to the employment of tones and semitones. The opinions held by so many natives, that pieces played upon the piano or harmonium are to them discordant, can be easily accounted for thus: they are simply confused—being unaccustomed to anything but simple melody—when they hear five or six notes played in chords. The chief difference seems to me to be that the Hindus prefer melody simply, while to European ears melody is preferred when clothed, as it were, with harmony of some sort."

Comparatively few Indian airs have found their way to Europe. Those few that have been published are mostly from either Bengal or Northern India, so that there is but small resemblance in them to the national music of the Deccan or the South; for there is a marked difference between the music of the various parts of India, which to even the most casual observer is evident.

The following examples of songs—though a mere handful from so vast a storehouse—will, it is hoped, aid in filling the vacancy, and thereby afford some help to those who may care to make further research.

Many of these melodies in themselves are extremely beautiful, and their simplicity adds an additional charm that no words can express—the airs of different country districts are but a reflex of the character and feelings of the people to whom they belong. Some are pathetic and melodious—music that exactly reproduces the feelings inspired by the words; others are gay and bright—true accompaniments to the daily pursuits and occupations of life; and in many of them may be found a vein of repose, slightly tinged with melancholy, that offers a curious contrast to either of the former; indeed, so much variety may be

---

[2] The *Athenæum*, Jan. 4, 1890. Review of "Musical Instruments and their Homes." M. E. and W. A. Brown, New York.

[3] T. M. Venkatas'esha S'astri.

found that it is unnecessary to notice in detail merits that must be evident to the musical reader.

But yet, though the melodies themselves are so beautiful, it is but seldom that we hear them well sung; indeed, singers of the ordinary type often entirely ruin the effect of the music; for native singers appear to have an idea that the highest form of their art consists in introducing as much grace as possible, whether it adds to the beauty of their songs or not; in fact, they try to disguise the real melody as much as possible by embellishments of their own, and so in nine cases out of ten it is quite impossible to follow either the air or the words of a song, since the singer is only anxious to exhibit what he fondly imagines to be his skill.

Native singers rarely practise, for they think that practice, to even a moderate extent, ruins their voices. The treatment of the voice, too, is quite different to what experience in Europe has proved to obtain the best results.

The voices of Indian singers are almost always weak and deficient in volume—one result doubtless of their system of training, by which a full clear tone is made to give way to incessant small inflections. Girls, too, are taught singing when much too young, so that their voices either break or become harsh and shrill.

A singer rarely stands while he sings, and instead of using his proper range of voice, he prefers a most unnatural falsetto, which he can rarely control, and his endeavours to make himself heard generally cause him to make the most ludicrous grimaces. Singers of this kind it is who bring Indian music into disrepute, and cause it to be regarded with contempt by European audiences.

But still there *are* singers in India whose voices are wonderfully sweet, and when they sing their own songs in their simple form, no hearer can doubt that, like other national music, that of India possesses a charm peculiarly its own.

The various styles of Indian compositions, consisting as they do entirely of melody, do not present to the casual observer differences as clearly marked as in those of European music. Nevertheless these melodies are classified systematically, and in their construction are subject to certain definite rules of composition. Almost all consist of a burden or refrain called Pallevi, a kind of answer to this refrain styled Anupallevi, and stanzas (called Charanam) of which there is usually an uneven number. These parts are in the several compositions arranged in different ways, and by this means the style of composition is determined. Rhythm is usually very marked, but differs largely from that of most European music from the fact that the times are frequently irregular.

Between vocal and instrumental music the difference is slight, the vina, the only instrument of any large capability, being considered to be but an imitation or reproduction of the human voice; and if an air be accompanied by that instrument, it is usually only played in unison with the voice.

The different exercises, compositions, &c., are usually classified under the following heads:—

Sâralas	Kruthis
Gentuvérsis	Kirthanas
Alankâras	Vérnams
Gítas	S'ankâvérnams
Prabhandas	Pathams
Thânas	Javadis
Svarajotas	Râgamâlika

A râga, when performed by itself, contains two movements—(i.) Alâpa and (ii.) Madhyamakâla.

Pallevi, a kind of fantasia upon some theme abounding in imitation, and with a well-defined rhythm.

The rhythm existing throughout all the different styles of composition is worth careful notice; and it is interesting to compare it with that employed by other nations. The similarity of that of the Turks and other Eastern nations is remarkable.

As in European music each period is complete in itself, being clearly marked by the tâlas, which divide the different periods into regular or irregular sections, as the case may be, following each other in definite and regular order. The periods differ only from those commonly found in European music in that they may consist, if necessary, of an uneven number of sections or measures, the tâla itself often being irregular, owing to the employment of mixed times. Hence when Indian music is written in ordinary notation there will be a regular rotation corresponding to the tâla, of bars each of which *may* have a different time signature. A reference to the list of tâlas upon page 36 will explain this more readily than any words can. These periods or phrases are often extended by the addition at the commencement of a few notes leading up to the commencing note of the phrase, or by being terminated with a small cadence or codetta which may be either a repetition or imitation of what has gone before, or may lead up to the next phrase.

The rhythm of the Pallevi and Anupallevi is usually a great deal more marked and regular than that of the stanzas, where the phrasing is frequently irregular, the periods being interwoven by means of, as it were, abbreviaturas, or extended by the prolongation and "rekhu," a species of turn or transient shake upon a note in the middle of a roulade with which all Hindu music abounds. This is especially the case in the performance of râga as a *solo*, which in certain cases is absolutely timeless.

Hence the great difficulty of expressing such music correctly by means of ordinary notation. The peculiarity of the scales or modes employed in Hindu music often raises a difficulty in determining the real tonality of many of the melodies, the Hindu Sa, taken by native musicians as the "Khuruj" or keynote of their scale, not necessarily corresponding to what is the real tonic of the scale. Indian music has been compared to that of Scotland, but the resemblance can be traced principally to the frequent employment by both nations of a somewhat similar scale of five intervals, the fourth and seventh being omitted; and possibly also from the fact that a similar motive is often found in both, where the first note has one-fourth of the duration of the second, as—

In reviewing the national music of any country, we cannot help being struck with the way in which special scales are employed, special graces worked in, all more or less varying in the music of different nations. In the music of India, owing to the multitude of scales or modes which it employs, a resemblance here and there can be traced to the music of nearly every country.

The chief characteristic, for instance, of Hungarian music is that it usually employs a scale with two superfluous seconds, or the harmonic minor with a sharp fourth. This scale is in every respect similar to the Indian scale called S'rinhandra, and nearly similar to one much employed and called Sábhapántovarâli, both of which will be found among the list of scales upon pages 32-35.

Many of the graces and embellishments employed in the gipsy music in Hungary are to be found in Indian melodies.

Mr. Carl Engel[4] has drawn attention to the employment of the minor seventh in both Servian, Wallachian, and Scotch music. This interval is employed both in Arabic and Indian music. Some idea of the plaintive and impressive effect of which it is productive can be gained from the song, "Seki yénaka thaké," given upon page 80.

Mr. J. A. Kappey, in his collection of "Songs of Eastern Europe,"[5] draws attention to the characteristics of Turkish songs, and to the fact that they employ a scale having a minor third with an augmented fourth, and a minor sixth

[4] "An Introduction to the Study of National Music." Carl Engel. London, 1866.
[5] "Songs of Eastern Europe." Edited by J. A. Kappey. London, 1881.

with a major seventh. A comparison of the examples he gives with songs of India will be of great interest; and the similarity of both melody and rhythm is striking. One of the songs quoted—a song of sorrow by Nihad Bey—might be from India; it appears to be written in much the same form, and it is also to be noticed that it employs a mixed time of $\frac{3}{8}$ and $\frac{2}{4}$, precisely the Indian Triputa Tâla, already noticed.

In a previous chapter attention has already been drawn to the resemblance that Indian music bears to that of Greece, and this is still more fully borne out by a careful study of modern Greek national airs. In a work not long published, by M. Bourgault-Ducoudray,[6] the construction of the peculiar scales found throughout the East have been made the subject of most careful research, and the use of what the author terms the "chromatique oriental" is especially noticed. This scale is no other than the Indian Máyamâlavagaula, and to its frequent use attention has been drawn elsewhere. M. Bourgault-Ducoudray's work to students of Eastern music is especially interesting, and the careful analysis that is given of each air renders the work most valuable. The resemblance between Indian songs and the examples of melodies from the Levant is so striking that, in many cases, it is difficult to believe that their origin is not identical.

Mr. Engel calls attention to the fact that Chopin, in one of his studies for the black keys (Douze grandes Études, No. 5), has given some idea of the beautiful effect that may be produced by a melody which employs a limited number of intervals; only in this case he notices that as the accompaniment employs other intervals, the pentatonic effect of the whole is somewhat marred. In Indian music, too, a frequent use is made of the pentatonic scale, as has been already remarked. Again, in Spanish national music, embellishments are of constant occurrence, especially in descending the diatonic scale; the same predilection can be observed in Indian melodies; indeed, a further resemblance can be traced in the occasional employment of endings of the following nature—

which in the common songs, such as are heard in the jungles and country districts of many parts of India, are not unfrequent.

The following observations by Captain Willard are short and to the

6 "Trente Mélodies Populaires de Gréce et d'Orient." L. A. Bourgault-Ducoudray. Paris, 1876.

point, and seem to apply equally well to Southern as to Northern Indian melodies :—

1. The melodies are short, lengthened by repetitions and variations.
2. They all partake of the nature of what by us is called a Rondo, the piece being invariably concluded with the first strain, and sometimes with the first bar, or at least with the first note of that bar.
3. A bar or a measure or a certain number of measures are frequently repeated with slight variations, almost *ad libitum.*
4. There is as much liberty allowed with respect to pauses, which may be lengthened at pleasure, providing the time be not disturbed.

The times employed in Indian music are peculiar ; simple times are of most frequent occurrence, mixed times are largely employed ; true triple time, curiously enough, is of the rarest ; but there is a time, the accentuation of which is upon the first and second beat, which may be said to be a kind of triple time (although in reality a mixed time of $\frac{2}{4}$ and C), and is much used for love songs.

The *tempo* in which the various melodies are sung is sometimes irregular, and from being exact sometimes changes into a recitative or *ad libitum* in the middle of a song. The peculiarities in the working out of the motives are striking, and the employment of rests of short duration is noticeable.

The endings are often not definite, the last few bars leading up to the commencement ; the reason for this is probably that it is usual to repeat the melodies, and when the performer wishes to end, he generally leads up to the note upon which he wishes to conclude, and prolongs it in this manner—

Indeed, it seems more natural to regard all endings of Indian melodies rather as different forms of *Da capo* than as real closes, the object in most cases being a return to the commencement of the song. The fact so often noticed by those who have endeavoured to collect Indian airs, that almost every interval of the scale can be found used as a close, can possibly be thus accounted for. The words of most of these songs, particularly those sung by the common people, such as lavanies and javadis and svarajotas, are generally a long ballad, so that a definite ending is not required after each stanza. Many singers indeed, as a variety, improvise their words, so that after each stanza closes on intervals of all kinds are found. But when the real ending is reached, the performer frequently leads up to the key-note, or what he regards as the key-note of the Indian scale. Judged from a European point of view, it appears that closes on the intervals of the third and fifth should be regarded more as *half* closes upon the intervals of the tonic chord; those on the second and seventh as upon intervals of the dominant chord; whilst those on the sixth or minor third betray the relative minor; sometimes the third may be looked upon as the fifth to the relative minor. This view can of course be equally well applied to the national airs of any country, but it appears to be specially applicable to those of India.

Some of the melodies in their conclusion imply a modulation into the relative minor, showing thereby a trace of the old pentatonic scale. Examples will be found among the following melodies of endings with the fifth, the sixth, the seventh, the second, and (like those of the Servians) with the third. Closes on the fourth are rarely if ever employed. An example will nevertheless be found in the Khyal upon page 88.

In the examples following an endeavour has been made to point out some of the chief peculiarities and characteristics of the different râgas in which the melodies are composed.

The first exercises taught to pupils are called Sâralas, they are always in the scale of Máyamâlavagaula; similar exercises called Gentu-versis, containing repeated notes, are next taught, after which Alankâras—exercises upon time—are learnt, several in each tâla.

The simplest melodies are called Gíta, and are of two kinds—Pillârigíta and Ganarâga-gíta. The first-named are four in number and are hymns to the god Pillâri or Ganésha. The Sangíta Pârijâta mentions four Pillârigítas, and it is believed that these are the four that are still in use. The following is an example of one of these ancient Pillârigítas:—

Râga Malahâri.
Tâla Rupacca.

Ganarâga-gítas are very similar to the above.

Somewhat similar to gítas are Prabhandas, only that they are usually longer, and are divided into two or three parts by breaks called Khándam. Skilful performers are fond of playing such pieces in order to exhibit their proficiency to an audience.

Thânas are studies for the vina, teaching special styles and difficulties met with in the performance of the various râgas. They are particularly intended as an introduction to the difficult movement called Madhyamakâla of a râga. Thânas are in no particular tâlas, the time being taught orally, and left in a great measure to the performer's discretion. Great attention is bestowed upon proper accentuation and grace; the *tempo* is usually very rapid—

Râga Nâta.

Râga Ârabi.

Râga Gaula.

Some of the most popular ballads of Southern India are called Svarajotas, and are sung by almost everyone. The words are usually odes to some deity or popular hero of the country. A song of this kind commences with a kind of refrain termed pallevi; following in quick succession is the anupallevi, a kind of short stanza, the words of which are an addition to a comment upon those of the pallevi. After this the pallevi is again repeated. The stanzas, which may be dissimilar both in metre and melody, follow in order, each concluded by a repetition of the refrain. There is an almost entire absence of superfluous grace in these songs, and their marked rhythm renders their execution within the attainment of nearly all. The following examples of these melodies are interesting, and display the fluent and decisive nature so characteristic of them all to the greatest advantage—

This air is one of the most popular in Southern India ; it is usually known only by the name of the râga in which it is composed, as the words vary in different parts of the country. Its origin is not known, but it is believed to be very old.

The following, a song peculiar to Mysore, and in praise of the goddess Parvati or Châmandi, is in a râga that is very little employed—

Allegro.
Pallevi.

"PARVATI PATE."

Râga Purna-chandrika.
Tâla Adi.

As an example of a melody confined entirely to the pentatonic scale and with an undefined conclusion the following is interesting. The apparent want of a distinctly indicated key-note is evident, and it might be harmonised equally well in several different keys. Some musicians would doubtless treat it as in a minor key, and harmonise it therefore in E minor. The Hindus, however, regard it as pertaining rather to the Mesolydian mode, and therefore make G—the dominant of the natural scale—the tonic.

This melody is also worthy of note as it is considered to be one of the oldest songs of the kind remaining—

"RÂMA NA MORÂ ALINCHERA."

Râga Kamachi.
Tâla Rupacca.

The above air displays a good example of the peculiar effect of a rhythm of three measures. More than one example of what is styled "Vishama tâla" by the Hindus may be found here, where a note at the end of a bar is tied to one at the commencement of the bar following.

The two songs following are of a similar kind to the foregoing, and both are exceedingly popular. They are of quite recent date, and were probably composed by some Telugu pandit at the court of Mysore. I have given them precisely as they are sung, and without attempting to divide the parts (*i.e.*, pallevi, &c.)

composing them. The parts can, however, be easily distinguished, and also the small codettas and cadenzas which separate them—

"SUVI, SUVI,"

Râga Behag.
Tâla Rupacca

"KAMINI VINAISA."

Râga S'ankârabharna.

Sacred songs, called Kruthis, are very popular. The airs of some of these hymns are very old, and have been handed down by successive generations for hundreds of years. Kruthis are, as a rule, in the more difficult râgas, the characteristics of which are made as prominent as is consistent with the melody. They consist of a pallevi, anupallevi, and one stanza. Some few have three stanzas, and this number is never exceeded. The pallevi is sung at the commencement, then the anupallevi, after which the pallevi is repeated with a slight variation at the option of the singer, followed by the stanza, and concluding with the pallevi again. The *tempo* is rather of an *Andante con moto*, and the whole is sung in a dreamy way, with a great deal of expression, and as much grace as is wished.

These hymns were revived by the Râjah Sarabhoji of Tanjore, and were greatly improved in style by the celebrated musician Tiâgyarâj of that place, who composed a large number which are still popular.

Other famous composers of kruthis have been Siama S'astri, Diksitalu, and Subbaraya S'astri.

As will be noticed from the following example, kruthis have a curious mixture of pathos and hilarity, and the words are always in accordance with the emotions expressed by the music. The peculiarly plaintive effect imparted to these melodies by the employment of grace embracing intervals less than semitones, and its special charm so readily shown upon the vina—the usual companion to these hymns—no notation can be found capable of expressing—

"UPACHARAM CHESAVARU."

Râga Bhairavi.
Tâla Rupacca.

The scale of this melody is "Nâta-Bhairavi," which, as can be seen, corresponds exactly to the ancient Hypodorian mode. The peculiarities of the râga Bhairavi, in which it is composed, admit of E being taken either as ♮ or ♭ at will. Hence this melody, although partaking partly of the nature of a minor key, should be regarded as founded upon the dominant of the major key; and, therefore, if harmonised to preserve its character, written in one flat only, and harmonised with the triad of the dominant as the principal chord. The vibrato upon B♭ is characteristic of the râga, and is never omitted.

The composer of this melody was Tiâgyarâj.

The composition of the next melody is attributed to Kolashekara, a former Maharajah of Travancore, which, perhaps, accounts in some way for its wide popularity.

One great peculiarity of the compositions of the Maharajah is the copious insertion of what are called "Svaraksheras" in them. To make my meaning clear—the Hindu gamut, as has been stated, is signified by the syllables "Sa, ri, ga, ma, pa, dha, ni." The composer has adroitly introduced these syllables at the very place where the notes signified by them occur in the song, without interfering with the sense of the words. This is the more difficult to do when we remember that in Hindu music the notes must follow each other in a particular order, according to the râga, and not exactly according to the composer's fancy. In the following piece the words are "*Sa*rasa *Sa*mamukha para nava*ma*," &c. The syllables Sa and Ma are introduced at the very points where the notes C (Sa) and F (Ma) stand in the song. The Hindus regard, in this song, C and not F as the key-note, though the latter is clearly the real tonic, and there is apparently no difference in the tonality of this and the melody "Smaranâ Sukâm," in which they allow the tonic to be F. The other two melodies, also from Travancore, are compositions of Kolashekara Maharajah—

"SARASA SAMAMUKHA."

MELODY FROM TRAVANCORE.

Râga Bilahâri.

MELODY FROM TRAVANCORE.

Râga Mohanna.

"SMARANA SUKAM VO RAMANAM."

Râga Gârudadvâni.
Tâla Eka.

An example of an irregular melody is shown below. The two first periods consist of nine and seven bars respectively. This frequently occurs in Indian music, and is probably produced simply by rests having in course of time been either lengthened or disregarded; or by a bar imitated, repeated, or overlapping; so that a symmetrical period is transformed into one of an uneven number of bars. The effect produced is original, and often very pleasing. That this has been fully recognised by musicians in Europe is well known, and many examples might be quoted from the works of classical composers to prove that this has been largely appreciated as an important element of variety—

"NANNA GANNA TALLI."

Andante.
Pallevi

Râga Manohari.
Tâla Eka.

The two melodies following are both in the scale called Máyamâlavagaula. The intervals of the scale are so peculiar and so many harmonical combinations can be formed from them that it well deserves attention, especially when it is remembered that this is a scale largely used by the Hindus, and that all elementary exercises taught to pupils are invariably upon this scale, instead of, as would be supposed, the diatonic major, which is by us commonly regarded as natural.

These melodies are again irregular in construction; the râgas in which they are composed, though much alike, differ, in that the third is not admitted as a real note in the ascending mode of the second example. A characteristic of the râga Purvi is shown in the "glisse" from D to G in the sixth and seventh bars of the first air—

"TRILOKA MÂTA."

Râga Purvi.
Tâla Adi.

"NAGÂDHERA."

Râga Nâdınâmakrya.
Tâla Rupacca.

Very similar to kruthis are Kirthanas. They consist, like the former, of a pallevi, anupallevi, and stanzas, the tâla being regular throughout. The râgas in which they are composed are for the most part popular ones, and there is little grace essential to their performance. The music of kirthanas is very simple, and the words, addressed to some deity, plain and easy to be remembered.

The following are examples of popular kirthanas—

Allegretto.
Pallevi.

"BÂLA NANNA CHALA BROVAVA."

Râga Kambódi.
Tâla Adi.

Vérnams are songs very similar to svarajotas, merely differing in that the several parts of which they are composed are not arranged in quite the same manner, and that they are more difficult of execution. Vérnams are, as a rule, much longer than svarajotas, and contain a larger amount of grace throughout. They are usually in the more uncommon râgas, and the time is purposely made as catchy as possible. Their performance is therefore seldom attempted by other than skilled musicians.

A vérnam consists of an introduction to which there are words, usually concluded by a "Sol-fa" passage. Following this are stanzas generally merely "sol-fahed." After each stanza there is a short refrain to which words are sung. The words of vérnams treat mostly of the deeds of favourite heroes or warrior deities.

The following is an example of one of the simplest vérnams. In performance a musician would treat this as a kind of theme which he would expand, vary, and embellish according to his own taste and skill—indeed, grace is sometimes employed to such an extent that the original air can hardly be recognised.

This melody is the composition of some pupil of Tiâgyarâj of Tanjore; it displays two of the characteristics of the râga Sâranga very prominently—viz., the *glisse* from B to G and the *vibrato* upon D—

The following is another well known song of this kind—

S'ankâ-vérnams are somewhat similar to vérnams, only that the *tempo* is less rapid. They are usually very elaborate in style, and abound with graces of all kinds. They are commonly sung at Nautches and are intended to give full scope to convey "bhavas"—the gestures and sentiments conveyed by the dancer as she sways to and fro to the music.

Javadis are songs of a light and pleasing nature, such as love songs, cradle songs,[7] &c. They are much sung by both Nautch girls and all, especially women, of the higher classes in domestic life. They are of two kinds—ordinary ballads and songs of a more or less indelicate nature, sung during the performance of a peculiar dance called Kârwar. Javadis consist usually of a pallevi, anupallevi, and stanzas, sung in the usual manner as described before, and are chiefly in popular râgas. The *tempo* is in accordance with the words, and not too slow, the favourite measure being Rupacca. Consequently, many of these songs bear a resemblance to a waltz, only that they are taken at a slightly slower pace.

The words of javadis are often very beautiful; and those upon the loves of Krishna and Radha are always popular. Musicians as a rule sing these songs more in their naked form, and with less grace than is their usual custom. Each stanza is sung to the same air.

These songs are of comparatively recent introduction, being first sung by the Kanarese musicians of the Court of Surapuri, a petty state near the celebrated Humpé ruins. The popularity of songs of this kind increased rapidly, and they are now to be heard throughout almost the whole of Southern India, where they take the place of the Tappa of Hindustan.

Among the following examples the air "Anthalona Telavari" is perhaps the most popular—the accompanying rhythm of the tâla falls upon the first and second beat of each bar; this is much noticed when it is accompanied by instruments, such as the small tinkling cymbals and drums, which mark the time strongly. This song seems to be known throughout Southern India—the version varies slightly in different places, but, on the whole, the air is much the same everywhere.

The air "S'ri Sâratha" is very popular both in Mysore and Tanjore; the modulation into the relative minor is noticeable as it shows traces of a pentatonic scale—

Andante. Pallevi. "YIVANA PIRDIDU." Râga Biag. Tâla Adi.

"KAYALÂGA DÂVANA." Râga Janjuti. Tâla Rupacca.

[7] Simple cradle songs, called "Palna," are very common, and answer to the lullaby songs of Europe.

"ANTHALONA TELAVARI."

Râga S'ankârabharna.
Tâla Rupacca.

Pallevi.

"JÉNAKA VANEANATHA."

Râga Janjuti.
Tâla Rupacca.

"SEKI YÉNAKA THAKÉ."

Râga Kapi.
Tâla Eka.

Pallevi.

"S'RI SÂRATHA."

Râga Kamachi.
Tâla Rupacca.

Very similar to javadis are songs called Pathams; they are exclusively love songs, and are sung largely both in the native drama and by Nautch girls. The music is very much varied, and the performers frequently leave the air and improvise cadences and embellishments, rejoining the melody at will. The *tempo* is slower than that of javadis, and is varied according to the expression the singer wishes to put into the words; the tâla is generally irregular, a mixed time of $\frac{3}{4}$ and C is the commonest.

The most popular composer of pathams was Kshattrya, whose songs are largely sung, and contain some of the most beautiful and poetical sentiments that can be found; but, like all Oriental love poetry, they employ imagery too luxuriant for exact translation—

"YALLA TELLA VARA."

Râga S'ankârabharna.
Tâla Druva.

In the above melody the characteristics of the râga S'ankârabharna are well shown. The glide to the upper C is never omitted in this râga. Another peculiarity of this air should be noticed: at the sign ‡ it will be seen that B is tied; the string is *twice* slightly deflected and shaken upon the fret, so as to sharpen the note to a degree less than a semitone, with a trembling effect.

This song is very well known in the Mysore country. The pace is moderately quick but not hurried, and the melody is sung in a soft, dreamy manner, that, coupled with the gestures of the singer and the tinkling of the accompanying cymbals, is peculiarly fascinating, especially when heard for the first time.

Here is another example of these songs—

{ Râga Mukâri.
{ Tâla Triputa.

Religious hymns, called Yallapathams and Tathvams, are largely sung by the lower orders. They are very lugubrious and monotonous, and are invariably in the râga Yedukula-Kambógi. The former are funeral dirges, the latter allegorical chants sung at religious gatherings. The following example of a Yallapatham shows the nature of these songs—

Râga Yedukula-Kambógi.
Tâla Adi.

The ordinary folk-songs of the country are called Lavanis, and will be familiar to everyone who has heard the coolies sing as they do their work; the women nursing their children; the bullock drivers; dhooly bearers; or sepoys on the march. The airs are usually very monotonous. The words, if not impromptu, are a sort of history or ballad in praise of some warrior or "burra Sahib." Some have a kind of chorus, each man in turn singing an improvised verse. There is no employment of râga.

At the time of the Kâma festival in honour of the Indian god of love, special lavanies called Saval are sung. The words of these are sung by two parties—one called Turai and the other Kalki—intended to represent the god Krishna and his mistress Radha. Questions of a metaphorical nature are sung by one party and answered by the other. These were formerly sung extempore, but their performance is now usually rehearsed beforehand. This species of entertainment is also practised in Northern India under the name of Kabi.

The two following are examples of popular lavanies—

Allegro moderato.
No. 1.

No. 2.

A composition called Râga-mâlika, or "garland of râgas," is occasionally heard. As the name implies, it is a song that modulates into many different râgas. A râga-mâlika consists of a pallevi or refrain, and stanzas. The pallevi is employed only at the beginning and at the conclusion. The stanzas are usually uneven in number. Each stanza employs a different râga, the name of which must be mentioned in the words, in order that the audience be able to follow and appreciate the performer's skill. The tâla remains the same throughout.

Somewhat similar to the above is a Pallevi. This word signifies literally "a creeping plant," and hence the name is given to a kind of fantasia upon some theme worked out in accordance with certain rules, and containing a large amount of grace and imitation. As this kind of composition is extremely popular it well merits some attention.

A stanza or sentence of some poetical nature is sung to any air that the performer may improvise, and in any râga and tâla. This opening melody is taken as the theme of the pallevi, and is varied, imitated, and answered subsequently according to the skill and inclination of the performer. Occasionally a kind of counter theme is introduced, and a skilful musician will keep the two parts distinct. If this is done the counter theme is, as a rule, introduced upon a fourth or sixth lower. But it is not intended to imply that there is any employment of counterpoint as understood in Europe; for though in certain cases these two parts may be actually going at the same time, yet the native musician is guided by no *contrapuntal* laws, but by his ear, and the rules of *râga*, entirely. Much greater license is given as to râga in a pallevi than in any other composition.

There are usually three movements—viz., an adagio, a moderato, and an allegro or scherzo.

The first movement commences with the subject being given out in any râga or tâla that may be called for. The space of time occupied by this is termed an *avatâr*, and constitutes the chief rhythmical division or period into which the pallevi is divided. Each succeeding avatâr, though consisting of several short phrases, either linked together or separated by rests, must be of equal length to the original. Each avatâr differs essentially from those preceding, and if the voice is employed, commences invariably with the first syllable or word of the original theme.

The second movement follows with or without a short pause between. The measure remains the same, but the duration of the movement is less.

The third, or concluding movement, follows; the only difference being that the *tempo* is much increased. In this it is usual for the performer to modulate into different râgas (called for at the time by the audience), taking care that the special characteristics of each shall be made clear; each avatâr is, however, ended in the original râga. This movement is brought to a close by a repetition of the original theme in the original *tempo*, after which a few bars in the same râga are given *ad libitum* by way of a *Finale.*

In the performance of a pallevi no harsh or discordant instruments are employed. For marking a rhythmical accompaniment the hands are employed, or sometimes a Mridang or Gatha. Occasionally another performer hums softly a kind of accompaniment to syllables (ta, di, ti, ka, &c., as if sol-fahing) intended to represent the beats of a drum ; this is called konnagólu, or tâlavinyasa.

Songs of salutation or hail, called Mangala, are sung at the conclusion of all performances. Melodies of this kind are usually in either the râgas Surati or Saurâshtra. The following is one of the most common Mangalas. The chief peculiarity in songs of this kind is evident here—the beats of the tâla falling upon tied notes at the commencement of a bar—

"PARAMANA SUTTU BATTU PADARA." Râga Saurâshtra. Tâla Adi.

Hindustani music in some respects differs from the system previously described, and which is called Karnâtik. It has been much copied from the latter, but its professors are not often men of much education ; and though many of them are skilled executants, their knowledge of the theory of their art is, as a general rule, but small. In Hindustani music more attention is paid to the minute distinction between the various râgas than to the actual melody itself. To melodic form the same importance is not attached. The nomenclature of Hindustani and Karnâtik râgas differs, but musicians everywhere quote the Sangíta Ratnâkera as their principal authority. They also say that, apart from Arabian and Persian innovations, the difference between the systems of music prevalent in the North and South of India is accounted for by the fact that in the former that of Hanumân is preferred, while the Southern music is a relic of the earliest system of Nârada.

In Hindustani music the elaborate arrangement of scales previously described is not used, but merely twelve ; all of which, however, are found, and are in common use, though under different names, in the Karnâtik system. The tâlas, or measures, employed in Hindustani music are similar to those previously described upon page 36. As regards the *form* of Hindustani melodies, in place of what has been styled "pallevi," "anupallevi," and "charanam," or stanzas, all their songs consist of distinct parts. The pallevi is styled *asthayi*—the anupallevi *antâra*—and the charanam *abhōg*. As the differences between the two systems consist mainly of technical points, which would be of slight interest to the reader, the following observations will, perhaps, be sufficient.

The Dhrupad—perhaps the most admired of all Hindustani songs—is a heroic song, with a slow and dignified style, and sung almost exclusively by men. It consists of three parts—*i.e.*, asthayi, antâra, and abhōg. Great scope is given to variations upon the actual theme, and the time cadence is very complex. Other songs are called Tilanas and Sarigams (or svaragrâmas), and are in particular tâlas; they contain only two parts.

Ghuzals—songs of the same nature as Kshattrya's pathams of the Karnâtik—are very popular; they consist of only asthayi and antâra. Of a similar form to ghuzals are Tappa, resembling the Karnâtik javadis, and consisting of two parts. There are also Thungri, Dadra, Hari; Gurbah, sung at the Dassera festival; and Palna, or cradle songs. Songs called Khyâls, somewhat like the Karnâtik kruthis, which display a great deal of grace, and have a slow time cadence, were introduced by Sultan Shirki of Jounpur; they consist of two parts only. Many Hindustani lavanis are very pretty, though most melancholy.

The tuning of instruments used by Hindustani musicians differs from that employed by Karnâtik professors, in that the interval of the fourth is always admitted upon the open strings; the modulation therefore of these instruments is less confined; hence frequently, though the melody itself is less pleasing, *accompaniments* to Hindustani songs are preferred to the ordinary Karnâtik accompaniments, and music played in the Karnâtik style upon instruments tuned thus is much liked. Hindustani musicians practise singing more than do Karnâtik. They have better voices, and take more pains to cultivate them. Karnâtik singers, as has been said before, appear to have an idea that practice is hurtful to their voices, and from attempting to sing when too young, before the voice is formed, they are apt to ruin their singing entirely; while Hindustani singers practise much, and sing in a more manly style; hence Hindustani music is much admired in Southern India, chiefly as a variety—the softness of the language itself, and the ease with which it lends itself to singing, giving it an additional charm. A careful study of the Hindustani melodies given below will amply repay the time given up, and their great beauty and inherent passion can hardly fail to enchant one.

The following examples, gathered principally from the Deccan, Guzerat, and

Rajasthân, display some of the chief characteristics of these melodies. The names of their respective râgas have, in some cases, been omitted, the names of Hindustani râgas being different from Karnâtik. Several of them modulate into different râgas. Such technicalities are not of much general interest. Examples, however, may be found below. The ghuzal given is popular in Guzerat, and is sung quickly, but with great expression and varying *tempo*. It should be remembered that, in all cases in performance, the airs are much varied by grace, and rarely are sung in their naked form. All singers, both Hindustani and Karnâtik, make great use of a slide akin to the *portamento*.

GHUZAL.

IN RÂGA S'ANKÂRA.

LAVANI.

THUNGRI.

KHYAL. Râga Kedara.

PATHAM.

THUNGRI. Râgas Pilu and Désh.

KHYAL. Râga Kaliân.

DADRA. Râgas Kâfi and Désh.

LAVANI. Râga Gauri.

GURBAH.

Râga Kâfi.

GURBAH.

Râga Mând.

GURBAH.

THUNGRI.

SCALES USED IN HINDUSTANI MUSIC AND STYLED "THÂTS."

(The numbers in brackets refer to the corresponding Kârnatik scales upon pages 32-35.)

THE NAHABET. FROM A NATIVE DRAWING.

CHAPTER VI.

Musical Entertainments—Music and the Drama—Influence of the latter upon songs of the country—Of the Indian orchestra—Religious music—Temple music—Employment of bells—Street music—The Nahabet—Nautch music—Dancing.

MUSICAL entertainments among the higher classes are very popular and much in vogue. Upon such occasions a company of musicians are hired for the evening. The Vina is the favourite instrument, and is generally accompanied by either a Mathala or Tabla, or else by a kind of earthen pot called Gátha, much like the ordinary "chatty," which, in the hands of a skilful performer, is beaten with wonderful dexterity. Sometimes, but rarely, two vinas of different sizes are employed. In this case, if the players are skilful, the effect is very pleasing, especially in the performance of an Alâpa, a kind of rhapsody or fantasia impromptu, in any râga; each instrument keeps its part distinct, and the theme is cleverly imitated and tossed about from one to the other much as is done in a modern orchestra. Such imitation is, however, purely at the fancy of the performers, and not contrapuntal imitation as understood in Europe.

Throughout Southern India the native drama is exceedingly popular; the actors are generally well educated and of a high caste, and a good company always attracts full houses. Music is largely employed upon the stage, and there is a kind of orchestra attached to every native theatre. The songs sung at performances of the kind do not, as a rule, differ much from the ordinary music of the country, and of late years there has been a tendency to imitate foreign music, such as Arabian or Persian, and the English, Scotch, or other airs played by military bands at all large stations. These naturally find their way from the theatre into private houses—boys learn them and sing them in the street—and so their influence gradually extends and makes itself felt upon Indian music in general. The old melody types, or râgas, are being less jealously adhered to, and the better educated classes of Hindus are beginning to see that music is not necessarily confined to one or two particular systems, but that, like nearly everything else, it is capable of improvement and further development.

A marked change for the better in the manner of singing is evident. This, indeed, could not fail to be the case when it is remembered that if a voice is intended to be heard by a large audience in a theatre or other building of the kind it must be thrown out to the full extent of its volume, instead of being contorted and its sweetness spoilt by the continued small inflections of tone and unnatural falsetto notes so much practised by native singers of the ordinary class.

The native orchestra is usually made up of the following instruments, or of a somewhat similar combination :—

Sârangi (*string*)	2	Mathala or Tabla (*drums*)	1
Tamburi (*string*)	1	S'ruti (*drone*)	1
Mukavina (*native oboe*)	1		

The use of the Sârangi in Southern India—except in conjunction with Nautches—is rapidly being discontinued, and an English fiddle tuned as a vina or sârangi is often substituted for it. Farther North the instrument appears likely to hold its place for a long time to come. A clarinet is sometimes preferred to the Mukavina.

In musical performances cymbals and bells of different kinds are used, according to taste, and the occasional use of a harmonicon of little bells or plates of metal (Septaghantika), or of porcelain cups or glasses (Jálatharángini), is much admired.

It is a common custom for the members of particular castes, sects, &c., to meet together at stated intervals for the purpose of worship, either in each other's houses or in temples. On these occasions music forms a prominent feature, and consists of hymns of different kinds, accompanied by a variety of instruments. Music of this nature is called Bhazana, and its use is almost universal.

Among the higher castes great trouble and expense is incurred in procuring good performers for this purpose. The songs are generally pretty and well sung to the accompaniment of the vina or sitar and tamburi, with, perhaps, a small drum to mark the rhythm. The Bhazana of the common people is a great contrast to this, and in their assemblies melody is often sacrificed to mere noise. Each man, in order to show his devotion, sings in turn, frequently with no regard for time or tune, whilst the others beat drums or blow a kind of whistle called Sillu, with other instruments, just as it pleases them, and, as can be imagined, the effect of this is discordant in the extreme.

The instruments commonly employed in Bhazana consist of one of the following combinations—

Tamburi	2	S'ruti	1
Sârangi or Fiddle	2	Sitar	1
Mathala	1	Tabla	1 pair

Tamburi	1	Sitar	1
Sârangi	1	Tâla (*cymbals*)	1
Mathala	1	Tabla	1 pair

Or, if the means of the worshippers be very limited, a single tambouri, with, perhaps, one pair of little cymbals and a common drum, or tabor such as Khanjeri, is found.

The music performed for Bhazana usually consists of kirthanas, gítas, and kruthis.

In temples, chiefly those of Lingayet or other Saivite sects, there is a peculiar kind of music in use called Kâradísaméla. It is so-called because a large conical kettle-drum called by that name is the principal instrument employed in it. The Kâradísaméla carries with it a special rhythm of its own; for lively airs—♫ ♫ ♫ | ♩. ♩. | —; for those of a mournful nature—♫ ♬ 𝄾

A system of music called Sopânam is found in Malabar, where it is confined to temple services. In every temple of any importance in Malabar and Travancore it is usual to have both instrumental and vocal music at the steps leading to the principal shrine during the performance of certain services. The word sopânam, in its literal sense, means "steps," and hence gives its name to this particular kind of music. The Sopânam system varies in many respects from both the Karnâtik and Hindustani; a detailed description of it would, however, be unnecessary, since it is much akin to the Karnâtik system and differs only in technical points, which would be uninteresting to the reader.

The use of the gong and bell in temples is universal. Colonel Meadows Taylor, in speaking of this, remarks that the gong is not used as an accompaniment to any but the loud crashing and generally dissonant music of the temple ceremonies. No ceremony of sacrifice or oblation is ever performed without a preliminary tinkling of the bell, repeated at certain intervals according to the ritual.

There can be no doubt that the practice of using it is as ancient as Hinduism itself, and the ritual liturgies and works on ceremonial observances define the use to be made of it.[1] In fact, the use of bells for religious purposes

[1] "Proceedings, Royal Irish Academy." Vol. IX., Part i.

seems to have been from the earliest times so universal amongst almost all nations that it is only necessary to point out that the exact counterpart of the Hindu Ghante is to be found at the present day in the Sanctus bell in use in Christian Churches, and it is perhaps worthy of note that in the great sculptured Trimurti or Hindu trinity at Elephanta one of the figures holds a bell.

The Dasaris, a mendicant class of temple servers of Vaisnavite persuasion, usually employ a little side-drum, with one head only, called Dinni, not unlike the modern Egyptian "Tabl Shâmî"; other mendicants, called Andis, outcasts from Saivite sects, play upon a small gong called Semakkalam, which they beat with a stick. Both Dasaris and Andis often carry a horn as well, and support themselves by singing doleful ballads or hymns at street corners and by begging. Work of any sort they decline. The ordinary native band of discordant wind instruments, drums, and cymbals found throughout Southern India is called Méla. The players in these bands are mostly taken from a caste of Telegu-speaking barbers called "Mángala-vândlu," who make this their special profession and provide the music, so-called, commonly heard at temple ceremonies, weddings, festal gatherings, and all street "tamâshas." The composition of these bands varies greatly, the number of instruments in some cases being as many as thirty and in others perhaps only three or four; generally one or two nâgasâras—a s'ruti or drone—a drum such as the dhol—and a pair of cymbals (called Jhanj), about ten inches or a foot in diameter, are found. Sometimes a méla, consisting of a single mukavina, a flute, a flageolet, a drone, and a small side-drum called Dhanki is employed.[2]

The effect of a méla can hardly be called pleasing, unless to those whose chief delight is discordant noise. The air, such as it is, is generally drowned by the clanging of cymbals and the incessant drumming, which, added to the prolonged and shrill drone of the s'rutis, produce an effect considerably imposing. But, as Captain Willard pithily enough remarks,[3] it is heard to advantage "from a distance."

A peculiar institution of Indian music is known as the Nahabet,[4] and is so called from that being the name of the largest drum associated with it. There are certain persons—Hindu or Mahomedan noblemen—who are privileged to have attached to their service bands of professional musicians, who perform at certain stated hours of the day or night. This privilege is sometimes extended to certain temples and shrines of saints, or to spiritual princes—gurus or swâmies. To these

[2] Preference seems to be given to instruments of European manufacture, and it is not unusual to find old clarinets, flutes, and fifes used in these bands.

[3] "A Treatise on the Music of Hindustan." Captain N. A. Willard. Calcutta, 1834.

[4] This word is commonly pronounced "Nōbut."

bands the name of Nahabet is given, and they are usually placed in balconies over the gateways of cities or palaces, or in other elevated places elsewhere, and these places are known as the Nahabet Khaneh. The music played is, of course, traditional, but it possesses a distinct character of its own that is entirely different to any other music heard in India, and the effect, especially among mountains or in the hill fortresses, such as are found in Central India or Rajputana, is very striking. Usually care is taken to retain the services of the best performers for the Nahabet, and when heard from a little distance upon a still Indian night, and the sound is subdued, there is a good deal of wild beauty about it that possesses a charm peculiarly its own.

In the time of the Mogul Empire, we learn from the "Ain-i-Akbari,"[5] the Nahabet was held in great esteem, and the Emperor Akbar himself was even a performer. There were then in the palace Nakkera Khaneh some eighteen large Nahabets, twenty smaller kettledrums (Nakkeras), four Dohl, four Kurna or large trumpets, nine Surnais or pipes similar to the Nâgasâra, and their accompanying drones, two S'ring or horns, and three pairs of cymbals of large size, besides several Nafirs (a smaller kind of trumpet, similar to the Tuturi); and in those days the performances of the Nahabet occupied a prominent place in the daily palace routine. The general practice then was that the Nahabet played first at midnight and the second time at dawn. An hour before sunrise the musicians commenced to play the Surnais, an hour later there was a short prelude, which in turn was followed by pieces introducing the Kurna, Nafir, and other wind instruments, with the occasional use of the largest drum of all (Damama or Nahabet), but which did not introduce the Nakkera. After this the Surnais and Nafirs were played alone; an hour later there was a general *crescendo*, and then followed seven distinct performances, brought to a conclusion by the chanting of various prayers for blessings upon the Emperor, and then the day's service was finished by the Surnais players playing softly to a *pianissimo* of the drums.

In the present day the large number of different instruments formerly found in the Nahabet Khanehs of fortresses and palaces do not exist, and the effect of the modern Nahabet is therefore less imposing. There are, however, to be found in most Nahabet Khanehs one pair of large Nahabets, a couple of pairs of smaller kettledrums (Nakkera) and possibly other drums with a Kurna, one or two Tuturi, a pair or two of cymbals, one or two Nâgasâras and their accompanying drones, with perhaps a couple of Nuy or flutes-à-bec.

---

[5] "Ain-i-Akbari." Translated from the original version by H. Blochmann, M.A. See Vol. I., Ain. 19.

The Kurna is not always found, for only nobles of the highest rank are considered able to use it; and by Brahmins it is still held to be the most ancient and sacred instrument of music in existence, and they consequently give it a prominent place in their temple ritual.

Nautch music is termed Taffa or Kéylika and is performed exclusively by a caste of Nautch people called in Southern India Mélakâra-jâti. This is a composite class of dancing women and male musicians, distinguished by a marked social division from the higher orders of the musical profession. The dancing men and women of the Mélakâra caste, who together form a complete chorus, constitute what is called a Chinnaméla (or smaller music), in distinction to the Peryaméla (big music), which is a band of male musicians who play upon the Nâgasâra with drums and accompaniments differing from those of the dancers.[6] The Peryaméla, or Pathamélam as it is also called, is the ordinary native band formed by the Mángalavândlu caste and already described.

At Nautches the usual arrangement of instruments is as follows:—

Sârangis, or English fiddles tuned in the native manner	2
Mridang or Tabla (*drum*)	1
S'ruti-upanga (*drone*)	1
Tâla or jâlra (*cymbals*)	1

The Hindu art of dancing is treated of at great length in the Sanskrit work "Bhârata S'astra." Its origin is ascribed to the god Brahma. The science of dancing is usually considered under three heads—viz., nritta, vatya, and nrittya. Of these nrittya is what is understood by dancing as seen at a Nautch; nritta comprises only rhythmical movements without gestures; vatya has to do with stage action only. The masculine and feminine aspects of each of these three heads are fully treated of, and are styled *Tandava* and *Lasya.* There are rules for numerous motions of the head, eye, brow, and neck, to say nothing of those of the body, arms, and feet, that have to be carefully attended to. Each movement or look is described with an exactness that is almost incredible. All these various gestures and expressions are regulated by the tâla or rhythm of the dance, and are centred in the stamp of the feet upon the ground at intervals, or in the tinkling of the bells worn by the dancer. Indian dancing, like that of most Oriental nations, consists of gestures, slow, and more or less dignified, in time to the music, rather than actual dancing as understood by a ballet. To an Englishman a Nautch is therefore apt to be a rather disappointing entertainment, there being little real grace or symmetry of movement about the performance.

[6] "Manual of the Tanjore District." T. Venkasami Row. Madras, 1884.

And like Indian music, Indian dancing should be judged entirely from an Oriental standpoint. A Nautch usually commences with the singing of a Mangala or "song of hail" (generally in the Râga Nâta), the words of which are intended to do honour to the principal personages present. When this is concluded, the leader or conductor of the troupe, who invariably plays the tâla or jâlra, hums or sings a kind of accompaniment, called Konnagólu, to this one of the girls dances, keeping time with the soft tinkling of the bells tied round her ankles. During this the other instruments are independent of the leader and are played softly and without time in any râga that may be chosen, the chorus, if any, being much subdued. And when the dance is finished, songs—such as javadis or pathams—follow, one voice singing the solo and the whole of the voices taking up at intervals a soft refrain. Dances or gestures, in character with the words of the song, are made by the girls performing in front of the musicians.

Sometimes Sanskrit slokes, called "Astapathi," are sung by one voice, the instruments playing a kind of soft, dreamy accompaniment without any well defined time, either with or alternately with the voice.

The performance is brought to a close by the singing of a Mangala, in either the râgas Surati or Saurâshtra.

A Musical Party.

CHAPTER VII.

Of instruments—Decoration—Materials—How susceptible of improvement—Chief defects in construction—Eastern origin of many European instruments—Descriptions of instruments in common use.

MOST of the early Indian musical instruments remain still in use. Since the time of the Mahomedan invasion, about a thousand years ago, some Arabian and Persian instruments have been adopted, and have become almost naturalised; but their use has never become universal, and is mostly confined to the North of India or to Mussulman musicians.

The people of India have always been conservative in their tastes, and in nothing do we find this more evident than in their music and musical instruments. Descriptions of them all are found in many of the old Sanskrit treatises, and show that the forms of the instruments now in use have altered hardly at all during the last two thousand years; old paintings and sculptures, such as those of Ajanta, prove this even more conclusively.[1] There are many musical instruments to be found among the sculptures existing upon various old temples, cave temples, and ancient Buddhist topes and stupas in different parts of India. Those at Amravati and Sanchi are especially interesting.[2] For in the Amravati sculptures, which were visited by the traveller, Hiouen Thsang, and called by him Dhanakacheka, about the year 640 of our era, we find several representations of musical instruments. One of peculiar interest shows a group of eighteen women playing upon drums, a shell trumpet or s'ankha, one much like a surnai, and two instruments, apparently quanūns, of a shape very similar to

---

[1] *See* "The Industrial Arts of India." Sir C. M. Birdwood. London, 1880.

[2] "Tree and Serpent Worship." James Fergusson, F.R.S. London, 1868. *See* plates LXII., XXXVII., XXVIII. These sculptures are now in the British Museum.

the Assyrian harps. But there is another instrument represented that would seem to have been especially popular, but which is never met with in India now, nor can descriptions of it be found in the Sanskrit treatises upon instruments. This again figures in Assyrian and Egyptian sculptures and paintings. It is somewhat like a harp, and much like an African instrument called Sancho, and still used in some parts of that continent. Mr. James Fergusson notices strong Bactrian influences in this monument at Amravati, and is of opinion that the expression of the traveller Hiouen Thsang that this tope was ornamented with all the art of the palaces of Bactria is borne out to its fullest extent. This peculiar harp is again found amongst the sculptures at Sanchi; where also is seen an instrument resembling the Roman tibiæ pares. But the tibiæ pares are there shown without the capistrum or cheek bandage, and it is known that this instrument was also used by the Greeks. It is worthy of note that a form of the tibiæ pares is still common in Northern India, where it consists of a pair of flutes-à-bec. At Sanchi, too, is found a figure of a man blowing a kind of trumpet—the s'ringa—of much the same shape as that now employed in Bengal.

Perhaps the most reliable proofs of the antiquity of Indian instruments can be found, not so much in the Sanskrit, but in the Pâli works remaining. For to these Buddhist treatises it is an easier matter to assign dates that can be tolerably accurate. In the Milindha Panha,[3] a Pâli work, written a little after the Christian era, is a description of the vina, also of the shell-trumpet (s'ankha) and the flute (here rendered vañsa—a reed). And in the Mahaparambhana Sutta, a still older work of about 400 B.C., we find mention of the Bheri, a word still used for the Nâgara, or large kettle-drum, and also of the mridang (here rendered muttinga; *cf.* mathala, the Southern Indian name of the mridang). The same work contains mention of the vina and pañava, the latter being a drum. And these same instruments, with the addition of one called dendima, are found in a contemporary work called Sāmañña-phale-sutta, and in the Vimāna-vatthu also. The dendima is possibly the modern dinni, a small side-drum used by religious mendicants in Southern India at the present day.

The materials of which musical instruments are made are for the most part those that are found readiest at hand in the country—bamboo, or some similar cane, and large gourds are much employed. These gourds are used for many

---

[3] *See* Milindha Panha, Sacred books of the East, Vol. I., page 84. Vina is here translated *mandoline*: also page 48. *See* Buddhist Suttas. Oxford, 81. Translations of Mahaparambhana Sutta, page 101; also of Sāmañña-phale-sutta, § 90, and of Vimāna-vatthu, § 81, 10. Two kinds of tâla are mentioned in Digha I., 1, 13—*i.e.*, metal tâla and hand-tâla. The word for hand-tâla is found in many Pâli works. The thanks of the Author are due to Professor T. W. Rhys Davids for much valuable help and information.

purposes, and the best are trained in their growth to the shape for which they are required.

In the manufacture of certain instruments earthenware is employed; the common country "blackwood" is largely used; in fact, whatever is found by the instrument makers, that from its natural shape, or the ease with which it can be worked, can be adapted with the least possible trouble to themselves, is readily seized upon, whether its acoustical properties are suitable or not, purity of tone being sacrificed to appearance. The natural consequence of this is that many instruments are badly put together in the first place; faults in their construction are glossed over by outward ornamentation, and, from want of proper material, the tone, which should be the first consideration, is frequently sadly deficient in volume and quality.

The reason why this is so appears to be that the manufacture of musical instruments is chiefly in the hands of ordinary carpenters, most of whom are totally ignorant of the most elementary principles of music, and who, even if they possessed the requisite knowledge, could seldom afford either the time or money to spend upon experiments tending to improve their instruments: their principal consideration seems to be quantity instead of quality.

Most musicians therefore prefer to patch and mend their old instruments, even though it will be slightly detrimental to their tone, to procuring fresh ones of a quality of which they are doubtful, and which they cannot test practically before they make their choice.

A musical instrument, to be of any real practical good, requires in its construction not only skilled labour, but an experimental knowledge on the part of the maker of the principles of acoustics; he must know of the best materials, and the best known methods of building up an instrument from these materials. Such knowledge as this can only be attained by much study and the experience of a regular apprenticeship to the art. All this is, of course, obtained easily enough in Europe, where there is a ready sale for good instruments, and instrument making is a trade profitable enough for a supply to be kept on hand. In India, where, until comparatively recent times, music has been an art almost neglected for some hundreds of years, it is clear that there has been little scope for instrument makers of any ability, the supply being always far in excess of the demand.

The chief defect apparent in the construction of Indian instruments, besides what are mentioned above, is one which affects them all—viz., that without altering the tuning a change of keys is impossible. This may at first sight seem incongruous, for the vina is semitonic. But it must be remembered that the third and fourth strings of that instrument, though they pass over the finger-board, are seldom stopped, and such devices as shifts are *absolutely* unknown. There is likewise no method of tuning to any fixed standard of pitch. Willard, in speaking of this, makes the following observations:—"A drum or tabor, the sound of which is necessarily monotonous, is an ever attendant and inseparable companion to Indian songs, whether any instrument be present or not. Its sound is taken as the keynote, and all other instruments that may be present and the voice are regulated by it. From this it appears that as long as the use of the drum or tabor is not laid aside there will be no necessity for change of keys, and the rhythmical nature of Indian music renders a liberal use of the drum more essential, in order to mark the time distinctly, than any other accompaniment."[4]

Many of our own instruments, such as are in use at the present day, have their prototypes still in existence in the East.

The ancient Pâli and Sanskrit treatises would appear to contain the earliest reliable description of any musical instruments, and from these it seems clear that those of most Asiatic nations were originally derived from the same source.

The Persians still use an instrument called quanūn, much like that of the same name found now in India—a kind of dulcimer, strung with gut or wire strings, and played upon by plectra fastened to the fingers of the performers. This is a development of the kattyayana-vina or shata-tantri (*i.e.*, hundred-stringed) vina, as it was formerly called. This Persian quanūn, the prototype of the mediæval psaltery, afterwards became the santir, which has strings of wire in place of gut, and is played with two sticks, and in the West it eventually took the form of the dulcimer. Hence the origin of the complicated pianoforte of the present day can thus be traced to the Aryans. And so with many others. The violin, the flute, the oboe, the guitar, all have an Eastern origin. One of the earliest stringed instruments was called "pinaka," and had one string twanged by the fingers; its invention is ascribed to the god Siva.

The violin bow is claimed by the Hindus to have been invented by Râbana, King of Ceylon, who, according to tradition, lived five thousand years ago.

The earliest instrument played with a bow was called râbanastra or râbanastrana. What this instrument was like is rather doubtful, but at the present time there exists in Ceylon a primitive instrument played with a bow, called "vinavah," which has two strings of different kinds: one made of a species of flax and the other of horsehair, which is the material also of the string of the

[4] "A Treatise on the Music of Hindustan." Captain N. A. Willard. Calcutta, 1834.

bow, which with bells attached to it is used as a fiddle-stick. The hollow part of this instrument is half a cocoa-nut shell polished, covered with the dried skin of a lizard, and perforated below.[5]

The vinavah is rarely met with except in the hands of strolling musicians, who support themselves by means of it. Whether this is the primitive râbanastra or not it is impossible to say, but it seems extremely probable that if not absolutely identical it bears at least a very strong resemblance to it. Another very ancient instrument which resembled the râbanastra was called amrita.

Numbers of instruments still in use in India have not altered in the smallest particular their ancient forms. The vina, the tamburi or tamburu-vina, and the kinneri still remain just as they are described in the ancient books, even down to the very details of the carving with which they are adorned, so conservative are the people who use them of all connected with the art they hold to be so sacred. The peculiar shape of instruments of the viol and violin tribe appears to have a prototype among Indian instruments; and this can be seen in the rabôb, which is made with distinct *upper, lower, and middle* bouts, and in a less degree in the sârangi, sarōde, and chikâra.

The rebec, once popular in Europe, was a form of the rabôb, brought to Spain by the Moors, who in turn had derived it from Persia and Arabia. Here again the Aryan origin is evident, the rabôb being, according to old Sanskrit works, a form of vina. And it is still popular in the North of India and Afghanistan.

The use of instruments of percussion of definite sonorousness, such as the harmonica, does not seem to have entered into Indian music at any time until quite of late years.

But this is rather an open question, for the harmonicon of cups called Jâlatharángini is by some ascribed to a very remote origin.

Wind instruments, although perhaps of earlier invention than those with strings, are nevertheless looked upon as of secondary importance. Possibly this may have some reason in the fact that Brahmins are not allowed by their religious laws to use them, excepting only the flute blown by the nostrils, and one or two others of the horn and trumpet kind. And so men of low castes are employed as players of wind instruments. But all unite in ascribing to wind instruments a very high antiquity. The conch shell, still used in the daily temple ritual in almost every place in India, is said to have been first used by the god Krishna, and it is mentioned in the great epic of the Ramayana, where it is called

---

[5] "An Account of the Interior of Ceylon and its Inhabitants." J. Davy, F.R.S.

Devadata. We also find it under the name of Goshringa, both in the Ramayana and the Mahabhârata.

The horn (s'ringa) is also said to be of Divine origin, and it is mentioned in the earliest writings. But the flute (murali) is still held to be peculiarly sacred, for this flute was the companion of the god Krishna in all his wanderings, and in Indian mythology this flute is looked upon with much the same veneration that the lyre was by the Greeks, and by Brahmins it is still used occasionally and blown by the nostrils. In all sculptures and pictures the god Krishna is represented as standing cross-legged playing the flute.

Reed instruments, although doubtless of a very remote origin, appear to have been invented at a later period than instruments of the flute species, and their use is, as has been stated, confined to either low caste Hindus or Mahomedans. For the Indian reed instruments are mostly harsh and wild, far too powerful and shrill to be used in concert with the delicate vina or sweet tamburi, and so their use is chiefly confined to out-of-door performances, where their sound is better heard and where they become fit adjuncts to the Nakkera Khaneh or band already described.

Instruments with double reeds appear to have been originally brought from India, and the double reed is found in the primitive oboes used there as well as in Persia, Arabia, and Egypt. There seems to be no trace of the *single beating* reed ever having been known in India, but the single *free* reed is found in the bagpipe of the country. Indeed, the bagpipe would itself seem to have an Eastern origin, and although its use in Southern India and the Deccan is chiefly confined to a drone-bass, yet in the Punjâb and Afghanistan pipes are sometimes found containing both drone and chanter. And I have heard them played with a dexterity that would do credit to a Highland piper.

The pungi, now used almost entirely by snake charmers, is said to have once been blown by the nostrils and called " Nâsajantra."

The jew's-harp (murchang) is mentioned in most of the Sanskrit works upon musical instruments, and its use is common all over India.

The use of the gong and bell are universal, and need no particular description. The gong—called sometimes Tâla, but more generally Ghari—is found in almost all Hindu temples, and is used both in the daily ritual and also to note the hours of the day. It is usually about a foot in diameter and $\frac{1}{5}$-inch in thickness; it is made of bell metal, and sounded by a wooden mallet. Indeed, the tone more nearly resembles that of a bell, and has certainly nothing in common with the Chinese gong. In Southern India a light instrument of this kind called Jâgatay or Semakalam is found, which is sounded by a curved bone striker. The small bell—called Ghante—is used in every Hindu temple, and is familiar to everyone. Bells of any size are not known in India, but the antiquity of the bell in India has been proved beyond doubt; specimens of curious old bells have been discovered in cromlechs and cairns in different parts of India.[6] And among the Todas, the aborigines of the Niliri Hills, the bell is still an object of especial veneration.[7]

The little ankle bells used by Nautch dancers are called Gūnguru or Gajelu, and are tied in strings round the ankles. They produce "a faint clashing sound as the feet move in steps, which mingles not unmusically with the dance music or songs which accompany the dance; and they not only serve to mark the time, but to keep the dancer or singer in perfect accord with the musicians. These bells are the symbols of their profession with all dancers and singers, and to some extent are held sacred. No dancer ties them on his or her ankles before performance without touching his or her forehead and eyes with them, and saying a short prayer or invocation to a patron saint or divinity—Hindu or Mahomedan. Nor is it possible, after a female singer or dancer has once been invested with them—a ceremony which is very solemnly performed and attended with much cost—to abandon the professional life so adopted. He, or she, *has tied on the bells*, is even a proverb to signify that the person alluded to has devoted himself or herself to a purpose from which it is impossible to recede. Strings of these small bells are also used for horses and tied round the fetlocks of prancing chargers, with gay tinsel ribbons or pieces of cloth; also round the necks of lap dogs; and some of a large size round the necks of favourite plough or cart bullocks. The latter are identical with sleigh bells. No post runner in India travels without a string of them tied on the end of his pole on which is slung the leather bag he carries, and on a still night their clashing sound, besides being heard at a great distance, serves to scare away wild beasts and to cheer the runner on his lonely path."[8]

And here it may be well to mention two instruments sometimes met with in Southern India—viz., the cup-harmonica and the Gatha.

The Jâlatharángini[9] is a harmonicon of cups of porcelain or earthenware tuned to the particular scale required by means of pouring in more or less water. It is played with two thin sticks, covered with felt or tipped with cork; and in company with other instruments the contrast of tone that its use effects is not unpleasing. The Septasvarab, called also Septaghantika, or Indian Glockenspiel,

---

[6] "Bells of the Church." H. T. Ellacombe. Exeter, 1872.

[7] "A Phrenologist amongst the Todas." Colonel Marshall. London, 1873.

[8] "Proceedings of the Royal Irish Academy." Vol. IX., Part i.

[9] This instrument is *said* to be mentioned in a Sanskrit work—the name of which the author has been unable to ascertain—believed to have been written about A.D. 700.

is somewhat similar, but more musical; it is made either of metal plates or bells, struck with a small felt-covered hammer. The employment of both instruments is rare.

The Gatha resembles a large spherical jar or "chatty" in shape, and is largely used by Telegu musicians as an accompaniment to the vina. It is about 18 inches in height, and has a very small aperture and short neck, which is held downwards when it is in use. It is beaten with the hands and wrists, much like the drum called mathala, of which it takes the place, and the players manage to produce sounds of different pitch by striking it in different places. The performer usually sits cross-legged, and holds the gatha between his thighs, striking it with his finger tips, flat of his hand, or fleshy part of his wrist.

Players upon the gatha display great dexterity, and often vary their performance by throwing the instrument up into the air and catching it again, beating it as they do so: this they keep up for almost any length of time. At the conclusion of the piece they let it fall into their hands (or upon the ground, so as to break with noise) at the exact conclusion of the measure (tâla), which they never for a moment lose.

In some performances it is not unusual for the player upon the vina to change the measure suddenly, as often as he wills, so that the gatha player may better show his dexterity.

Instruments of the trumpet kind—in which tones are produced by the lips vibrating within a cup-shaped mouthpiece—appear to be of very great antiquity, for mention is made of them in both the great Hindu epics—the Mahambhârata and the Ramâyána. There are large curved horns which in tone much resemble the Alp-horns of Switzerland. There are both straight and bent trumpets. The method of making an instrument of this kind more portable by being turned back, but without shortening its length of tubing, would seem to be very ancient. It is difficult to describe any definite scale for these instruments, for they are, with one or two exceptions, rarely used by any but men of low caste, and their proper compass is not employed or understood. The great similarity between the shape of the modern trumpet and the Indian tuturi is very striking, especially when it is remembered that this shape has not been copied from the European instrument, but has existed in India from remote ages.

Indeed, so many points of resemblance might be noticed, and the development through ages of so many instruments traced, that it would be inadvisable to enlarge this chapter by so wide a digression from the subject.

Indian musical instruments are usually classified under the following four designations, just as they were by Bhârata two thousand years ago :—

I. Tata-yantra—Comprising all stringed instruments.

II. Shusira-yantra—Comprising all instruments of percussion (not being covered with skin or parchment, such as drums), and includes cymbals, gongs, bells, castanets, &c.

III. Ghana-yantra—Comprising all instruments covered with skins, such as drums, tabors, &c.

IV. Anuddha-yantra—Comprising wind instruments of all kinds.

In different parts of India there is of course a preference for particular instruments, but it is impossible to assign definite districts to them, as all kinds are to be found more or less throughout the country.

In the following pages an endeavour has been made to give as far as possible some mention of all these instruments, together with the names by which they are known in different parts, and descriptions of those in most common use.

If details are given sometimes which at first sight are apparently unnecessary, it has been done because in similar cases of musical investigations, if many things which appeared to be of little moment at the time had not been left unnoticed, much interesting light would have been thrown upon several questions of great interest which are still involved in darkness.

In the tunings for stringed instruments given later, the position of the strings is as if the instrument were held upright, body nearest the ground, with the finger-board facing the reader. It is to be noted that in instruments of the vina kind the order of the strings is reversed from that of sitars and the like, where the first string or *chanterelle* is always on the right.

A PLAYER ON THE KARNÂTIK SITAR.

PLATE I.

A BÎN PLAYER.

THIS plate shows the position of a player upon the Bîn or Vina[10] of the North of India. The vina of the South, described in the next plate, is sometimes called the Rudra vina, in distinction to the bîn or Mahati vina. As will be seen, this is a fretted instrument, the frets being arranged at semitonic intervals. The tuning differs from that of the Southern vina, and two gourd resonators take the place of the wooden pear-shaped body. It is worthy of note that an instrument of this description was described by Mersenne in 1636.[11]

The average total length of the instrument is 3 feet 7 inches, in which case the dimensions are as follows :—

The first gourd is fixed at 10 inches from the top, and the second about 2 feet 11$\frac{1}{2}$ inches.

The gourds are usually very large, about 14 inches in diameter, and each has a round piece cut out of the bottom to act as a sound hole.

The finger-board is 21$\frac{6}{8}$ inches in length and about 3 inches wide, and upon it are placed the frets, exactly in the same manner as in the vina, and at the same semitonic intervals.

The frets are nineteen to twenty-two in number, that nearest the nut usually being $\frac{1}{8}$-inch above the finger-board, and that at the other extremity about $\frac{7}{8}$-inch, the decrease gradual.

---

[10] This instrument is very fully described as "The Indian Lyre." "Asiatic Researches." Vol. I.
The bîn has been described by Mr. Carl Engel as "the vina of the Indus"; this is, however, an error on his part, it being but a form, and far from the best form, of that instrument, popular chiefly because of its comparatively low cost. Drawings of this instrument will be found in his "Musical Instruments," in "Asiatic Researches" above-mentioned, and in Hipkins and Gibb's "Musical Instruments."

[11] "Harmonie Universelle." Fr. Mersenne. Paris, 1636.

The strings are seven in number, four of which pass over the frets, the remainder being side strings, placed two on the left side and one upon the right.

The instrument is tuned as follows :—

but a very much more common tuning is—

the wire X upon the right side being tuned to either Ga (E) or Dha (A), according to the requirement of the râga performed.

The strings upon the left side and the two highest upon the finger-board are usually steel, the remainder brass or silver.

The instrument is held over the left shoulder, the upper gourd resting upon it, and the lower gourd on the right knee.

The frets are stopped with the left hand, the little finger of which is used occasionally to strike the side string on the left side.

The strikes are made by the right hand in a similar way to that employed in the sitar, except that the *two* first fingers are armed with wire plectra.

The notes are rapidly reiterated in the bîn as well as in the sitar by the plectra being passed backwards and forwards across the string ; this produces a kind of *sostenuto*.

The chief peculiarity of this instrument, as will be remarked, is the tuning, which employs additional intervals to that of the Southern vina, and so renders the instrument less confined in its modulation. The tone is rather thinner than and not so pleasing as that of the vina of the South, on account of the greater tendency of the strings to jangle. The instrument is nevertheless very popular, and when found in Southern India is used chiefly by Hindustani musicians. Instruments of this kind are sometimes made with moveable frets, like those of a sitar, in consequence of the greater facility with which they can be played by less experienced performers.

An illustration of a bîn of this latter kind is shown in Plate IV.

PLATE II.

SOUTHERN INDIAN VINA. SMALL SITAR.

THE instrument to the left of the plate represents the Vina in common use in Southern India. Though in Northern India and the Deccan the use of the vina, or bîn, is restricted to professional musicians or skilful performers, we do not find this to be the case in the South. This instrument is taught in the schools in many places, and is a very favourite one with amateurs of the higher classes. The specimen here represented is about 250 years old, and is from the collection at the Tanjore palace. The delicacy of the carving and the great wealth of decoration bestowed upon this instrument are remarkable, and prove it to have belonged to some very distinguished personage—probably to one of the Maharajahs of Tanjore.

The vina is a stringed instrument, with frets, played with the fingers, or rather finger-nails, somewhat in the same manner as a mandoline or guitar.

Its construction, however, renders it for purposes of melody a far more perfect instrument than either of the latter, and although its tones are not so full and rich, its compass is larger, and it is, in skilled hands, capable of producing a much greater variety of effects.

Its tone, judged from a European standard, is rather thin, but curiously soft and plaintive. It is somewhat like that of the Tyrolese zither, which, however, it exceeds in fulness, and it is capable of infinitely more expression.

The vina has seven strings, four pass over the frets (twenty-four in number), three shorter strings are placed at the side of the finger-board, and are employed chiefly as a kind of accompaniment or to mark the time used by the performer.

The four large strings are termed saranis and are named thus :—

Sarani	1st, thinnest	....	steel.
Panchami	2nd,	....	,,
Mandaram	3rd,	....	brass or silver.
Anumandaram	4th, thickest	....	,, ,,

The three side strings are termed pakha-saranis and are of steel.

The names of the various parts of the instrument are as follows :—

(*a.*) Kayî or body, formed of thin wood and hollowed out of the solid.

(*b.*) Gvantu, a projecting ledge, often of ivory, separating the body from the stem.

(*c.*) Langaru,[12] metal fastenings which secure the strings to the attachment. These fastenings have rings sliding upon them which can be used in tuning to alter the pitch slightly, without turning the tuning pegs.

(*d.*) Dhandi, neck, made hollow.

(*e.*) Yeddapalaka, or belly. Small sound holes, in circles of about 2 inches diameter, are placed on each side of the strings, about 1 inch above the bridge.

(*f.*) Dhandipalaka, a piece of thin wood covering the hollow of the neck underneath the frets.

(*g.*) Mâruvapalaka, two ledges, each about ½-inch in height, projecting from the dhandipalaka and to which the frets are secured.

(*h.*) Metlu, or frets, formed of "half-round" bars of brass or silver about ⅙-inch thick.

(*i.*) Cupé, a cup or socket of some metal into which the burra or calabash is fastened; these cupés are often of silver and richly chased.

(*j.*) Burra, or calabash, a kind of hollow gourd attached to the underside of the neck, near the head, to increase the volume of sound.

(*k.*) Pallumanu, or nut, a piece of ivory over which the strings pass, placed between the pegs and the finger-board.

(*l.*) Mogulu, small ivory pegs answering the purpose of nuts, over which the side strings pass.

(*m.*) Gurram, bridge.

(*p.*) Bhirtu, tuning pegs.

[12] Strings are sometimes secured to the attachment directly, as described for those of the tamburi.

The burra or calabash is secured to the neck by means of a nut and screw, and is detachable at will.

The instrument is tuned in one of the three ways following:—[13]

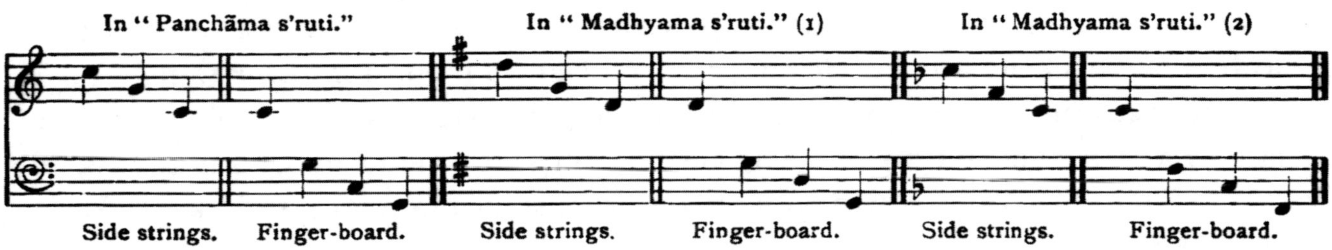

The construction of the bridge is peculiar and deserves notice.

A wooden arc supports a slab of wood 1 by 2½ inches. A resinous cement is poured upon this, and a piece of metal passing underneath the second, third, and fourth strings is laid above and manipulated until the strings produce a clear tone free from all buzz or twang; a wet cloth is then applied, or a little cold water poured over the upper surface, so as to harden the cement. Under the first string a similar piece of metal, in this case of a superior quality—either polished steel or bell metal—is fixed in the same way.

This process is considered very important, as the least carelessness affects the tone of the instrument and gives it a most unpleasant twang.

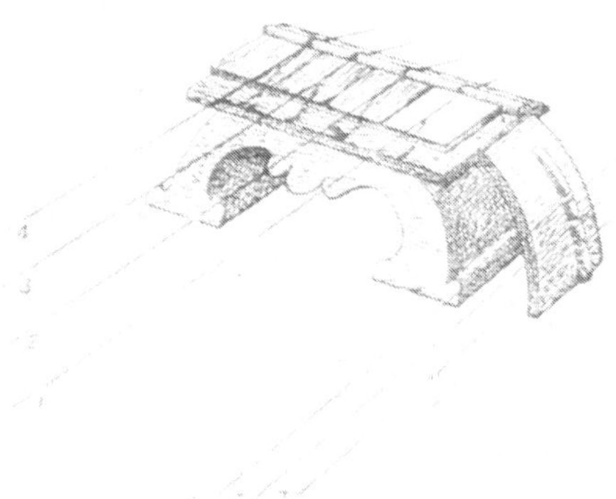

No. 1 is the thin string.
,, 2, very slightly thicker.
,, 3, thicker again.
,, 4, thicker again.

No. 5, ,, 6, ,, 7 — The same gauge as No. 1.

[13] A native musician would say for Panchãma s'ruti, "Pa, Sa, Pa, Sa"; and for Madhyama s'ruti, "Sa, Pa, Sa, Pa": hence the change of keys is shown.

The side string bridge is secured to the main bridge and the belly of the instrument and is made entirely of metal; it consists of an arc of brass with a projecting rim upon the side nearest the attachment.

The strings pass across the flat of the arc through three saw cuts in the rim. Pieces of silk or quill termed "jivalam," placed beneath the strings and the bridge, are occasionally employed to correct any inclination to buzzing.

Most instruments of this description require steel strings of a quality specially made for the purpose. The best strings are made at Channapatna in Mysore, or Bareilly in the North, where the process of manufacture is kept secret and is in the hands of a particular caste.

The price given for such strings is high, on an average Rs. 6 for a *sîr* of twenty-four rupees weight, when sold wholesale.

The fretting of a vina requires great care, and most musicians prefer to fix their own frets.

The frets are fixed to the mâruvapalaka by means of small spikes, and additionally secured by a resinous cement poured in between them, and moulded neatly as it hardens.

When finished the finger-board resembles a ladder, there being a space varying from ½-inch at the head to 2 inches at the end nearest the bridge between the frets and the dhandipallaka, or piece of wood covering the hollow stem.

The vina is held in one of the three following positions:—

(*a*.) The performer sits cross-legged upon the ground, and holds the vina so that the calabash almost touches the left thigh, the left arm passing round the stem so that the fingers rest easily upon the frets. The body of the instrument is upon the ground, partially supported by the right thigh.

(*b*.) The calabash almost touches the left thigh as before, but the right knee is bent upwards, the body of the instrument being in front and resting upon the ground, touching the right leg, which prevents it slipping away.

(*c*.) The performer sits cross-legged upon the ground as before, but holds the body of the instrument in his lap, the finger-board being vertical.

The method of playing upon the vina is rather different from that of other Indian instruments. The left hand is employed to stop the strings on the frets, the right hand to strike with.

Strikes are called "mehtu," and are of three kinds, viz.:—

Kutra—mehtu.

Toda—mehtu.

Gotu—mehtu.

The right hand is employed thus: the wrist is laid almost upon the edge of the belly, and the hand is slightly arched upwards; the first and second fingers are above, and are used to strike the large strings, all strikes being made with the *nail downwards.* Players upon the vina purposely allow the nails of the right hand to grow rather long, for this instrument is never played with plectra. The side strings are sounded by the third and fourth fingers of the right hand moved *upwards.*

The first exercise that a pupil learns is to strike one of the large strings (downwards) simultaneously with one of the side strings (upwards), a more difficult feat to accomplish than might be at first supposed.

These simple strikes are called gotu mehtu. The kutra mehtu is accomplished by striking the same string twice—first with the forefinger and then with the second finger—so as to produce a repetition of the same sound.

The toda mehtu, or etouffe, is made by striking a string with the forefinger and then gently stopping the vibration with the second finger so as to produce a staccato sound.

The left hand is used for all work upon the frets.

As was the case with the lute, the melody is chiefly played upon the first string—the chanterelle, in fact—which is commonly stopped by the first and second fingers placed together.

The fourth string is stopped by the thumb—the others, when required, by the middle and third fingers.

The least difference of pressure upon the frets causes a variation in the pitch, of which use is made in all grace and embellishments.

A species of transient shake styled "rekhu" is of frequent occurrence; it is produced by the string when stopped being slightly pressed, and at the same time pulled out of the straight line. This will raise the pitch to any degree required, not exceeding a major third, beyond which it is found that the string usually breaks.

The performer can thus produce graces of all kinds, embracing intervals less than semitones, which can be clearly distinguished by the ear.

Another effect called "rava" is produced by the string being stopped upon one fret and being beaten by a finger upon the next fret above.

This, when combined with rekhu, adds considerably to the capability of the instrument, and it must be remembered that the string can be kept in a state of vibration very much longer than in the guitar, owing to its thinness in proportion to its length.

The use of glisse, as with the guitar, is frequent.

The small sitar shown on the right of the plate is of Deccan manufacture. It is ornamented prettily with ivory carving, and the body of the instrument is formed from a cocoa-nut. Sitars of this kind are much used by native ladies, and their tone is singularly sweet and plaintive, though, of course, not so powerful as that of the larger sitars. The method of arranging the frets and of playing the instrument is precisely as that described for the larger sitar in Plate III.

ANNA GHARPURE (A SITAR PLAYER IN THE SERVICE OF H.H. THE THAKORE SAHIB OF WADHWAN).

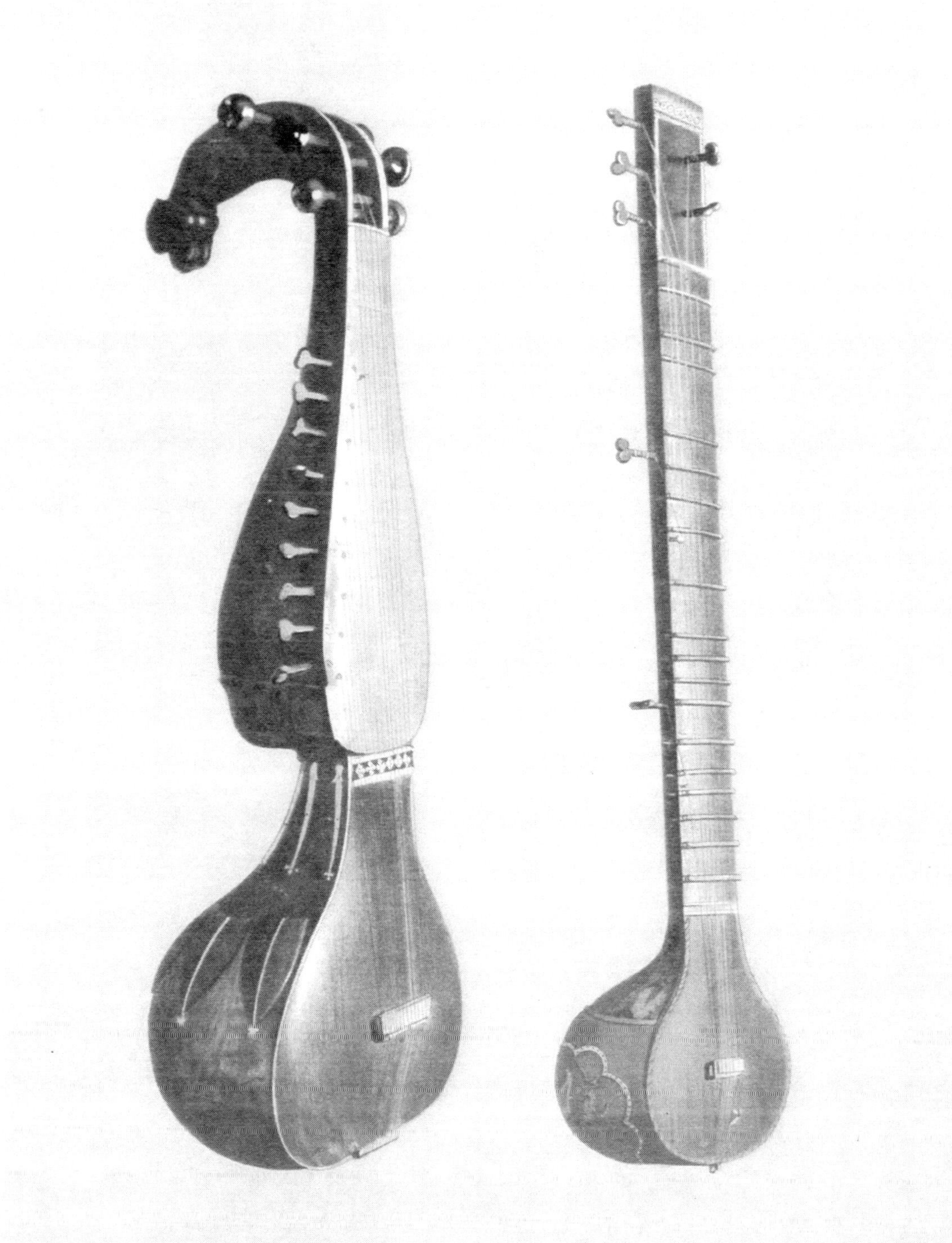

PLATE III.

SUR-S'RINGÂRA. LARGE SITAR.

THE instrument shown upon the right of the plate is the Sitar.[14] This specimen has been adorned with paintings, representing the avatars or appearances of the god Vishnu, and is the work of a Poona maker. The sitars commonly found are only different from this in that the bodies are unpainted.

The sitar is called also Sundari, and is perhaps the commonest of all the stringed instruments of India, being much admired. Its use in Southern India is not so frequent as in the Deccan and farther North, and is chiefly confined to those who practise the Hindustani in preference to the Karnâtik system of music.

In general appearance the sitar is not unlike the tamburi, described later.

The finger-board is about three inches wide, the frets are of brass or silver, eighteen (sometimes sixteen) in number, and flatly elliptical; they are secured to the finger-board by pieces of gut passing underneath—this arrangement admits of their being shifted so as to produce intervals of any particular scale (thât), hence the capability of the instrument is naturally limited.

---

[14] The invention of the sitar is commonly credited to Ameer Khusru, of Delhi, in the twelfth century. Captain Willard states that the instrument derives its name from *si*, سه, signifying in Persian three, and *tar* تار, a string, as that number was commonly used.

The body of the sitar is usually of gourd, cut in half in the direction of the core, with a belly of thin wood pierced with a certain number of sound holes fixed upon it.

The tone of medium-sized sitars is considered preferable to that of large ones.

The nut, or ledge, over which the strings pass on their way to the pegs from the frets is peculiar, and is made double; that nearest the pegs having holes through which the strings pass, and that nearest the frets having simply small notches. The number of strings varies, instruments being made with from three to seven strings.

They are tuned as follows—

These tunings are considered to be " Panchãma s'ruti." If the G strings be lowered a tone the sitar will be in " Madhyama s'ruti."

The instrument is played by means of a plectrum of wire placed upon the forefinger, the thumb being usually pressed firmly upon the edge of the belly, so that the position of the right hand shall change as little as possible.

Sitars, called Taraffedar, with sympathetic strings underneath those played upon, are sometimes found.

The sitar is fairly easy to learn, and much can be made of it by experienced performers; but there is a peculiarity in its tone when played at all loud which greatly mars the effect, the tender charm and colouring of that of the vina being completely absent. To be heard with advantage a sitar should be at a little distance from the listener, the unpleasant jangle of its strings will not then be so apparent, and the melody will be more clear.

According to the common custom, the methods of shifting the frets are five. The five methods, called thâts, are as follows. These thâts have no names, but are usually known from the râgas that are commonly played upon them :—

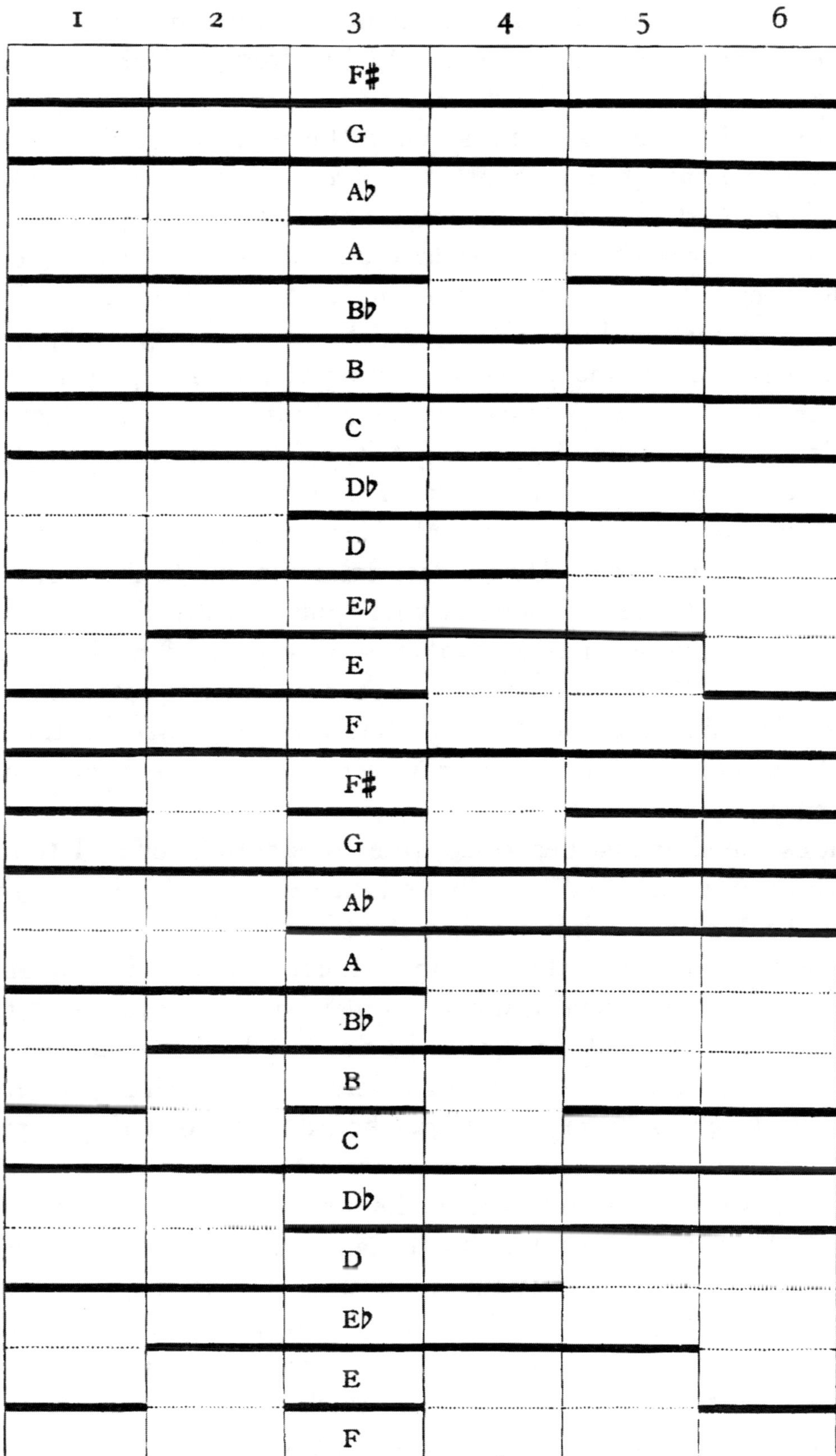
1
2
3
4
5
6
F♯
G
A♭
A
B♭
B
C
D♭
D
E♭
E
F
F♯
G
A♭
A
B♭
B
C
D♭
D
E♭
E
F

Nos. 1, 2, 4, 5, 6 are the arrangements of frets in different thâts for an eighteen-fretted sitar. No. 3 is for a twenty-four-fretted sitar, in which there is no need to alter the frets.

The intervals given represent those upon the F string or chanterelle.

In Taraffedar sitars the sympathetic strings are tuned to the intervals obtained by the F string, and the frets over their respective nuts. All instruments with moveable frets (other than sitars) are arranged according to one of the above thâts. The sympathetic strings are arranged in various ways, but very commonly thus—G, A, B, C, d, e, f, g, a, b, some of the intervals being flattened or sharpened according to the râga played.

Some sitars are so constructed that the body is almost flat, instead of pear-shaped. This is accomplished by cutting the gourd body in a peculiar manner, so that the calix shall be at the back of the instrument. To such sitars the name Kachwar is given. Some people give the name Kachapi-vina to them. A rather uncommon instrument of this description is called the Surbehar, which is merely a large-sized sitar or kachapi-vina, played with a steel plectrum, and specially used for the performance of alâpas or râgas. The body is of wood, with a flat back, and there are usually sympathetic strings attached. The tone is rich and mellow like that of the vina, but the large size of the instrument renders its use fatiguing, while the cost is very high. It is tuned, of course, as the ordinary sitar.

But besides the sitar just described, there is another form of the instrument to be met with in Southern India. This might be called the Karnâtik-sitar, and it differs from the ordinary sitar in that it is confined in its intonation and is generally made with a much thinner and shorter neck. Its capability is, of course, much less. It is usually shaped somewhat like a tamburi, the body of the instrument being made either of gourd or of wood. The manner of stringing is peculiar. The first and second strings only pass over frets, which are about ½-inch wide, and raised from the finger-board; these strings are tuned in unison, and they are placed very much nearer together than the other strings. The third string is tuned in unison with the first, but does not pass over frets. The fourth string passes round a small ivory bead about half way up the finger-board, whence it passes obliquely under the strings to its tuning peg. The fifth string is placed in a similar way, the ivory peg being in this case a little nearer to the bridge. The sixth and seventh strings pass straight up the finger-board in the ordinary manner. With the exception of the seventh, which is of brass, the strings are of steel, and are secured either as those of the tamburi or vina.

The frets are of wood, with an upper edge of metal, only about ¼-inch in width, and fixed to the finger-board; the strings cannot therefore be pulled so as to produce "rekhu" without their coming off the frets. The number of frets is usually fourteen, placed at the intervals of the diatonic major scale; occasionally there are two extra frets at semitonic intervals, placed between the third and fourth, and tenth and eleventh. Karnâtik sitars are sometimes found fretted throughout in semitonic intervals, the number of frets being the same as in a vina.

The instrument is tuned thus—

In the ordinary instruments the noise made by the accompaniment frequently drowns the air, the strings having a strong tendency to twang. But the tone of these Karnâtik sitars, when properly made, is soft and sweet, and, being confined in intonation, more nearly resembles that of the mandoline than any other Indian instrument.

The Sur-s'ringâra—shown upon the left of the plate—is somewhat like the rabôb in shape, but with a wooden belly, and played with an iron plectrum. There are, as a rule, two frets only, the finger-board below the frets being generally of metal, so that the fingers may slide easily over it. The length of the instrument is about 4 feet, and its tone is rich and mellow, somewhat like that of the pizzicato notes of the violoncello. It is tuned thus, and has usually seven sympathetic strings tuned to the intervals of the râga in which the performer is playing; the melody string is that upon the right, tuned to G:—

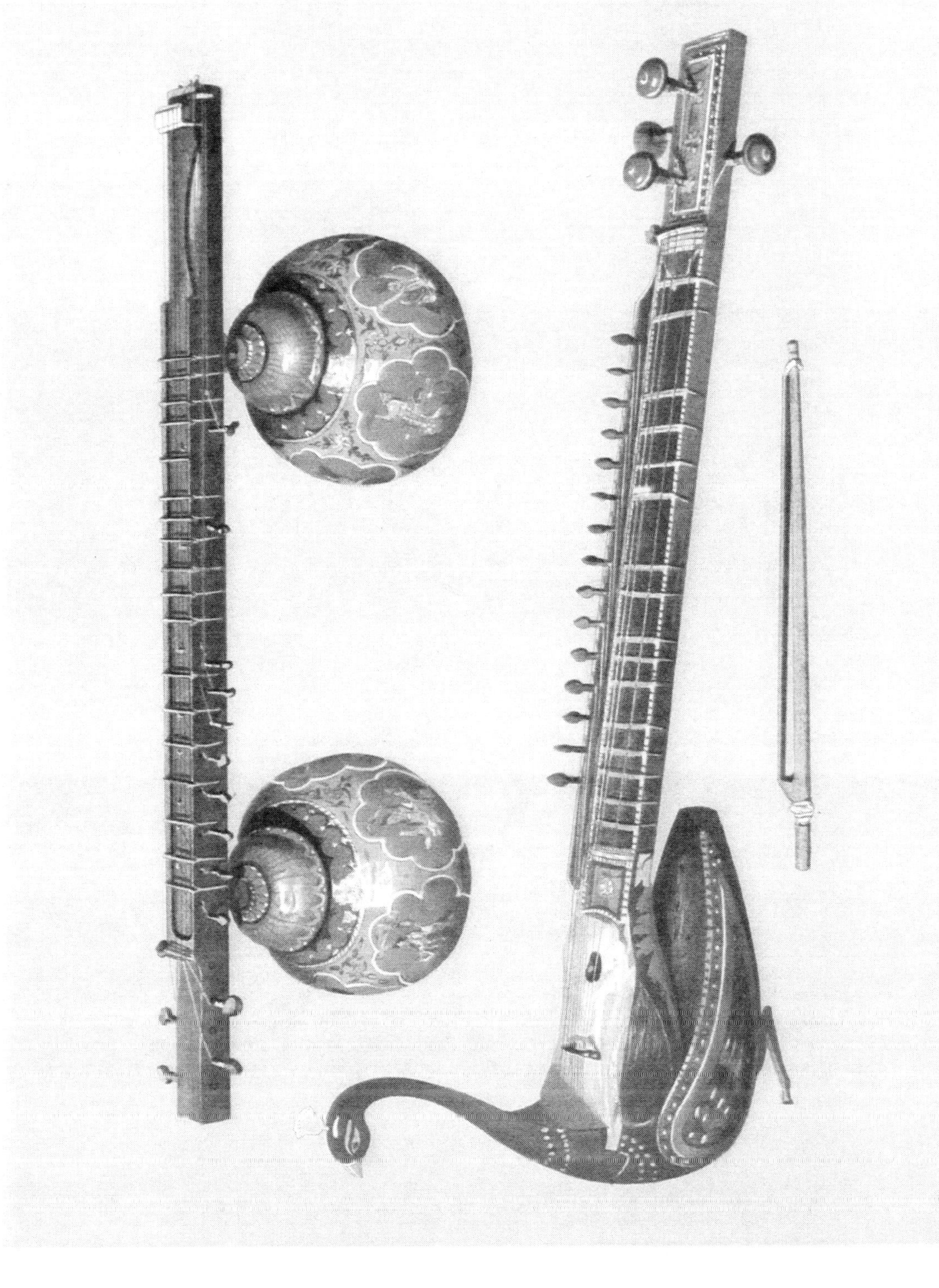

PLATE IV.

BÎN-SITAR. TÀÙS.

THE instrument to the left of this plate is the Bîn-sitar, in outward appearance very similar to the bîn previously described. It differs, however, in that the frets are moveable and are arranged precisely as given for those of the sitar. The strings are arranged as those of the bîn, and therefore reversed in order from those of the sitar. The Bîn-sitar is not a common instrument; indeed, the few specimens that I have met with have all been in Poona and the neighbourhood. The tuning is like that of the bîn.

The instrument to the right of the plate is the Tàùs or Esrar. Sometimes this instrument is called Mohur. It is merely a form of sitar with moveable frets. The Tàùs is not much esteemed by any but Nautch musicians, and it is rarely to be met with out of Upper India. As its name implies, it is usually shaped like a peacock. Its body is painted like that of the bird, and to the lower end a wooden neck and head, covered with feathers, are attached. It is sometimes played with a bow.

The tuning varies slightly, but never employs other intervals than the tonic, fourth, and fifth, and occasionally the third. There are usually sympathetic strings attached, tuned to the intervals of the râga played.

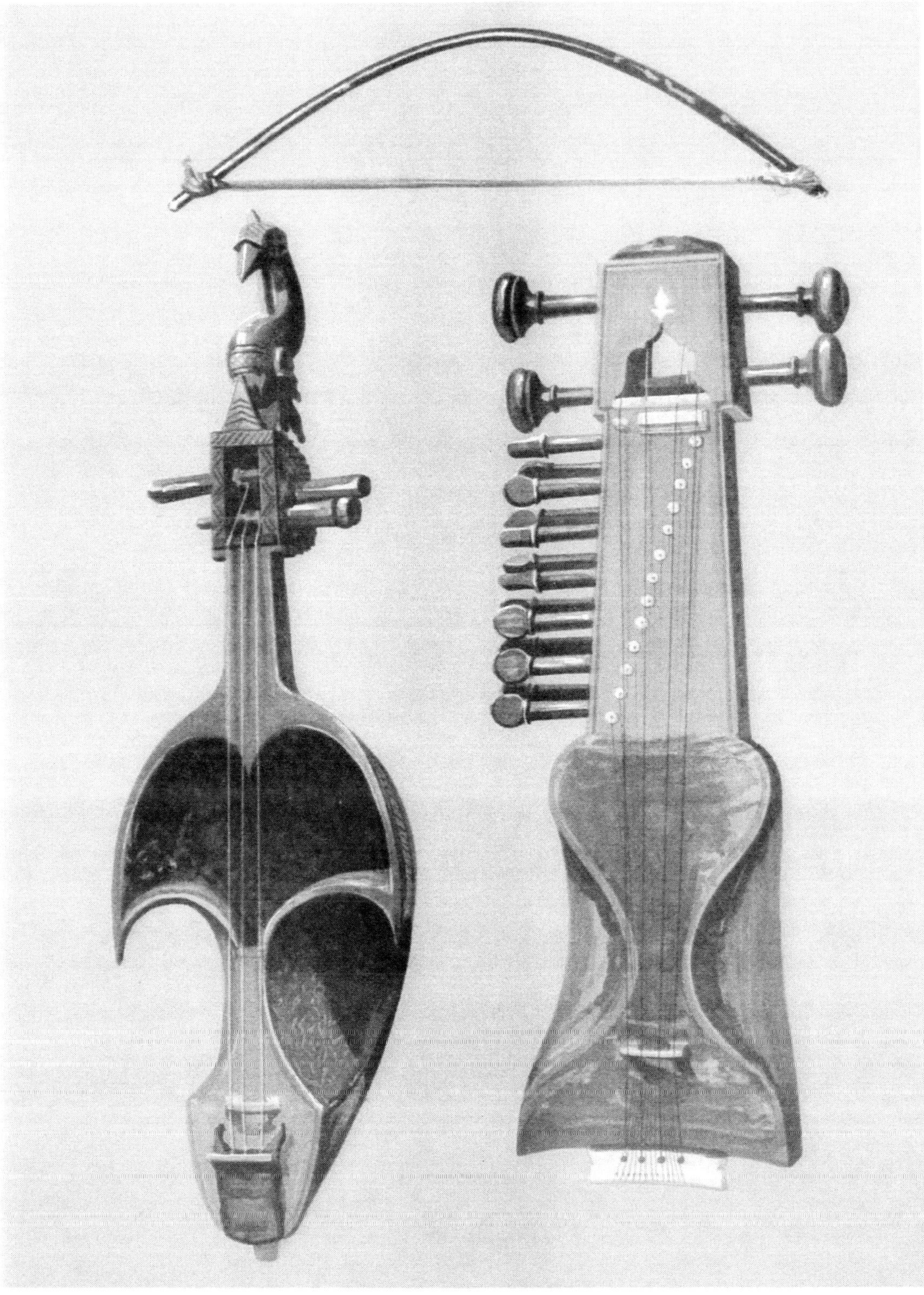

PLATE V.

SÂRÍNDA. SÂRANGI.

THE Sârangi, or fiddle of India, shown to the right of this plate, is usually strung with three strings of thick gut and played with a bow. Sometimes a fourth string of wire called *luruj* is added. The fingers of the left hand, in stopping the strings, do not press them down upon the finger-board, but press against them at the side in all the positions. The tone of the sârangi more nearly resembles that of the viola than any European instrument, and when well played there is a charm about the instrument that is not easily forgotten. The sârangi is frequently employed to play a sort of *obbligato* to a song, particularly in theatrical performances and by Nautch companies. There are generally in instruments of this kind fifteen sympathetic strings of wire tuned chromatically. The instrument is made from a single block of wood hollowed out, and has a parchment belly. When in use it is held vertically, head uppermost. Curiously enough, as was the case with the violin in England at one time, the instrument is considered to be rather vulgar, and hence musicians, though they admire and like it much, will usually employ either a low caste Hindu or a Mussulman to play it. The tuning is as follows:—

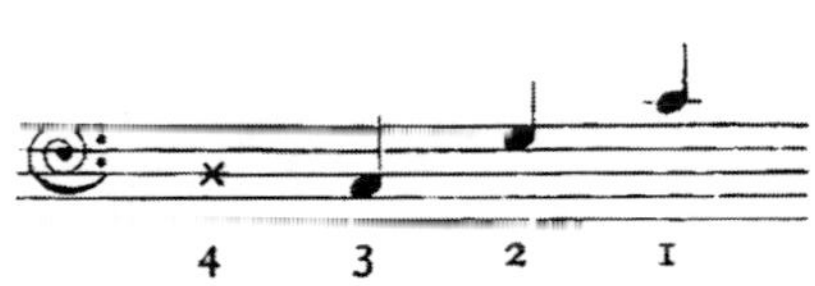

The string marked x is of brass, tuned either to E or F, according to the requirements of the râga played—this string is called *luruj*.

The illustration shows the instrument as commonly found in the South of India and the Deccan. The resin for the bow is ingeniously placed in the head.

The bow for the Sârangi is the same as that shown in Plate IV. for the Tàûs. In Upper India and the Punjâb a slightly different form of the Sârangi is found, and is generally more highly decorated and with a differently shaped head.

The three-stringed instrument to the left of the plate is the Sârínda, a bowed instrument common in Bengal. The decoration and carving are characteristic, although rough. The Sârínda is not a very high-class instrument, but is very popular with the lower classes. The tuning is like that of the chikâra, and the strings are of gut or silk. The bow used with it is that shown. The chief peculiarity of the Sârínda consists in the way that the belly, which is of parchment, is put on. As will be seen by the plate, it is made to cover only the lower part of the body, leaving the upper half quite open.

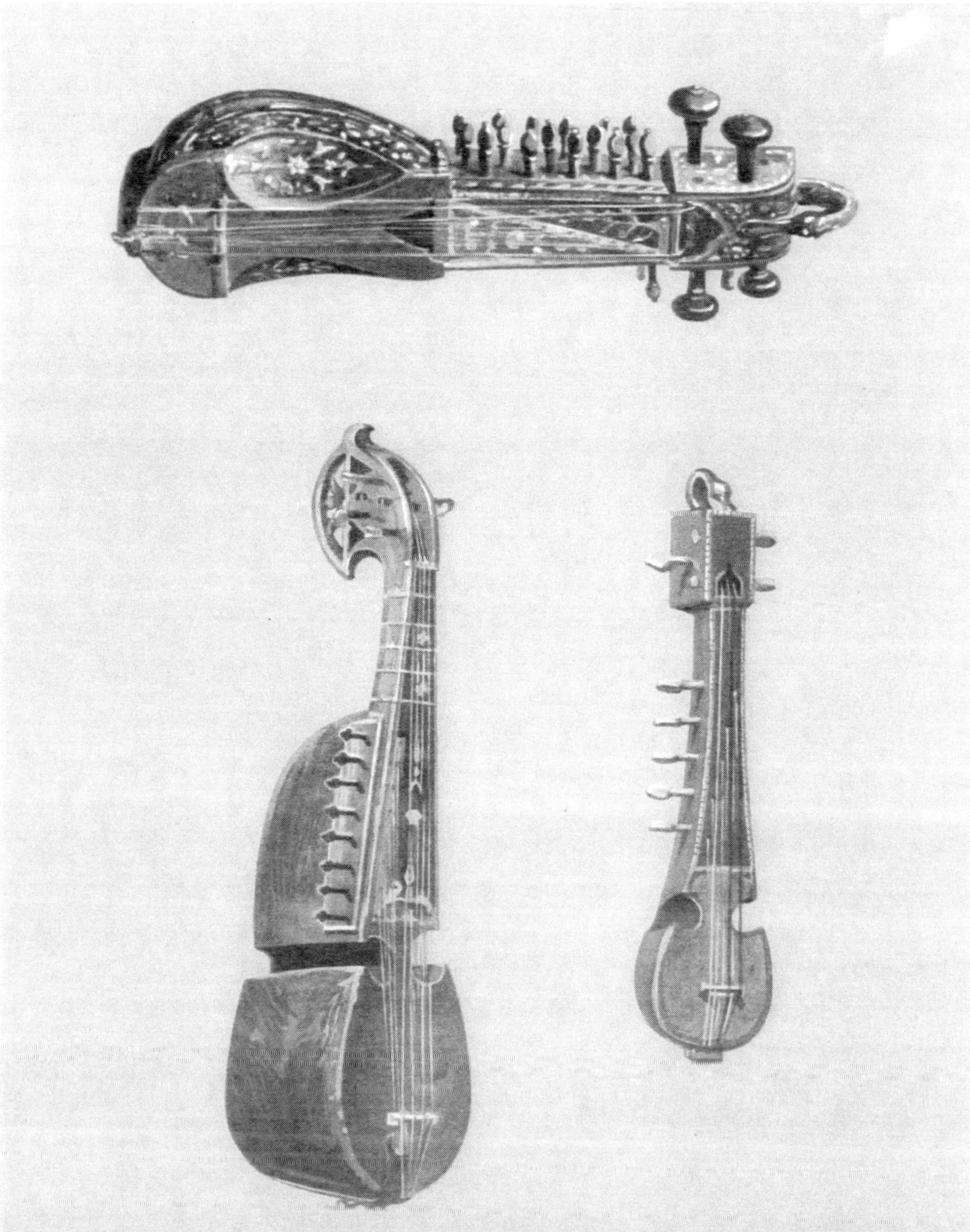

PLATE VI.

RABÔB. CHIKÂRA. SÂRANGI.

THE Sârangi found in Upper India differs slightly from that of the South and the Deccan. The head is generally carved to represent the neck of a swan, and the body is rounded instead of being square ; the number of sympathetic strings, too, is often less. The beautiful specimen shown in the upper part of the plate is in the possession of Mr. C. Purdon Clark, C.S.I., through whose kindness Mr. Gibb has been enabled to make this representation. The instrument is ornamented with ivory and inlaid with numbers of small turquoises. The tuning and the method of playing the Northern Sârangi do not differ from that of the instrument described under the preceding plate.

The Chikâra—shown to the right of the plate—is somewhat similar to the sârangi, but smaller, and is used by common people. It has three strings of gut or horsehair and five sympathetic strings of wire. The tuning is

commonly, or else like that of the sârangi. The sympathetic strings are generally tuned to G, A, B, c, d ; (any of these intervals being made ♭ or ♯ as required).

The other instrument in the plate is the Rabôb, which is found in almost all Mahomedan countries, and in various places differs only in shape. The Indian Rabôb is principally used in the Punjâb and Upper India ; its use in other parts is confined to Mahomedans. The instrument is made of wood, with a belly of parchment. In general there are four strings—three of gut and one of brass ; the two upper strings are sometimes doubled and tuned alike, in which case, of course, the instrument has six strings. Sympathetic strings of metal are usually attached at the side. Four or five catgut frets at semitonic intervals are sometimes found. The instrument is played with a wooden plectrum, and rarely with a bow as a sârangi. The Rabôb is a handsome instrument, and when well played is very pleasing. Its tone rather resembles that of the banjo.

It is tuned thus—

The specimen here shown is from Afghanistan. As usually found in India, the Rabôb is slightly different, and is made with a rather larger body, the lower part of which is wider in proportion than that of the illustration; but in the Punjâb a preference appears to be given for the Afghan form of the instrument.

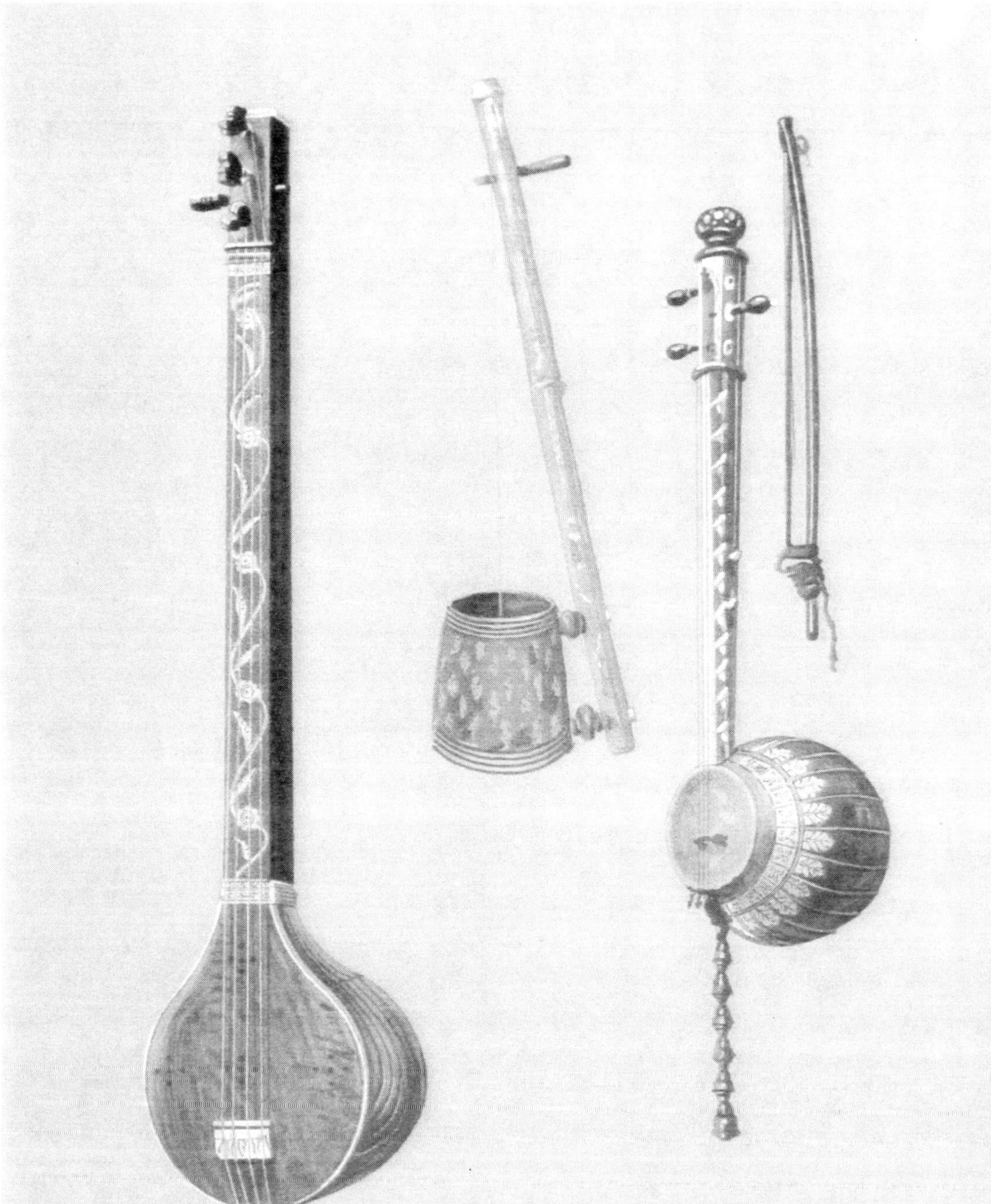

PLATE VII.

TAMBURI. YEKTAR. PERSIAN SITÂRA.

THE Tamburi shown to the left of the plate is used as a common accompaniment to singing, the strings are never stopped, but are always struck open by the fingers, which in this case are not armed with plectra. In outer form the Tamburi much resembles the vina, but is less complicated, having no frets or calabash affixed to the stem; and it is employed for accompaniments only.

There are four strings tuned thus—

The first, second, and third are of steel, the fourth of brass; the steel strings are similar to those of the vina. The Tamburi has no side strings; the tuning pegs are placed differently to those of the vina; those of the first and second strings being placed at the side, as in a violoncello; and those of the second and third strings being placed at right angles to the centre of the head as in a banjo or peghead guitar.

The bridge is moveable, and is entirely of wood or ivory, no metal being employed in its fitting. The tone of a Tamburi is slightly buzzing, and to procure this result pieces of quill or silk, termed *jivala*, are placed between the bridge and strings, and manipulated until the desired effect is obtained.

The nut is deeper than in the vina, the strings passing through holes instead of slits. In many tamburis there is a contrivance called *tekkah*, resembling in action the capo-tasto of a guitar, sliding on the finger-board, and by means of it the pitch of the instrument can be immediately altered to any degree required by the performer.

The strings are secured directly to the attachment, which is a narrow ledge fixed to the body, instead of to langarus as sometimes is the case in the vina. In place of langarus, and for the purpose of assisting in tuning, there are beads called *pusalu*, threaded upon the strings between the bridge and the attachment to which they are secured. These beads pushed down in the direction of the attachment act like a wedge between the belly and the strings, and thus stretching the strings serve to alter their pitch as required. This contrivance is found in many Indian instruments.

The method of fastening the strings to the attachment is worthy of note, and is as follows. The string is bent round the attachment and passed upwards through one of the holes; it is then bent round itself and passed back through the same hole when it is drawn tight, and the spare portion, if necessary, cut off.

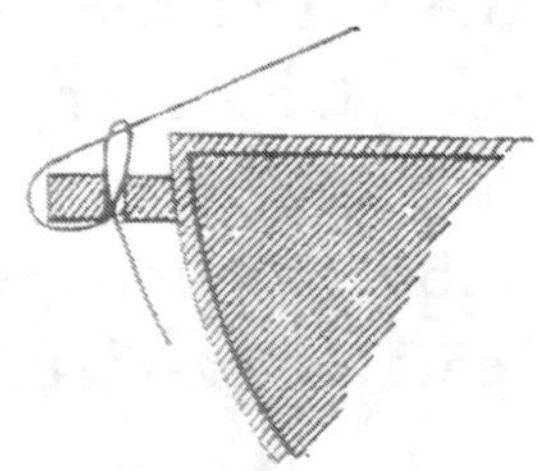

The belly of the instrument is usually slightly convex, and there are small circles of sound holes cut like those of the vina. When played the Tamburi is always held upright, the body resting upon the ground. The tamburis of the Southern parts of India are generally made with wooden bodies, beautifully carved and ornamented with ivory, as in the illustration; farther North they are found with bodies of gourd. Some of the finest instruments of this kind are made at Tanjore, where their manufacture has been made a subject of special study, and large prices are frequently paid for them.

All instruments of this kind are called Tamburis, and many varieties may be found; one kind frequently met with is made smaller and with a curved head like that of the vina, and is used by mendicant singers.

Those of the kind described are used only by musicians and are styled "Dasiri Tamburi."

The Yektar, or Tuntuni as it is sometimes called, shown in the centre of the plate, can hardly be called an instrument at all, since it has only one string and no frets.

It is made from a piece of bamboo, to the under side of which a large gourd or hollow cylinder of wood is attached, one end being closed by a piece of parchment. In the centre of the parchment there is a hole, through which the string is passed and tied in a knot to prevent its slipping back.

The Yektar is often used by mendicants, and is twanged from time to time as an accompaniment to their monotonous chanting. In villages and country districts in the Deccan and Central Provinces this instrument is very popular. It is used in conjunction with a drum of some kind, and the performers keep up a sort of monotonous dialogue upon some common topic of village interest, which is full of witty and rather broad remarks about the principal personages present.

The three-stringed instrument to the right of the plate is the Persian Sitâra. Its use in India is very uncommon, but it is sometimes met with in large native cities, such as Hyderabad or Jeypur, where it is admired chiefly as a variety. The body of the specimen drawn is of wood, ornamented with ivory, the back of the instrument being left open. As can be seen, the belly is of parchment, and the tailpin, which serves as a foot for the instrument, is of brass, rather curiously worked. There are usually three gut strings, tuned like those of the sârangi, and played by means of a bow.

PLATE VIII.

SVARAMÁNDALA.

THE Quanūn, or Indian Dulcimer, is an instrument seldom met with, and is to be seen mostly in the hands of Punjâbi musicians. There are usually twenty-one strings, some of brass and the rest of steel, and tuned to the intervals of any of the Indian scales as required by the râga played. Occasionally gut or silk strings are found. The kind of quanūn here drawn is called Svaramándala, and is generally larger and better finished than the ordinary instrument of this name. It is played with two wire plectra, worn upon the finger-tips of the performer. The capability of the instrument is much greater than might be supposed at first sight. The performer holds in his left hand an iron ring somewhat like a quoit, which he applies to the strings, so that it acts like a *nut* and thus enables him to produce all sorts of grace and embellishments. There is, of course, only one string to a note. The tone is sweet, soft, and reminds one rather of that of the clavichord, though it is louder and possibly more nasal in quality. The Svaramándala is rarely heard, both on account of its great difficulty and very high cost, and therefore good execution upon it is rarely met with.

The Santir, already mentioned as a Persian instrument, is also to be found occasionally. It, like the quanūn, is a kind of dulcimer, but has a great many more strings than the former, and is generally played by being struck with two sticks covered with leather or felt. Both these instruments are to be found in Afghanistan, Turkey, Persia, and Egypt, as well as Arabia. The Indian Quanūn and Santir do not differ much from the Egyptian and Arabian forms, drawings of which can be found both in Lane's "Modern Egyptians" and Mr. Carl Engel's "Musical Instruments." The Svaramándala here drawn is from Cashmere. The tuning pins are turned by means of an iron key, and the tension of the strings is usually very high. The beautiful decoration and the delicacy of the painting with which this instrument is so profusely adorned are evident.

The Hindus say that an instrument of this description was first invented by the rishi or sage Kattyayana; hence it is called the Kattyayana vina—and sometimes Shatatantri (or hundred-stringed) vina—in the Sanskrit treatises.

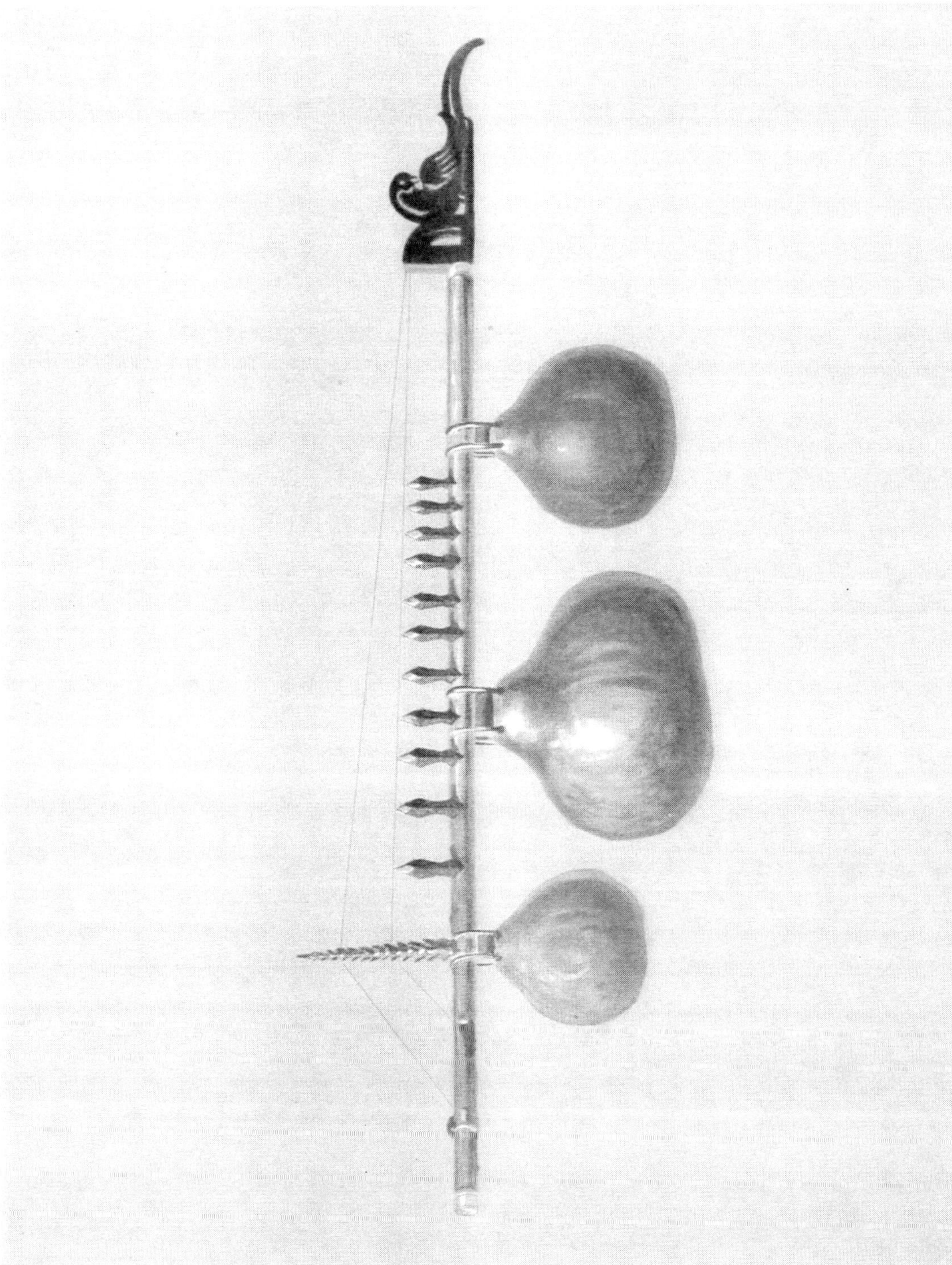

PLATE IX.

KINNARI.

THE Kinnari is a rude stringed instrument employed chiefly by the country people in South Kanara and Mysore. It is somewhat singular that a stringed instrument of much the same name—the Kinnor[15]—should have been mentioned in the Bible, and this leads one to conjecture that they may both have been derived from the same Aryan source; for the Kinnari is an instrument of great antiquity, and takes its name from the legend that it was invented by Kinneri, one of the gandhârvas or singers of Brahma-loka, the heaven of the god Brahma.

It is formed out of a piece of bamboo or blackwood, about 2 feet 6 inches in length, upon which are placed frets, sometimes made from the scales of the pangolin or scaly ant-eater (bone or metal however is generally used), and fixed by means of some resinous composition. Beneath this stem are fixed three gourd resonators.

The instrument possesses two strings only, made of wire. One of these strings passes over the frets, the other is fixed rather above the frets, and is tuned either a fourth or fifth below the former, according as the instrument is tuned in Panchāma or Madhyama s'ruti.

The frets are twelve in number, and are placed according to the intervals of some particular scale or scales. Hence the compass and capability of the Kinnari are naturally limited. The tone is weak and thin, and the twanging of the strings renders the instrument unpleasant to ears not accustomed to it.

Most of the Sanskrit treatises upon musical instruments contain some mention of the Kinnari, or kinnari-vina as it is sometimes called. It is worthy of note that the tailpiece of the instrument is still invariably carved to represent the breast of a kite, precisely as directed in all the old treatises; and in many of the old sculptures to be seen on temples and shrines in the Mysore country this instrument is so represented.

---

[15] *See* II. Chronicles xx. 28.

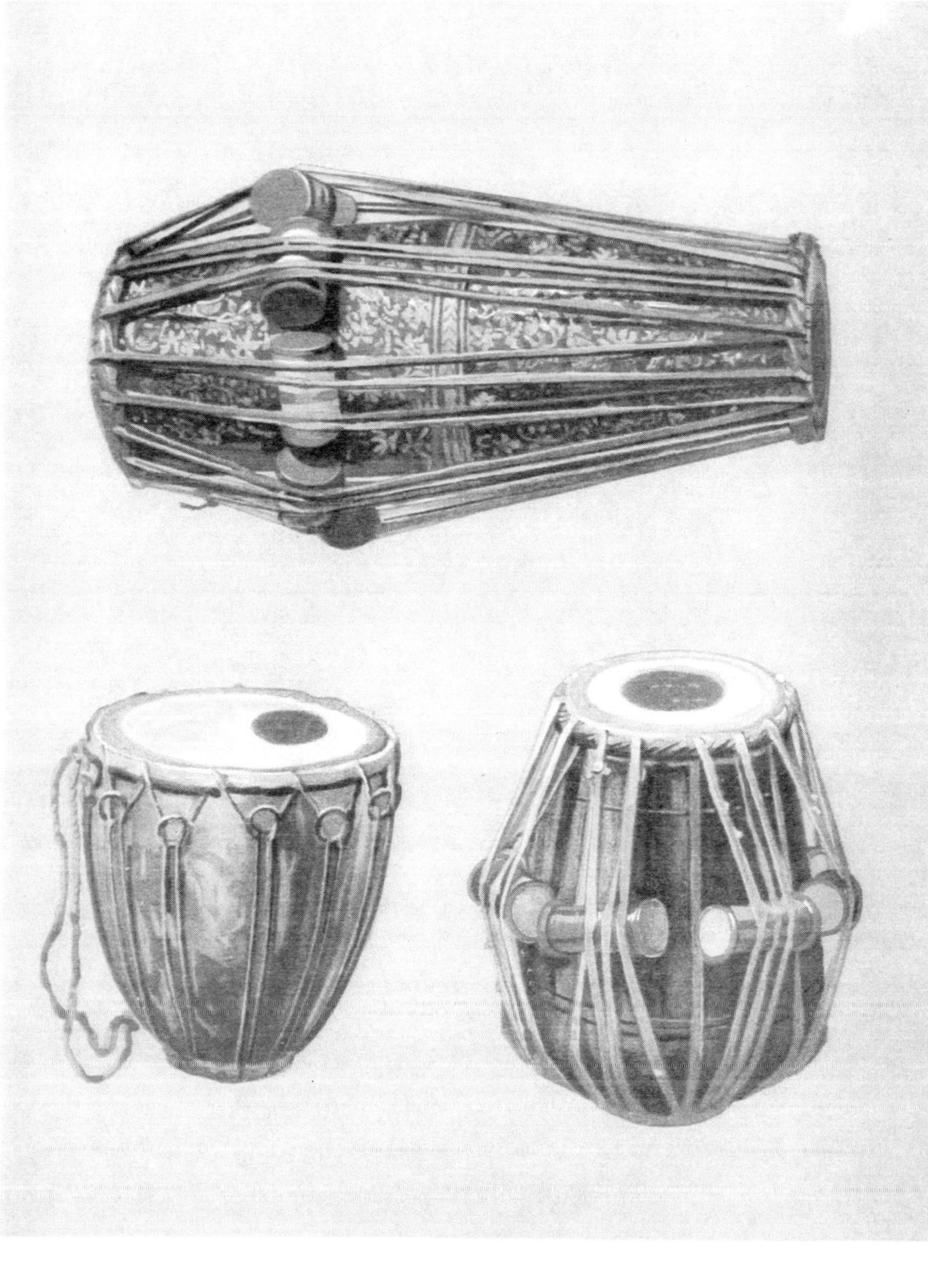

PLATE X.

MRIDANG. TABLA AND BAHYA.

THE Mridang, or Mathala, considered to be the most ancient of the Indian drums, is commonly employed by musicians in Southern India as an accompaniment to their songs and instrumental performances. It consists of a hollow shell of wood, larger at one end than the other, and upon which are stretched two heads of skin, fastened to wooden hoops and strained by leather braces interlaced and passing the length of the Mridang. Small pieces of wood placed between the shell and braces serve to tune the instrument. The two heads are tuned to the tonic and fourth or fifth, according to whether the music is to be in Madhyama or Panchãma s'ruti. The centre of the smaller head of this peculiar drum is coated with a composition of resin, oil, and wax ; and, by way of ornament, an embroidered cloth is commonly stretched upon the upper side of the shell.

The Mridang is beaten by the hands, finger-tips, and wrists in a very peculiar manner, drum playing being a great art among Indian performers ; indeed, years of study are required to ensure proficiency. The smaller head of the Mridang is struck by the right hand, the larger head by the left. This drum is considered to be the most primitive of all Indian instruments. Its origin, as described in the purânas, is as follows:—" When Mahadéva, elated by his victory over the invincible demon Tripurásura, began to dance, surrounded by Indra and other deities, Brahma is said to have invented the mridanga to serve as an accompaniment, and under his directions the god Ganésha first performed upon it. From the very import of the word mridanga, it appears that its body was originally made of clay.

The primitive classical mridangas somewhat resemble the khole and mardola found in use among the aboriginal hill tribes. With some the khole, even to the present day, passes under the appellation of mridanga."[16]

The specimen—drawn in the upper part of the plate—is from Upper India; the Mridang found in the South is usually less ornate, and the leather braces are thinner and more in number.

In the Deccan and farther North preference appears to be given to the Tabla, which are small copper kettledrums—tenor and bass—always used together, and which are tuned as the two heads of the mridang. The Tabla are generally tied in a cloth round the waist of the performer. Frequently a small wooden kettle-drum, rather longer in proportion to its diameter, called Bahya, and answering to the smaller head of the mridang, is employed with one of the tabla drums.

All these drums are tuned by braces and by means of the resinous composition already mentioned being applied to them. Both tabla and bahya are considered as instruments of chamber music, and their sound is consequently soft and subdued, very different to that of the kettledrums employed in the Nahabet described elsewhere. Sometimes wooden drums, called Pakhwaj—in appearance similar to the bahya—are used. The name Pakhwaj is occasionally applied to the mridang. The drum to the left of the plate is the Tabla, that to the right the Bahya.

---

[16] "Short Notice of Hindu Musical Instruments." S. M. Tagore.

TABLA AND TAMBURI PLAYERS.

PLATE XI.

NÂGARA DHOL.

THE Nâgara (sometimes called Bheri), or Nakkera, is a large kettledrum, much employed in temples.

The shells are of copper, brass, or sheet-iron, rivetted together; the heads, made of skin, are strained upon hoops of metal, and stretched by ropes or leather thongs passing round the underside of the shell. The usual size of these drums is from 2½ to 3 feet in diameter. They are beaten with two curved sticks. In the Râmâyana, Mahambhârata, and some of the purânas, this instrument is called Dundubhi.

The Mâha-nâgara, or Nahabet, is a very similar kettledrum, of larger size, employed in bands attached to the palaces of Mahomedan nobles in the Deccan and Upper India. These instruments are sometimes made as much as five feet in diameter.

A form of nâgara called Karadísaméla is in use in Lingayet temples in the Southern Provinces; this form only differs from the ordinary temple drum in that it is larger and the shell is conical, with the apex of the cone flattened, in place of being nearly semi-spherical.

In the Deccan and Central India two smaller kettledrums are often associated with this instrument in performance.

The method of bracing drums of this kind varies slightly in different parts. A very common way is to cover the shell with a kind of network of twisted leather thongs, to which the head is attached when wet, and then shrunk on to its place. This method is commonly applied to the smaller varieties of kettledrums.

The Dhol, drawn at the top of the plate, is a species of drum chiefly employed in the native bands that are usually heard at weddings and other festivities. The shell is of wood bored out of the solid, and usually about 18 or 20 inches in length, and 12 inches in diameter. The size however varies greatly. The thickness of the shell is from $\frac{1}{8}$th to $\frac{1}{10}$th of an inch. The heads, made of skin, are stretched round hempen hoops, fastened to the shell and strained by means of thongs of leather interlaced. A band of leather passed round the shell and over the braces serves to tighten the instrument up to the desired pitch. The Dhol is played both by hand and stick. Sometimes the left side of this instrument is left out altogether, in which case the right side is beaten with two sticks. Metal rings struck by the drumsticks are sometimes attached as shown.

The Dholkee is a smaller dhol, much used by women in the Deccan.

The Dholuk and Dâk are drums somewhat similar to the dhol, but are generally rather larger and vary slightly in shape in different parts of India.

PLATE XII.

KHANJERI. TAM TAM.

TAMBOURINES and tabors of all kinds are found throughout India, but are rarely used by professional musicians. The largest instrument of this kind is called Duff, or Duffde, and is an octagon frame of wood about 6 inches deep and 3 feet in diameter, covered upon one side with skin strained by means of a network of thin leather thongs. The Duff is struck with the fingers of the right hand; and a thin switch held perpendicularly over it by the fingers of the left is made to strike the instrument with the middle finger at certain intervals according to the tâla. The Daera is circular and not more than 11 or 12 inches in diameter. It is played with the right hand in a similar manner to the duff. The thumb of the left hand is thrust into a loop in the underside of the Daera. This forms a sort of rest for the left hand a little above the centre of the instrument, so that the knuckle of the middle finger can be pressed against the skin when a rise in the tone is desired. In the Southern provinces a large circular instrument of this kind, called Thambatté, is found; this varies from 3 to 4 feet in diameter. The Thambatté is played in a similar manner to the duff, and is commonly employed by the lowest castes, and usually associated with the Kahalay or Kombu, a horn similar to the s'ringa shown in Plate XVII.

The Khanjeri, or common tambourine, shown in the plate, consists of a piece of vellum or skin stretched upon a wooden hoop, 8 or 9 inches in diameter and about 3 or 4 inches deep, bored out of the solid. In the hoop are placed three or four slits containing pieces of metal strung together, which clash when the instrument is shaken. The lower edge of the hoop is sometimes bound with silver, chased with mythological devices, and the hoop itself is often carved in the same way.

Water poured upon the skin serves for tuning.

The Khanjeri is generally employed in *Bhazana*—described elsewhere—and by Nautch girls.

The small kettledrum drawn in the plate is the common Tam tam used by beggars and the like, and which is to be found at all street corners throughout India. A tam tam of rather flatter shape, called Dinni, is common in Mysore, and is generally carried by religious mendicants of Saivite sects. In shape it much resembles the modern Egyptian tabl-shamî.

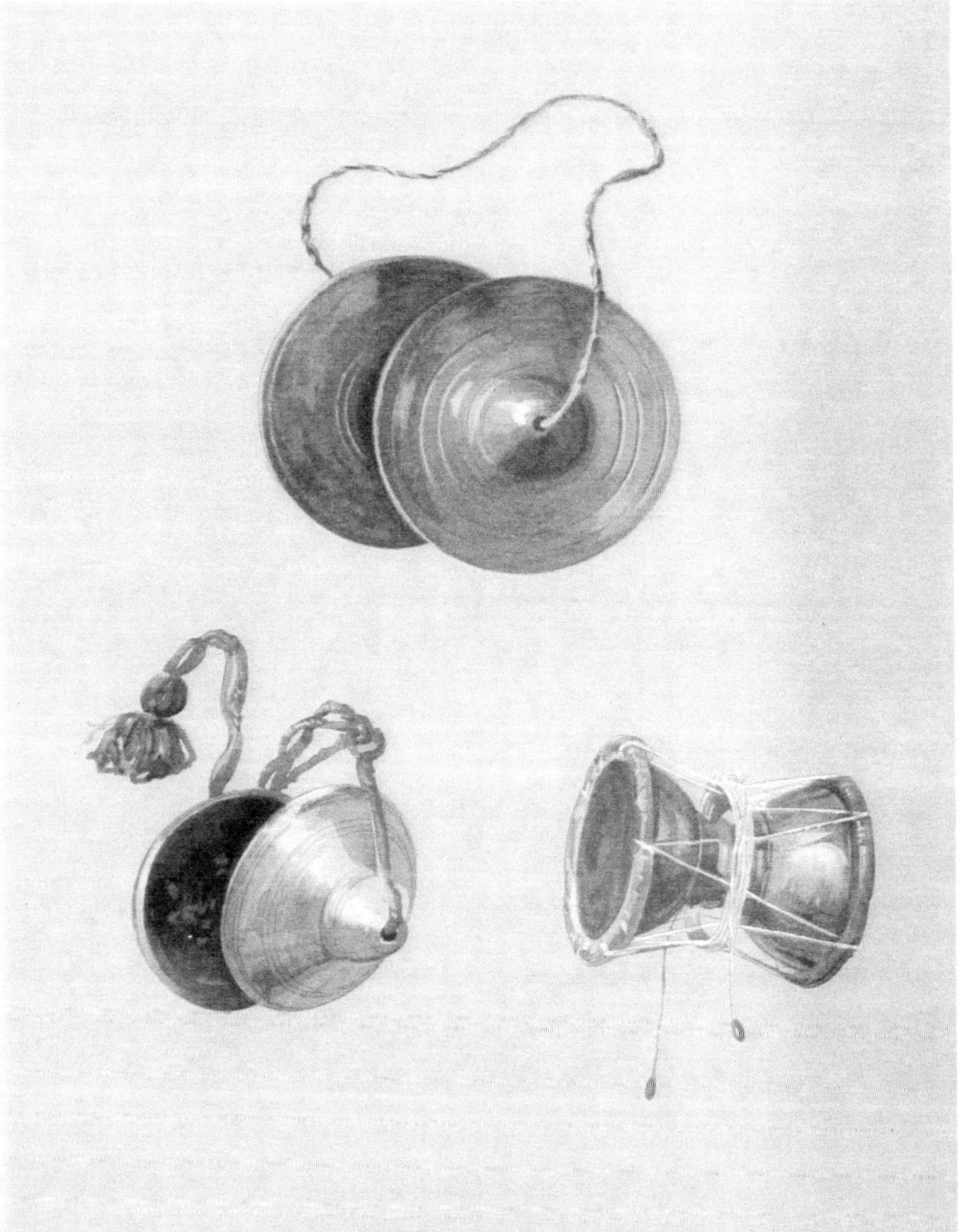

PLATE XIII.

TÂLA. JÂLRA. BUDBÚDIKA.

METAL cymbals of all kinds are used as accompaniments to native music. Farther North we find them chiefly in connection with music of a religious character, but in the South their use is universal. The larger kinds, called Jhanj, are much like the ordinary Turkish cymbals and are used in the Nahabet, and in company with the Tâla, or gong, in the wild temple music. The chief use made of all cymbals is to mark the time. The two small kinds of cymbals here drawn are peculiar to Indian music. The Jâlra—shown uppermost in the plate—are made in proportion a good deal thicker than the larger cymbals, and they are played so as to produce a ringing sound, somewhat like that of a trembling electric bell; they are usually connected by a cord passed through their centres. The cup-shaped cymbals to the left of the plate are called Tâla, and are so made that their edges only are struck.

Tâla are in size similar to Jâlra, but are not usually connected.

At the back of each a tassel of silk or wood serves for a handle. Colonel Meadows Taylor thus describes their use: "One is held in the left palm secured by a cord passed round the right, and is struck by the other, which is held loosely in the right. Players on these cymbals are extremely dexterous, and produce a not unpleasing accompaniment to the voice or to instrumental music, by striking the cups together in such a manner—outside, inside, and upon the edges—as to form notes in accordance with the voice or the other instruments by which it may be accompanied. This cymbal accompaniment is played with more execution than may be conceived possible from the nature of the instrument.

I have heard *professors* even play solos upon it, which, if not very intelligible as to tune, were at least curious in execution and diversity of *time*, as suited to the various style of music." [17]

The Budbúdika—shown on the right of the plate—is a small hand-drum from three to six inches in length, used by snake charmers, mendicants, &c. In shape it resembles an hour-glass, and in the centre a string is attached having a small ball of leather or cork at the end. When shaken in the hand the striker at the end of the string alternately touches each head.

A drum, somewhat similar in shape, called Edaka or Dudi, is common in Coorg. It is of metal, and about 1 foot in length and 8 inches in diameter; one end is beaten by a soft drumstick, the other by hand, like the dhol.

On the West Coast, and in Malabar, another drum of much the same shape is employed. It is usually very light and fragile, the shells being made of large gourds. Five or six of these drums are commonly used in religious services and the noise at certain seasons of the year resulting from this method of worship is almost incredible, and is continued for days together, by relays of performers, at certain festivals.

---

[17] "Proceedings, Royal Irish Academy." Vol. IX., Part i.

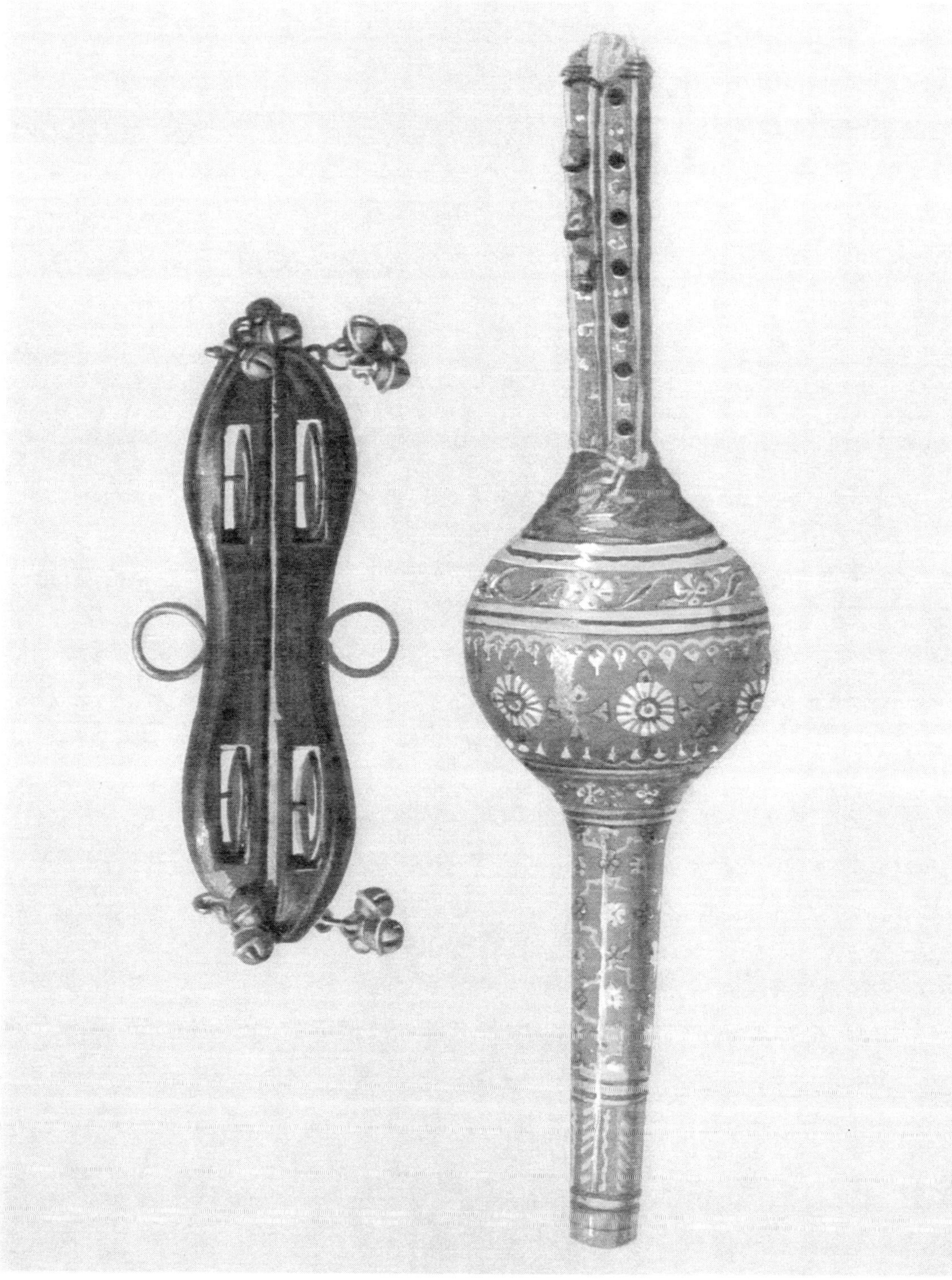

PLATE XIV.

PUNGI. KURTAR.

THE instrument drawn at the right of the plate is the Pungi, or Jínagovi, a reed pipe used exclusively by jugglers and snake charmers. The body and mouthpiece are formed from a bottle-shaped gourd, in which are inserted two pipes of cane, the interior ends of which are cut so as to form reeds. One of the pipes is pierced with finger-holes so that it can be played upon, the other being sounded in unison with the keynote as a drone.

The Pungi is invariably constructed in the scale of Hanumatódi (see page 33), and is played in the Nâgavarâli râga, a strain supposed to be specially pleasing to serpents.

The specimen shown here is beautifully painted, and is of Deccan manufacture, but the common pungi is of the roughest and simplest description, and hardly ever in correct tune.

Kurtar, or Chittika, are two pieces of hard wood about six inches in length, flat upon one side and rounded upon the other. They are held in the one hand and the flat surfaces beaten together by alternately closing and opening the fingers. A ring is usually inserted at the back of each for the fingers to pass through, and at the ends are placed little clusters of bells, or small pieces of metal which jangle when the Kurtar is shaken.

Circular wooden castanets, called Chacra, made with slightly concave surfaces, are frequently met with. To these the name of Khattala is sometimes given, and they are played with great dexterity.

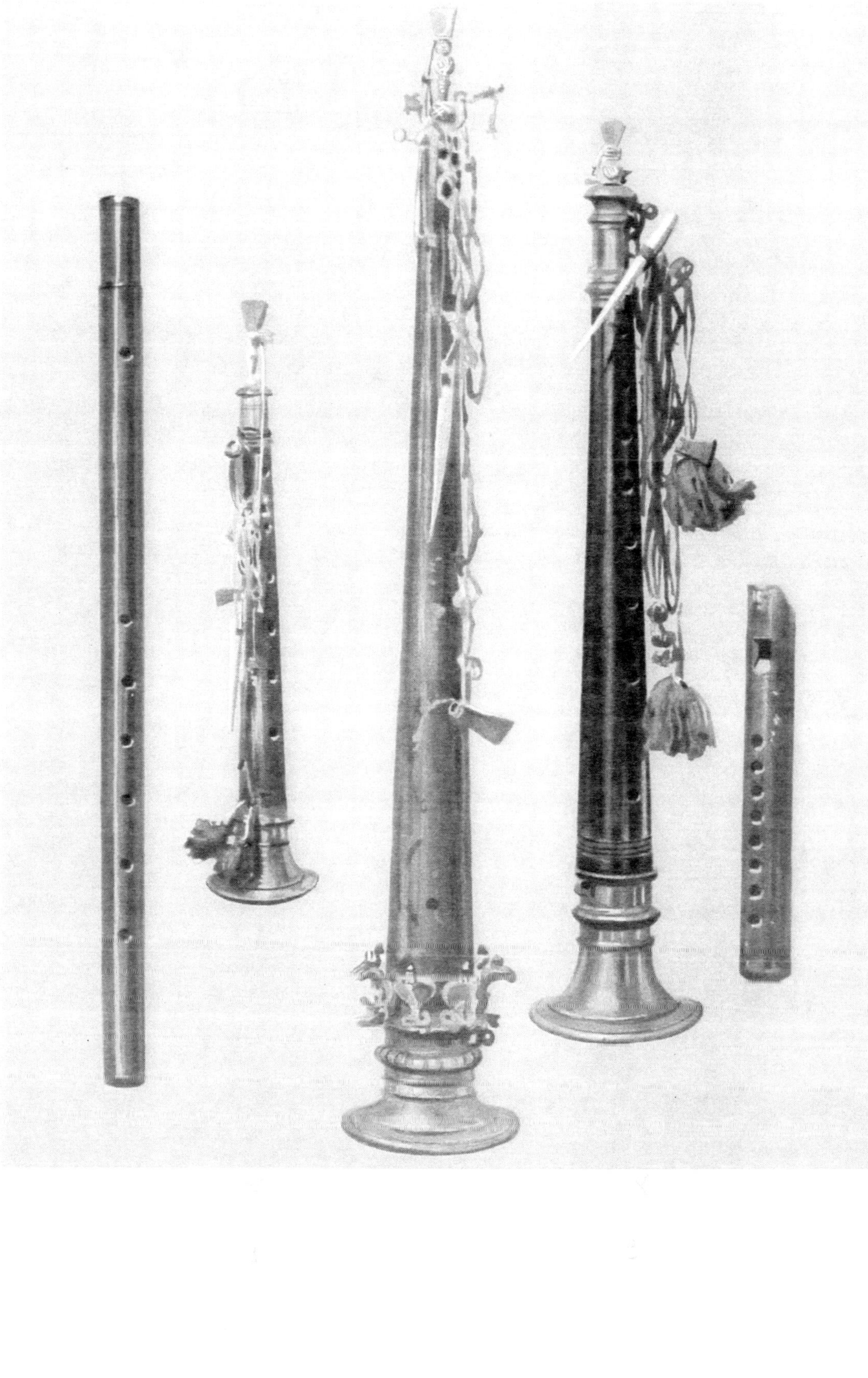

PLATE XV.

PILLAGOVI. MUKAVINA. S'RUTI. NÂGASÂRA. ALGOA.

THE three instruments in the centre of the plate belong to the same class, and are in general use in all parts of India.

The Nâgasâra—the second from the right in the plate—is a reed instrument with a conical bore enlarging downwards. It is usually pierced in twelve holes, the upper seven of which alone are employed in fingering, the others being stopped or otherwise with wax at the discretion of the performer, so as to regulate the pitch of the instrument. The holes are bored at intervals roughly corresponding to those of some Indian scale, but the native players often produce other and additional intervals by allowing the fingers to only partially cover the holes.

The reed somewhat resembles that of a bassoon, but it is very roughly made, and is wider in proportion to its length ; it is mounted like that of an oboe, on a short metal " staple."

The instrument is usually made of a dark close-grained wood called *chandanna*, and has a metal bell. Occasionally nâgasâras made entirely of metal are met with.

The tone is somewhat similar to that of a bagpipe, but is more shrill, and should be heard at a distance.

The Mukavina—the second from the left in the plate—bears a close resemblance to the nâgasâra, but is usually much smaller, about half the size.

It is an instrument of the oboe family, with a conical bore enlarging downwards. It is pierced in seven holes corresponding to the intervals of some scale, and is capable of the same inflections of tone. Its sound is naturally more shrill than that of the former, and is very piercing, which renders the instrument very unpleasant to ears not accustomed to it.

Both the nâgasâra and the mukavina when played in combination with other instruments are accompanied by the S'ruti, which forms a kind of drone bass. These drones are made in various sizes, and in outward appearance are very similar to the two instruments before-mentioned. The bore is conical and enlarging downwards, but more so in proportion to the length of the instrument than in either of the other two. Four or five holes are pierced near the bell at the fancy of the maker; and these holes, by being stopped wholly or partially with wax, serve to tune the s'ruti to the desired pitch.

When played in combination with other instruments they are tuned to the tonic and dominant; if only one s'ruti is employed it is tuned simply to the tonic.

The appendages to these pipes are spare reeds and an ivory bodkin for their adjustment.

Whether we may look to India for the origin of the drone bass is a doubtful point, but it is certain that the principle has existed there from very remote times.

"What bagpipes are to Scotland or Ireland, these pipes are to India. Their sound is precisely similar to that of bagpipes, only, perhaps, more powerful, and in the hands of good players more melodious. They have seven and eight holes respectively, and thus would appear to have no great compass; but in execution, whether from the effects of the lips and tongue upon the reed mouthpiece, or the manner of fingering upon the holes, combinations are formed which include semitones and quarter notes, and thus the expression of chromatic passages *ad libitum*, of which the native players are very fond, is given, which in reality are very effective. From their great power of sound these pipes are unpleasant if the performers be near; but at a distance, in the open air, and specially among the mountains, the effect is much subdued, and often attains much wild beauty and softness. They are in fact the only regular outdoor instruments of Indian music, and are employed on all occasions, whether in domestic or public religious ceremonials, processions, or festivals, temple music, and the like; and the music played upon them varies with the occasion on which they are used. Marches and military music exceedingly like pibrochs in character—pieces for marriages, for rejoicings, for funerals, welcomings, departures—familiar ballad airs and the stated music of the Nahabet have all separate modes and effects. In the Mahratta country, in which I know them best, the simple melodies of the people, joyous or plaintive, are performed with a style of execution often surprising; and combinations of musical effect are introduced which are equally curious and interesting."[18]

These pipes are also known as Holar-cha-Surnai and Hola-cha-Sur, or simply Surnai.

The flute to the left of the plate is the Pillagovi, or Murali, made of bamboo, and traditionally believed to have been invented by the god Krishna, who is usually represented as holding it or playing it. The name Bansuli is sometimes given to this instrument.

The Nuy, or *flute-à-bec*, resembles the pillagovi, but has the embouchure at the end, and is bored cylindrically. The tone is low and sweet, and the instrument is invariably played softly; indeed, notes of a piercing character could not be produced upon it. It is quite a pastoral instrument, and is much used by shepherds and cowherds. Many of the simple melodies of the country when played upon this instrument have a wonderful charm.

The Algoa—shown on the right of the plate—is a kind of flageolet of bamboo, with a tone and compass like that of the pillagovi. Instruments of this kind are found in the Punjâb and Upper India, played in pairs in a somewhat similar manner to the tibiæ pares of the Romans.

---

[18] Col. Meadows Taylor, " Proceedings, Royal Irish Academy." Vol. IX., Part i.

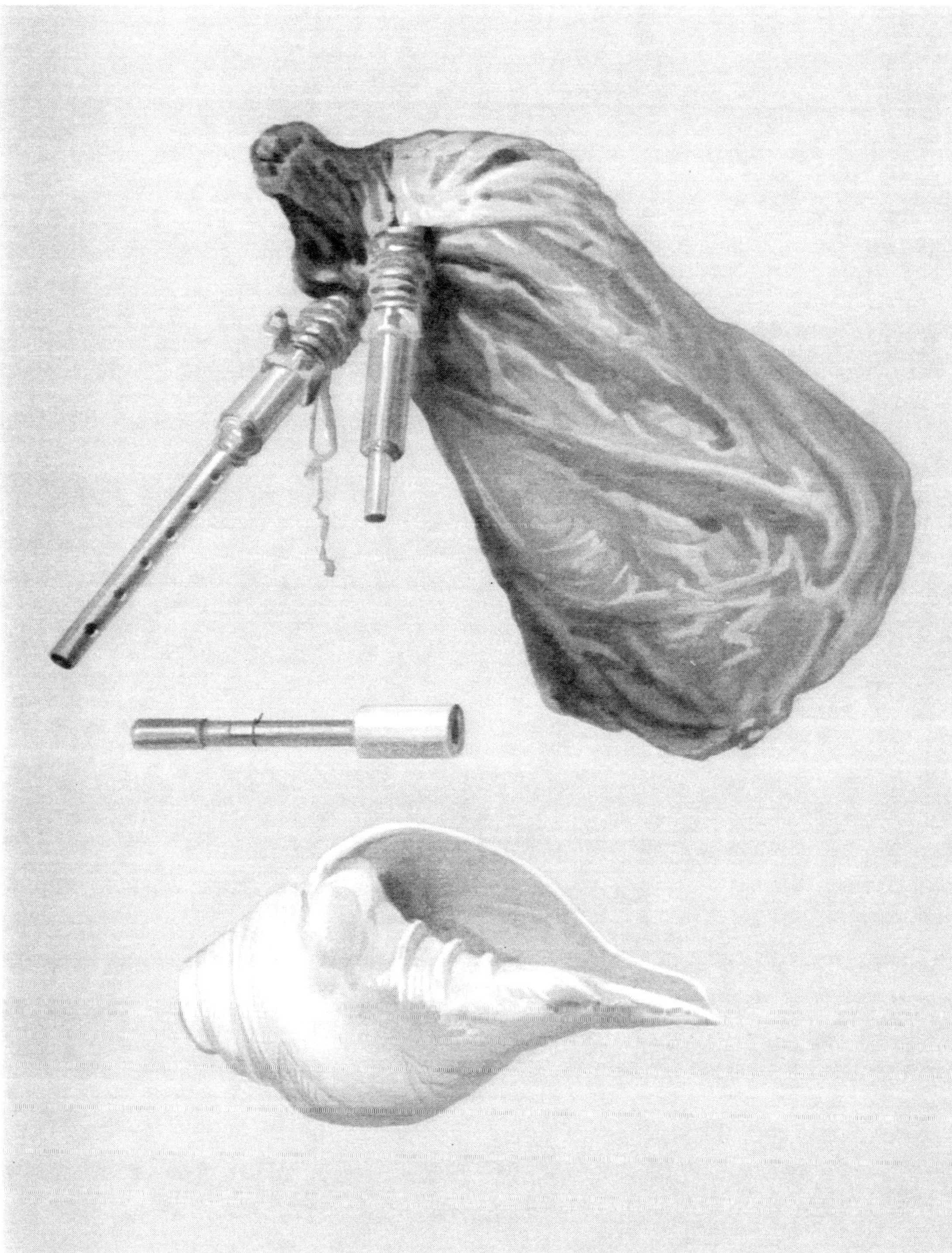

PLATE XVI.

MOSHUQ. S'ANKHU.

THE bagpipe here drawn is the Moshuq, or, as it is called in Southern India, S'ruti-upanga or Bhazana-s'ruti. It is used merely as a drone; the holes in the pipe are wholly or partially stopped with wax so as to tune the instrument to the pitch desired. The bag is made of the skin of a kid and is inflated from the mouth by means of the smaller of the two pipes shown. The drone is of cane, mounted in a stock of the same material, and which contains the reed. An enlarged drawing of the reed has been given in the plate, in order better to show its construction, and, as can be seen, the vibrations are controlled by a little piece of wire or fine twine tied roughly round the tongue. The whole reed is in one piece and is generally made of small cane or of the large marsh reeds found almost everywhere. Black wax is used to make the instrument wind-tight.

The Moshuq of Northern India does not differ much in outward appearance from this, but contains a chanter, with the addition sometimes of a drone.

The conch shell shown in the lower part of the plate is the S'ankhu. It is not in secular use as a musical instrument, but is found in every temple and is sounded during religious ceremonials, in processions, and before the shrines of Hindu deities. In Southern India the S'ankhu is employed in the ministration of a class of temple servers called Dâssari. No tune, so to speak, can of course be played upon it, but still the tone is capable of much modulation by the lips, and its clear mellow notes are not without a certain charm. A rather striking effect is produced when it is used in the temple ritual as a sort of rhythmical accompaniment, when it plays the part of *Konnagòlu* or *Tâlavinyasa*, described elsewhere.

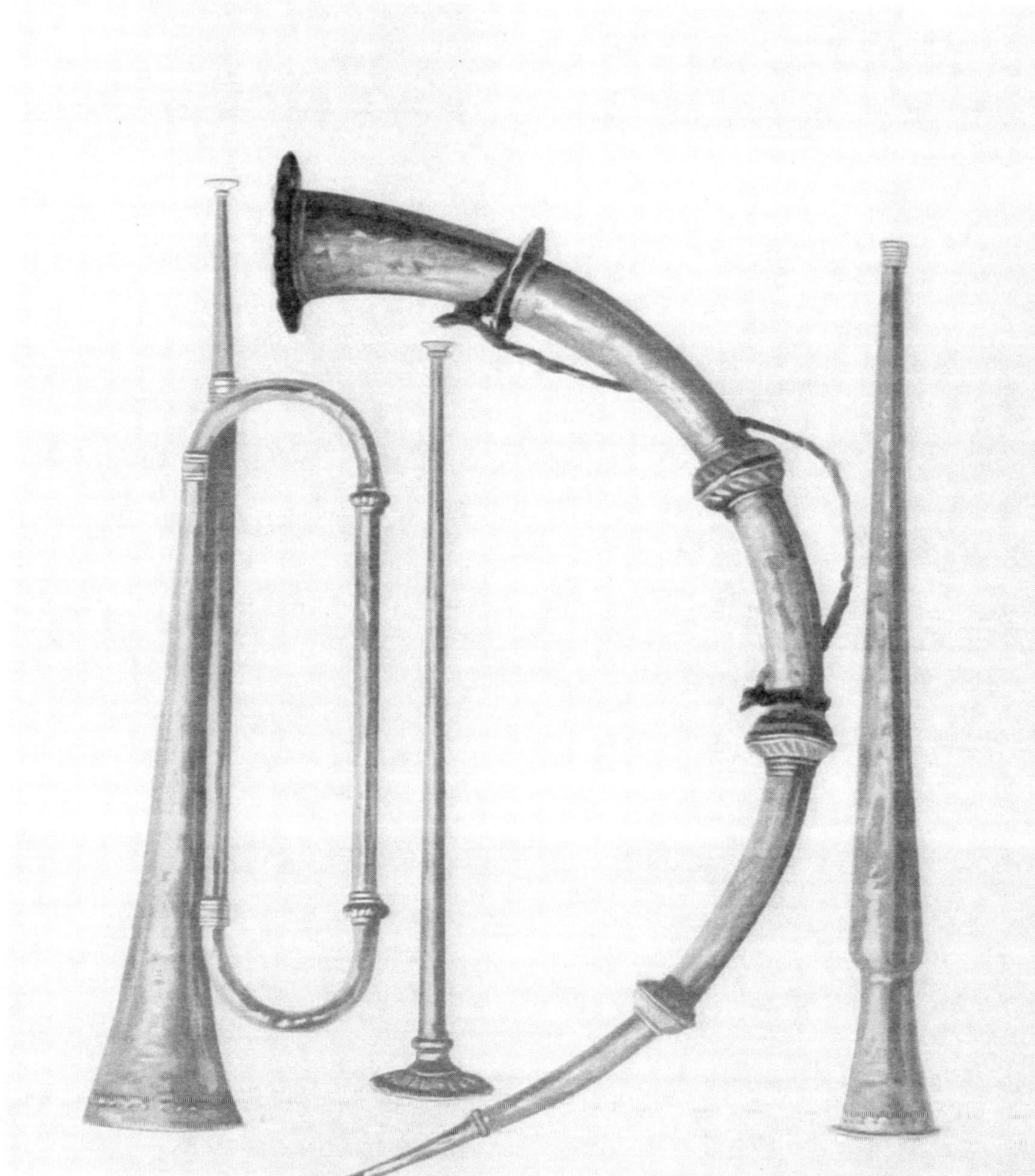

PLATE XVII.

TUTURI. NAFARI. S'RINGA. KURNA.

THE curved brass horn in this plate is the S'ringa or S'ing, called in Southern India Kahalay or Kombu. It is frequently found with a metal rod connecting both ends. This horn is "used universally through India for signals, watch setting processions, and the like, both by Mahomedans and Hindus, though the performers for the most part are Hindus of low caste. In every village of Central or Southern India it is the business of one or more of the watchmen to blow the horn at sunset, and again at certain hours of the night, or when the watchmen go their stated rounds. In large cities every *mahulla* or ward has a horn-blower attached to its night-watchmen or police, and there is seldom a guard or detachment of native irregular troops without one. In all processions, temple services, and especially at marriages and other festive occasions, this horn is indispensable, and wailing blasts for the dead are played upon it at the funerals of Hindus of the lower classes and castes, or equally so at the cremation of Hindu princes.

"No native authority traverses the country without one, frequently several, in his train, and as town or village are approached the great man's advent is heralded by flourishes of the instrument blown by the performer who struts at the head of the cavalcade. These blasts are answered by others from the town or village gate, whence the local authorities come out to meet the visitor and present their offerings of welcome. On these occasions the horn-blowers on both sides vie with each other in producing their grandest effects, and the discordance is generally indescribable.

"Itinerant mendicants of many classes use this instrument, both Hindu and Mahomedan, and by men in charge of droves of cattle carrying grain or merchandise, such as Brinjaris, Comptis, and others, it is sounded at intervals along the road to cheer up their bullocks and keep them from straggling, as well as at their departure from or arrival at one of their stages.

"In playing the high notes in many of the calls, shrill wavering cadences are produced, which have a startling and peculiarly wild effect, as heard from the wall of some ancient fortress, or from village tower and gates as night falls, and more especially in the otherwise unbroken stillness of night."[19]

The large trumpet with one turn is called the Tuturi. This name is usually applied to what might be called the tenor trumpet, as distinguished from the Kurna, the large straight trumpet drawn at the bottom of the plate. The tuturi—or turi—is made in various sizes and is used principally in religious ceremonies. The small straight trumpet is the Nafari.

The Kurna—called in Southern India Buruga or Banku—is used only on solemn occasions, and possesses but a few hoarse sounds. In fact, no Indian trumpets are capable of producing many notes, they are invariably of the most primitive description, and no attempt is made to play them scientifically: indeed, their proper compass is not even understood. Colonel Meadows Taylor, speaking of the Kurna, remarks: "These instruments are almost invariably played by Brahmins or priests attached to Hindu temples, and by persons attached to the retinues of Gurus, Swâmies or spiritual princes of the country, who possess large ecclesiastical jurisdiction, and are provided with them as a mark of high rank, which is not allowable in others. Occasionally also they are met with in the nobuts, or musical establishments attached by royal permission to nobles of high rank, Mahomedan as well as Hindu; but they do not exist in all cases, for there are distinctions in the classes of instruments according to the rank of persons privileged to play the nobut, which involve the presence or otherwise of the kurna. The kurna, or large trumpet, is esteemed by all Brahmins to be the most ancient instrument of music in existence."[20]

---

[19] "Proceedings, Royal Irish Academy." Vol. IX., Part i.
[20] See preceding note.

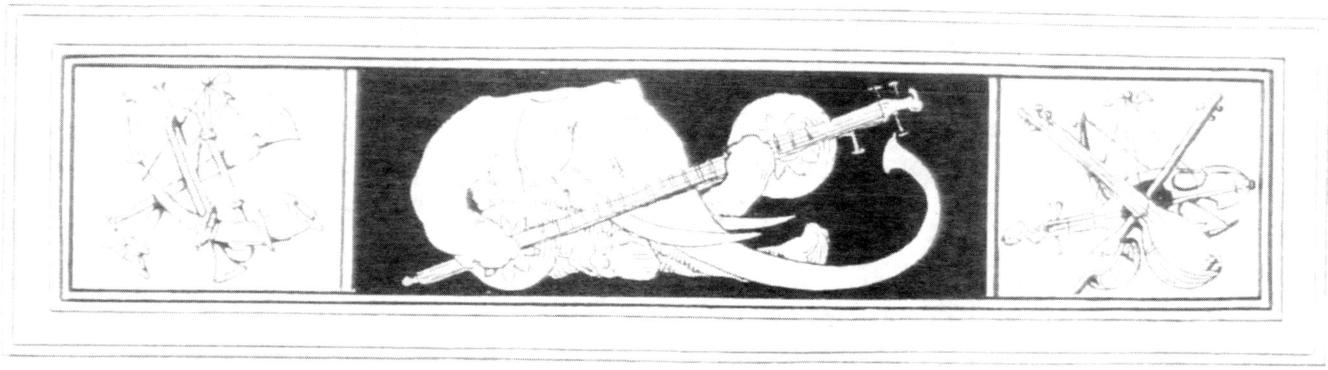

CHAPTER VIII.

Principal seats of music in Southern India—Famous Indian musicians of the South—Bibliography of Indian music—Sanskrit MSS. upon music.

FROM early times Tanjore has been the chief seat of music in Southern India and most of the best known Karnâtik musicians have either lived there or have received their musical education from musicians of the Tanjore school. Little information can be gathered as to what extent the art flourished there formerly, but it is certain that several centuries ago a regular school of music was established and patronised by the Maharajahs. In the reigns of the Maharajahs Sarabhogi, Surfogi, and Sivaji music flourished greatly, and the musicians attached to the palace received large emoluments. The native courts of Travancore and Mysore have also patronised music to a great extent, and it is believed that the art was originally brought to them from Tanjore. Some of the most celebrated musicians of Southern India will be found among the following :—

TIAGYA RAJ. A native of Trivadi, in the Tanjore district; a pupil of a musician called Venkatraman Iyer. He was a great composer of kruthis, many of which are exceedingly popular all through India. Tiagya paid special attention to the requirements of melody, and his songs are mostly free from the monotony and intricacies of the râgas as practised by Hindustani musicians. He flourished from about 1820—1840.

GOVINDASWAMI IYER. A contemporary of the above.

SIAMA S'ASTRI. A composer of kruthis and kirtanas, about the commencement of the present century.

SABHARAYYA S'ASTRI. A native of Pudukotta, a musician in the service of the Maharajah Sivaji of Tanjore.

PERTABSINGH of Tanjore.

SIVARAM IYER. A composer of "pallevi" in the service of the Maharajah Sivaji.

SABBHA RAO. Son of the above.

DIKSITALU of Trivalur, in the Tanjore district. Many of his compositions are still popular.

KSHETRYA. A poet as well as a musician. He was the composer of innumerable love songs called Pathams, which are widely popular. The words of these pathams are often very beautiful, and are full of imagery most poetical, set to music equally as plaintive and appealing to the senses. An example of one of these pathams will be found in the song "Yalla tella vara," upon page 81.

PAIDALA GURU MURTI S'ASTRI. A celebrated composer of "Ganarâga-gítas." Many of his compositions are popular at the present day.

NATHIVA VADIVELU. A singer of repute and composer of many Vérnams, Svarajotas. He is believed to have introduced the use of the European violin[1] into Southern India.

BIKSHANDAR KÖIL SUBBAYAR. A pupil of Sabharayya of Andalur. A singer of repute.

VARPAYA. A vina player in the service of the Maharajah Sivaji of Tanjore.

MADHEO RAO. A contemporary of the above.

PARIYA VAITI. A Malayalam musician of repute.

CHAL BALKRISHNAYYA. A musician of Tanjore.

KALASTRI IYER of Tanjore.

NILKANT IYER of Chingleput.

SABBHA KATTAYYA of Pudukota.

SAVYASACHI of Mysore.

SESHANA of Mysore. One of the best living performers on the vina.

SHAMANA of Mysore.

THE LATE MAHARAJAH KOLASHEKARA of Travancore.

RAGAVAYYA of Coimbatore.

SABBHAYYA of Andalur.

NARASAYYA of Salem.

KALYANA KRISHNA IYER of Pâlghât. Now in the service of the Maharajah of Travancore; a good vina player.

SÚRYANARÁYAN RAO PANTULU of Sitapur. A vina player, now "ASTHANA PANDITA" in the service of the Maharajah of Vizianagram.

VENKAYA of Vizigapatam. A vina player.

TIRUVÂNAKŌDIKĀVAL KRISHNAN. A violin player.

MAHADEVA IYER. Son of Parmísvara Bhagavata. A violin player in the service of the Maharajah of Travancore.

PARMÎSVARA BHAGAVATA. A singer in the service of the Maharajah of Travancore.

MAHAVAIDDI. A singer.

Besides these there are numerous Hindustani musicians in Southern India, Maharashtra, and the North, such as Maula Bux of Baroda, Bhande Ali of Indore, Anna Gharpure of Poona, Balkoba Nataka Sahib of Bombay. But to give a complete list of them would fill a volume. A detailed notice of many has been given in Panchari Banerjea's History of Hindu music, noticed briefly hereafter.

---

[1] Tuned and held in the native fashion, like a sârangi.

The following catalogue of works relating to Indian music has no pretence to completeness; it is merely a list of the names of works and passages written upon the subject. The names of some which contain only allusions that would be of no practical use to the reader have been omitted altogether. Some of the books in the list contain no musical notation, but are nevertheless of great interest to the musical enquirer. An endeavour to notice some of the various Sanskrit works upon music, and in some cases tables of their contents, has been made. It has not been thought necessary to notice each in detail, as for the most part they are written upon a very similar plan, and, as far as arrangement of contents, differ little from each other. These Sanskrit works exist chiefly in manuscript, and are to be found in almost all the libraries—such as those of Tanjore and the Sarasvati Bhandaram of Mysore—attached to the palaces of native princes. Many copies are also to be found in the hands of Pandits and Sanskrit scholars attached to the temples and religious houses throughout India. There are a number of valuable MSS. in the collection of H.H. the Maharajah of Bikanîr. Many too can be found in the Bodleian, the library of the India office, and also in the University library at Cambridge.

BANERJEA, PANCHARI. "History of Hindu Music." A lecture delivered at the Hooghly Institute, Bhowanipore, 1880. Contains a good deal of interesting information, also an elaborate table of râgas and râginis, with the essential notes entering into their composition.

BROUGHTON, Th. D. "Selections from the Popular Poetry of the Hindus." London, 1814. 8vo.

BOSANQUET, R. H. M. "On the Hindu Division of the Octave." "Proceedings, Royal Society, March, 1877, to December 20, 1877." London.

BROWN, M. E. & W. A. "Musical Instruments and their Homes." New York, 1888.

BURNELL, A. C., Ph.D. "The Saman Chants from Arsheya Brāhmana." Contains descriptions of the Sama Vedic chants and examples of their notation in plain chant. Mangalore, 1876.

BIRD, William Hamilton. *The Oriental Miscellany*, Calcutta. Printed by Joseph Cooper, 1789.

BIGGS. "Twelve Hindu Airs, with English words adapted to them by Mr. Opie, and harmonised for one, two, or three voices, with an accompaniment for the pianoforte or harp, by Mr. Biggs." London, printed by Rt. Birchall. N.D.

BIGGS. "A Second Set of Hindu Airs, with English words adapted to them by Mr. Opie, and harmonised for one, two, or three voices, with an accompaniment for the pianoforte or harp, by Mr. Biggs." London, printed by Rt. Birchall. N.D.

BLOCHMANN, H. "The Naqquerakhaneh and the Imperial Musicians, from the Ain-i-Akbari." Translated from the original Persian.

CAMPBELL, A. "Notes on the Musical Instruments of the Nepalese." *Journal of the Asiatic Society of Bengal.* Vol. VI., p. 953. Calcutta, 1837.

VON DALBERG, F.H. "Ueber die Musik der Indier. Eine Abhandlung des Sir W. Jones, aus dem Englischen übersetzt und mit erläuternden Anmerkungen und Zusätzen begleitet von F. H. von Dalberg. Nebst einer Sammlung indischer und anderer Volksgesänge und 30 Kupfern." Erfurt, 1802. 4to.

"Dramatic Amusements of Natives of India." *Asiatic Journal*, New Series. Vol. XXII., p. 27. London, 1837.

DUTT, Toru. "Ancient Ballads and Legends of Hindustan." London, 1882. Contains no music, but some songs which for imagery and Oriental colouring are delightful.

ENGEL, Carl. "An Introduction to the Study of National Music." London, 1866.

ELLIS, Alexander J., F.R.S., F.S.A. "On the Musical Scales of Various Nations." Paper read before the Society of Arts, March 25, 1885. See *Journal of Society of Arts*, No. 1,688. Vol. XXXIII.; also reprinted for private circulation by the author, with additions and corrections. April, 1885.

FOWKE, Francis. "On the Vina of the Hindus." "Asiatic Researches." Vol. I., page 295, Calcutta, 1788.

GLADWIN, Francis. "Ayeen Akbery." See Vol. III., "Sungeet." Calcutta, 1783.

GROSSET, J. "Contribution à l'Étude de la Musique Hindoue." Paris, published by Leroux. (Extrait de tome VI., de la Bibliothèque de la Faculté des Lettres de Lyons.) 1888.

HENDLEY, T. B. "Memorials of the Jeypur Exhibition," 1883. Peckham, W. Griggs. See Vol. III., plates clxxv., clxxix.

HEYMANN, W. "Ueber Bharata's Natyasastram." See Nachrichten von der Kœnigl. Gesellshaft der Wissenschaften und der G. A. Universitæt zu Gœttingen, February 25, 1884, pages 86—107.

HIPKINS, A. J., F.S.A., and GIBB, W. "Musical Instruments. Historic, Rare, and Unique." Edinburgh, 1887. Contains descriptions and very beautiful illustrations of several Indian instruments.

JONES, Sir William. "On the Musical Modes of the Hindus." See "Asiatic Researches." Vol. III., page 55. Calcutta, 1792. Also republished in "Works of Sir W. Jones." 6 vols., and Supplement, 2 vols. London, 1799 and 1801; together, 8 vols., 4to. See Vol. I., page 413.

MATEER, Rev. L. "Native Life in Travancore." London.

MAHILLON, V. C. "Catalogue Descriptif et Analytique du Musée Instrumental du Conservatoire Royal de Bruxelles." Gand. 1880.

NAUMANN, Emil. "The History of Music." Translated by F. Praeger, and edited by Sir F. A. Gore Ouseley. London, 1888.

OUSELEY, Sir W. "An Essay on the Music of Hindustan." Contained in "Oriental Collections illustrating the History, Antiquities, Literature, &c., of Asia." London, 1797-1800. 4to, 3 vols. See Vol. I., p. 70.

PORTMAN, M. V., Mus. Doc. "Andamanese Music, with Notes on Oriental Music and Musical Instruments." See *Journal of Royal Asiatic Society*, New series. Vol. XX., Part ii. London, April, 1888.

ROWBOTHAM, J. H. "The History of Music." London, 1885.

SAHASRABADHE, B. T. "Hindu Music and the Gayan Samaj." Published by the Gayana Samaj, Poona and Madras. Contains information respecting the recent revival of Indian music. Poona, 1888.

SCHROEDER, L. von. "Indiens Literatur und Cultur." Leipzig, 1887.

SOLVYNS (Balt of Calcutta). "The Costume of Hindustan elucidated by sixty engravings." London, 1804. Folio. Contains drawings of a number of musical instruments, chiefly those of Northern India and Bengal.

STACK, G. A. "The Songs of Ind." Calcutta, 1872. Contains a number of verses of more or less interest.

TAGORE, Râjah Sir S. M. "The Six Original Râgas."

——— "The Musical Scales of the Hindus."

——— "Some specimens of Indian Songs."

——— "Short Notices of Indian Musical Instruments."

The above four all printed by I. C. Bose & Co., Calcutta, for private circulation.

——— "The Eight Principal Râsas of the Hindus." Calcutta, 1879.

——— "The Dramatic Sentiments of the Aryas." Calcutta; 1881.

These two works contain much valuable information as to the sentiments conveyed by the various gestures (râsas, bhavas) made either upon the stage or by dancers.

——— "Hindu Music from Various Sources." Calcutta. A reprint of different writings upon Hindu Music. A most useful collection. Contains a reprint of Sir W. Jones' essay and Willard's treatise. But there are some misprints that are liable to mislead.

——— "The Twenty-two Musical S'rutis of the Hindus." Calcutta, 1886.

——— "Ækatana, or the Indian Concert." Calcutta. N.D.

TOD, Lieut.-Col. "Annals and Antiquities of Rajasthan." Vol. I., p. 538. London, 1829.

TWELVE HINDU AIRS, with English words adapted to them, with an accompaniment for the pianoforte or harp. Printed by R. Birchall, 133, New Bond Street. These airs appear to be chiefly from *The Oriental Miscellany.*

TRINKS. "A Collection of Hindoostanee Songs." Dedicated to Mr. Bristow, by C. Trinks, organist of St. John's Church, Calcutta. Folio.

WILLIAMSON. "Twelve Original Hindoostanee Airs." Compiled and harmonized by T. G. Williamson. London, 1797. Folio.

——— Second collection of "Twelve Original Hindoostanee Airs." Compiled and harmonized by T. G. Williamson. London, 1798. Folio.

WEBER. "Ueber die Metrik der Inder." See "Beiträge für die Kunde des Indischen Alterthums." Band VIII. Berlin, 1863. 8vo.

WILSON, H. H. "Select Specimens from the Theatre of the Hindus." Translated from the original Sanskrit. London, 1838. 8vo, 2 vols.

WALCKIERS. "A Collection of Twenty-four Hindoostanee and other Airs." Arranged for the pianoforte by L. Walckiers. London, Clementi.

WATERFIELD, W. "Indian Ballads and other Poems." London, 1868.

WILLARD, Captain N. Augustus. "A Treatise upon the Music of Hindustan, comprising a detail of the Ancient Theory and Modern Practice." Calcutta, 1834. 8vo. The following is the table of contents—

Preface.—A general view of the plan and contents of the work. *Introduction.*—Music; its power on the human mind. That of Hindustan. The opinion of the natives with respect to their ancient musicians. How a knowledge of it may be acquired. Not generally liked by Europeans. Reasons assigned for this. Native opinion with regard to its lawfulness. Musical instruments. Relation of music to poetry considered. Progress of music in Hindustan. The manner of life which should be led to ensure eminence in this science. Causes of its depravity. Date of its decline. The similarity which the music of this country seems to bear to that of Egypt and Greece. How a knowledge of the music of Hindustan might conduce to a revival of that of those countries. Comparisons offered. Whether the natives of Greece or Hindustan had made greater progress in music. Comparisons decide in favour of the latter. *Hindostanee Music.*—What it is termed in the original. The treatises held in the greatest estimation. Native divisions. What, and how many. The arrangement adopted in this work. *Of the Gamut.*—What it is called; the derivation of the word. The sub-divisions of tones. Resemblance of these to the Greek diesis. Opinions of Dr. Burney and Mr. Moore on the enharmonic genus. Names of the seven notes. Origin of these. The Gamut invented by Guido and Lemaire. Dr. Pepusch. S'ruti. *Of Time.*—The various measures used in Europe. Difference between them and those of Hindustan. Their resemblance to the rhythm of the Greeks. Similarity between the Greek and Sanskrit languages. The Hebrew unmusical, likewise the Arabic. Melody and metre considered. Tartini's objections against metre endeavoured to be controverted. The dignified prose in Sanskrit and tongues derived from it. Its superiority to the Oordoo. Probable origin of the modern musical measure. Tartini's deductions of measure from the proportions of the octave and its fifth opposed to the practice of Hindustan. Whether the rhythmical or the musical measure possesses greater advantages. Opinion hazarded thereon. Time table. Characters for expressing time. Their varieties. *Of Harmony and Melody.*—The origin of harmony in Europe. Opinions of several learned men on the subject of harmony with that of the author. Claims of melody. *Of Oriental Melody.*—Not generally susceptible of harmony. Limited to a certain number. Its character. *Of Rags and Râginis.*—The general acceptation of the terms supposed to be incorrect. Reasons offered why they are limited to season and time. Of the Ragmâla. Absurdity of limiting tunes to seasons. Division of the Rags and Râginis into classes. Rules for determining the names of the mixed Râginis. Table of compounded Rags. The Ragmâla copiously described. *Of Musical Instruments.*—Their present state susceptible of much improvement. Their classification. Detailed description of the several instruments now in use. *Of the various species of Vocal Compositions of Hindustan.*—Twenty different species described. *Of the peculiarity of Manners and Customs in Hindustan to which allusions are made in their song.*—Its characteristic nature. Reasons assigned for several of them which now no longer exist, and examples produced. Brief account of the most celebrated musicians of Hindustan. Glossary of the most useful musical terms.

The actual size of the work, notwithstanding this lengthy table of contents, is but small. The book is very interesting, and affords much valuable information upon Northern Indian music. The descriptions are, however, incomplete in many cases, and the author's meaning is in places rather vague, and apt to be misleading to those who have not studied the subject.

There are not a very large number of works relating to music in the vernaculars—some few are excellent, but the majority of them contain a very large amount of irrelevant matter, and are so full of inaccuracies that too great a reliance should not be placed upon them. Some of the most important of these works may be found amongst the following :—

"Svarasastra." An essay or tutor for the Sitar. A. Gharpure. Poona, 1880, in Marathi. Contains descriptions of the various kinds of Sitars, together with instructions for making, tuning, and keeping them in order. Contains also an elaborate system of notation invented by the author.

There are also works in Marathi upon the sitar by Viswanath Ramachundra Kale ; and by Vastâd Murabar Gonvekar.

In Bengali the chief works are :—

"Asurjanitatwar" on the Esrar. By Kshetra Mohun Gosvami.

"Sangit Siksha." By Sita Nath Boshak.

"Sangit Sâra." By Kshetra Mohun Gosvami. This work contains a good deal that is most interesting.

"Katakaumodi." By Kshetra Mohun Gosvami.

"A Treatise on the Mridanga." By S. M. Tagore. On drum playing, rhythm, &c.

"A Comprehensive Self-Instructor for the Setar, Esrar, violin, flute, and harmonium." Calcutta, 1868. An attempt to adapt Indian music to European notation. By H. D. Banerjea.

There are several Telegu and Tamil works of less interest. The only Telegu work that I have seen which is of any interest is a tract called "Sangíta Kaliânidhi," on the vina, with diagrams of the fingerboard. There is a Guzerathi work entitled "The Musical Instructor," by N. D. Apyakhtiar, Bombay, 1870. This work contains a certain amount of theory apparently extracted from the Sangíta Ratnâkera, and a number of coloured illustrations which, though poor, are not without interest. It contains also a large number of Guzerathi songs.

Of the more important of the Sanskrit treatises that are at present known to exist, some slight notice may be useful. The oldest of any is the Bhârata Nâtya S'astra by Bhârata Muni. This work is being translated by M. Grosset, of Lyons, who has procured and carefully compared several copies of the MSS., one of which is the property of the Royal Asiatic Society of London. The whole work is large, and consists of a great number of ādhyayas. The theory of music, of dancing, of the connection between music and the drama are treated of fully, as are also the various kinds of instruments. The antiquity of the lyric drama in India is most interesting. M. Grosset has published already the twenty-eighth ādhyaya of this work, containing the part relating to the theory of music, with a prefatory essay and copious explanations and notes, the results of his researches—a most valuable contribution to the study of ancient Eastern musical literature. The date of the Bhârata Nâtya S'astra is placed at some intermediate period from B.C. 200 to A.D. 100. An edition of this work has been printed, or partially so, at Poona recently. There is also a copy of the MSS. in the library of H.H. the Maharajah of Bikanîr.

Of the remaining Sanskrit treatises (excepting the work just mentioned) the Sangíta Ratnâkera is probably the oldest and the most valuable.

The work consists of seven ādhyayas, according to Dr. A. C. Burnell.[2]

I.—Svaragatādhyaya—treats of notes, scales, &c.

II.—Ragavivekādhyaya—of Râga.

III.—Prakirṇakādhyaya—of music in connection with the human voice.

IV.—Prabandhādhyaya—of musical composition.

V.—Talādhyaya—of times, pauses, measures, &c.

VI.—Vadyādhyaya—of musical instruments.

VII.—Nrityādhyaya—of dancing.

[2] "Classified Index to the Sanskrit MSS. in the Palace at Tanjore." Dr. A. C. Burnell. London, 1880.

An edition of the first ādhyaya, with a Commentary, was published at Calcutta in 1879. Its contents are as follows:—

CHAP. I.—Benediction upon music.
II.—Of sounds, notes, concordant and discordant relations.
III.—Of grâmas, murchanas, tâlas.
IV.—Of vérnams (ascending and descending successions of notes), alankâras or melodious successions of notes intended to impress upon beginners the idea of different pitches, and to cultivate a taste for pleasing combinations.
V.—Of certain subsidiary scales.
VI.—Materials and constitution of râga.
VII.—Describes certain ancient species of song called Kapâla and Kambala, and defines various styles of singing.

It appears quite impossible to assign any reliable date to this work. The author of it was Sarnga Deva, son of Sotala Deva, King of Karnata, and grandson of Bhaskara a Kashmirian.[3] Possibly, from this information, the date may be discovered at some future time.

In the Preface to the Calcutta edition of this work mention is made of only five ādhyayas, the other two (*i.e.*, the fourth and fifth) have apparently been discovered by Dr. Burnell.

The following authors or works are cited by Sarnga Deva in this work:— Anginayya, Kalinatha, Chudamanni, Pratibhavilasa, Manidurpana, Râganava, Vinoda, Sivakinkara, Sangítanava, Sarodhara, Haribhatta.

Perhaps next in importance to the Ratnâkera is the Sangíta Darpana, by Damodara Misra. This work, according to Aufrecht, consists of seven ādhyayas—

I.—SVARAGATĀDHYAYA.
II.—RAGĀDHYAYA.
III.—PRAKIRNAKĀDHYAYA.
IV.—PRABANDHĀDHYAYA.
V.—PADYĀDHYAYA.
VI.—TALĀDHYAYA.
VII.—NRITYĀDHYAYA.

Damodara took the greater part of his work from the Sangíta Ratnâkera and added a little from other authors and works. Sir William Jones tells us that the Pandits of Bengal preferred the Damodara in his time to any of the other Sangítas, but that he himself had never been able to procure a good copy of it.

---

[3] See Aufrecht's "Catalogus codicorum Manuscriptorum Bibliothecæ Bodleianæ" (Oxford, 1864), and Rajendralala Mitra's Catalogue of the Sanskrit MSS. in the library of H.H. the Maharajah of Bikanîr. Calcutta, 1880.

Here again the question of date must remain doubtful. The only information as to the author appears to be that he was the son of Lakshmidâra. Damodara mentions the following authors and works in addition to the Ratnâkera—Anginayya, Kalinatha, Chudamanni, Pratibhavilasa, Manidurpana, Râganava, Vinoda, Sivakinkara, Sangítanava, Sarodhara, Haribhatta.

Later than this work is the Sangíta Narayana by Narayana Deva.

This work consists of four parts :—

I.—SANGÍTANIRṆAYA.
II.—VĀDYANIRṆAYA.
III.—NRITYANIRṆAYA.
IV.—SUDDHAPRABANDHŌDARANAM.

The author of this work was the son of Padmanâbhai, and a pupil of Kaviratna Purushottama-misra. In this work Damodara is frequently quoted, Narayana Deva also quotes his master's work "Ramachandrodaya," as well as the following authors and works:—Krishnadatta, Kohala, Gitaprakasa, Chhandoratnâkera, Narada-Sanhita or Sanhita, Panchamasarasanhita, Mammata author of "Sangítaratnamala," Laksmanabhatta Gítagovindatikayam[4] S'riromani, Saivasavaswa, Sangítakaumodi or Kaumodi, Sangíta Sara, Hârinâyatta.

Sir William Jones, in his essay on the Musical Modes of the Hindus, inclines to the belief that the most valuable work that he had seen is the Râgavivodha, by Soma Raj. This is a later work than the Ratnâkera, which is mentioned in it frequently. It consists of five chapters.

I.—Of S'rutis, their divisions into svâras or notes—of suddha and vikrita notes—of octaves, definitions of notes essential to râga (*i.e.*, vâdi, samvâdi, &c.)—of grâmas—of murchanas—how râgas constituted of five, six, or seven notes.
II.—Of the Vina, and different kinds of vinas, measurement, and general directions for making.
III.—Classification of râgas.
IV.—The Ragmâla or list of râgas, with descriptions of each râga personified—hours of day appointed for performance of each râga.
V.—Râgas written in notation, with directions for the performance of each.

The Sangíta Pârijâta appears to be a very much later work than any previously described. The author of this work was Ahobala Pandit, and he seems to have been a native of Central India. The belief among pandits in India at the present day is that he lived not more than 250 years ago. The

[4] "On the Musical Modes of the Hindus." Sir W. Jones. "Asiatic Researches." Vol. III. Calcutta, 1792.

system described in the Pârijâta is a description of that practised at the period. The contents are as follows—

I. BENEDICTION upon music in general.
II. Of svâras or notes.
III. Of grâmas or scales.
IV., V. Of murchanas or permutations of notes, with examples.
VI. Of methods of tuning.
VII. Of gamakas, with a minute explanation of about sixty.
VIII. Of Suddhasvâras (or notes comprising their full complement of s'rutis) and directions for tuning the vina.
IX. Of gíta or melody.
X. Of râga and text of about 122 râgas, with directions for performance.

An edition of this work was printed at Calcutta in 1879.

There is a Persian work entitled Tohfuht-ul-Hind, by Mirza Khan. This work contains information extracted from the Sanskrit works Râganâva, Râgadarpana, and Subhavinodha. Of the present existence of these three works I have never been able to discover traces; still, it is to be hoped that they may eventually be brought to light. A copy of the Râgadarpana, with two works entitled Shams-ul-aswat and Hazar Dhrupad, was brought by Sir W. Jones to England; but these, with other MSS. that he is said to have deposited in the library of the Royal Asiatic Society, cannot be traced.

The following list of Sanskrit treatises upon music has been carefully compiled from catalogues of various Sanskrit MSS., and from information supplied by Pandits in different parts of India. Where no reference is made under the column of authorities, the information has been obtained from Pandits in India and is, perhaps, not always so reliable as the other authorities. When copies of any of the MSS. have been printed, the places and approximate dates of publication have been given.

The following abbreviations have been used in the column of authorities.

BIK = Catalogue of the Sanskrit MSS. in the library of H.H. the Maharajah of Bikanîr. Rajendralala Mitra. Calcutta, 1880.

AUF = Catalogus Codicorum Manuscriptorum Bibliothecæ Bodleianæ. Th. Aufrecht. Oxford, 1864.

TAN = Classified Index to the Sanskrit MSS. in the Palace at Tanjore. A. C. Burnell. London, 1880.

IND = Catalogue of the Sanskrit MSS. in the library at the India Office. Part II. J. Eggeling. London, 1889.

OPP = List of Sanskrit MSS. in Southern India. Dr. Oppert. Madras, 1885.

KIEL = Catalogue of Sanskrit MSS. in the Central Provinces. L. Kielhorn. Nagpur, 1874.

RICE = Catalogue of MSS. in Mysore. L. Rice.

BEN = Catalogue of Buddhist Sanskrit MSS. in the University Library at Cambridge. Cecil Bendall. Cambridge, 1883.

SANSKRIT TREATISES UPON MUSIC.

Name of the Work.	Author.	Name of the Work.	Author.	Authority.
आनंदजीवन	राजा मंडनपाल	Ānandajivana	Rājā Mandanapāla.	Bik, 1090.
अनुपसंगीतविलास टीकासहित	भावभट्ट	Anupa Sangīta Vilāsa with ṭīkā	Bhāvabhaṭṭa	Bik, 1091.
अर्जुनभरत	अर्जुन	Arjunabharatam	Arjuna.	
अष्टोत्तरशतताललक्षणं	......	Ashṭottaraṣata-tāla-lakshaṇam	......	Tan, p. 60, 12.
भरतभाष्यं	न्यायदेव	Bharatabhāshyam	Nyāyadēva.	
भरतनाट्यशास्त्रं	भरतमुनि	Bharatanāṭya-ṣāstram	Bharatamuni.	Bik, 1092, Poona, circa 1888.
भरतलक्षणं	......	Bharatalakshaṇam	......	
भरतशास्त्र संगीतं	......	Bharataṣāstra Sangītam	......	
भरतशास्त्रं	रघुनाथ	Bharataṣāstram	Raghunātha.	Tan, p. 60, 9.
ध्रौपदटीका	भावभट्ट	Dhraupadaṭīkā	Bhāvabhaṭṭa.	
गीतालंकार:	अनंतनारायण	Gītālankāra	Anantanārāyaṇa.	
हस्तरत्नावली	राघव	Hastaratnavali	Rāghava.	Auf. 483.
हृदयप्रकाश	हृदयनारायणदेव	Hṛidayaprakāṣa	Hṛidayanārāyaṇadēva.	Bik, 1093.
कल्पतरु टीका सुबोधिनी	गणेशदेव	Kalpataru with ṭīkā Subodhinī	Gaṇēṣadēva.	Bik, 1094.
मतंगभरतं	लक्ष्मण भास्कर	Matangabharatam	Lakshmaṇabhāskara.	
मेलाधिकारलक्षणं	......	Mēḷādhikāralakshaṇam	......	
मुक्तावलिप्रकाशिका	......	Muktāvaliprakāṣikā	......	
मुरलीप्रकाश:	भावभट्ट	Muraḷīprakāṣa	Bhāvabhaṭṭa.	Bik, 1095.
नाददीपिका	भट्टाचार्य	Nādadīpikā	Bhattāchārya.	
नन्दिभरत	नन्दि	Nandibharata	Nandi.	L. Rice.
नारदीशिक्ष	नारद	Nāradīṣikshā	Nārada.	Poona, circa 1887.
नर्तननिर्णय	पुंडरीक विठ्ठल	Nartananirṇaya	Pundarīkaviṭṭhala	Bik, 1096.
नृत्याध्याय:	अशोकमल्ल	Nṛityādhyāyah	Aṣōkamalla.	Bik, 1098.
नृत्यरत्नावली	गणपतिदेवसेन	Nṛityaratnāvali	Gaṇapatidēvasena	
पंचमसारसंहिता	नारद	Panchamasārasamhitā	Nārada.	See Auf. 480.

Name of the Work.	Author.	Name of the Work.	Author.	Authority.
रागचंद्रोदय	विमल	Rāgachandrodaya	Vimala.	
रागध्यानादि कथनाध्याय:	......	Rāgadhyānādikathanādhyāyah	......	Bik, 1099.
रागादिस्वरनिर्णय:	रघुनाथदासप्रसाद	Rāgādisvaranirṇayah	Raghunātha Dāsa Prasāda.	
रागकौतूहले नृत्यप्रकरणं	रामकृष्णभट्ट	Rāga-kautuhala, Nritya-Prakāraṇa	Rāmakrishṇa bhaṭṭa.	Bik, 1106.
रागलक्षणं	......	Rāgalakshaṇam	......	
रागमाला	पुंडरीक विठ्ठल	Rāgamālā	Puṇḍarīkaviṭṭhala	Bik. 1100.
रागमालावारत्नमाला	क्षेमकरण	Rāgamālā or Ratnamālā	Kshēmakaraṇa.	Auf. 481, Ind. p. 319, Bik. 1101.
रागमंजरी	पुंडरीक विठ्ठल	Rāgamanjari	Puṇḍarīkaviṭṭhala	Bik. 1102.
रागनिरूपणं	नारद	Rāganirūpaṇam	Nārada.	
रागप्रस्तार	......	Rāgaprastāra	......	
रागरत्नाकर	गंधर्वराज	Rāgaratnākara	Gandharvarāja.	Tan p. 60, 6. Kiel. p. 96, Bik. 1129.
रागतत्त्वबोध	श्रीनिवास	Rāgatatvavibodha	Ṣrīnivāsa.	Kiel. p. 96, Bik. 1103.
रागविचार	श्रीराम	Rāgavichāra	Ṣrīrāma malla.	Bik. 1104.
रागविबोध	सोमनाथ	Rāga-vibōdha	Somanātha.	Auf. 475, Poona, circa 1888.
रागविवेक	......	Rāgavivēka	......	Kiel. p. 96.
रुद्रडमरु भवसूत्रविवरणं	......	Rudraḍamaru-bhava Sūtravivaraṇa	......	Bik. 1107.
संगीतचिंतामणी	कमललोचन	Sangītachintāmani	Kamalolōchana.	Kiel. p. 96.
संगीतदामोदर	शुभंकर	Sangītadāmōdara	Ṣubhankara.	Ind. p. 318, Kiel. p. 96.
संगीतदर्पण	दामोदर	Sangītadarpaṇa	Dāmōdara.	Bik. 1108 et seq., Auf. 476 et seq , Poona circa 1887, Calcutta 1879.
संगीतदर्पण	हरिवल्लभ	Sangītadarpaṇa	Harivallabha.	Bik. 1110.
संगीतदीपिका	तिप्पभूपाल	Sangītadīpikā	Tippabhūpāla.	
संगीतकल्पतरु	......	Sangītakalpataru	......	
संगीतमकरंद:	वेदकृत	Sangītamakarandah	Vēda.	Bik. 1111, Tan. p. 60, 2.
संगीतमिमांसा	कुंभकर्णमहिमहेंद्र	Sangitamīmāmsā	Kumbhakarṇamahimahēndra.	Kiel. p. 96.
संगीतामृतं	कमललोचन	Sangītāmritam	Kāmalalōchana.	Kiel. p. 96.
संगीतमुक्तावली	देवान्नाचार्य	Sangītamuktāvali	Dēvannāchārya.	
,, ,,	देवेन्द्र	,, ,,	Dēvēndra.	Bik. 1112.

Name of the Work.	Author.	Name of the Work.	Author.	Authority.
संगीतनारायण	पुरुषोत्तममिश्र	Sangītanārāyaṇa	Purushottama-miṣra.	
संगीतनारायण	नारायणदेव	Sangītanārāyaṇa	Nārāyaṇadēva.	Auf. 480.
संगीतपारिजात	पंडित अहोबल	Sangītapārijāta	Pandita Ahōbala.	Calcutta 1879. Poona, circa 1887.
संगीतपाठ	......	Sangītapāṭha	......	
संगीतपुष्पांजली	......	Sangītapushpānjalī.	......	Bik. 1113.
संगीतराघव	वोमभूपाल	Sangītarāghava	Vōmabhūpala.	
संगीतराज	कुंभकर्ण	Sangītarāja	Kumbhakarṇa.	Kiel. p. 96.
संगीतरत्नाकर	शार्ङ्गदेव	Sangītaratnākara	Sārṇgadēva.	Bik. 1114 et seq., Auf. 471 et seq., Ind. p. 315, Calc. 1879, pt. 1 only
संगीतरत्नाकर टीका	शार्ङ्गदेव	Do. ṭikā	Do.	
,, ,,	कल्लिनाथ	Do. do.	Kallinātha.	Bik. 1120.
,, ,,	सिंहभूपाल	Do. do.	Simhabhupāla	
,, ,,	कुंभकर्णनरेन्द्र	Do. do.	Kumbhakarṇa narēndra.	
,, ,,	गंगाराम	Do. do.	Gangārāma.	
,, ,,	हंसभूपाल	Do. do.	Hamsabhūpāla.	
संगीतरत्नाकर	वनरक	Sangītaratnākara	Vanaraka.	Bik. 1121.
संगीतरत्नमाला	मम्मट	Sangītaratnamālā	Mammaṭa.	See Auf. 480.
संगीतरत्नावली	सोमराजदेव	Sangītaratnāvalī	Somarājadēva.	
संगीतसमयसार	......	Sangītasamayasāra.	......	
संगीतसारसंग्रह	......	Sangītasāra-sangraha	......	Rice.
संगीतसारामृत	तुलजेन्द्र	Sangītasārāmṛita	Tulajēndra.	Tan. p. 60, 4.
संगीतसर्वार्थसारसंग्रह	......	Sangītasarvārthasā-rasangraha	......	Opp. p. 656.
संगीतसारोद्धार	हरिभट्ट	Sangītasāroddhāra	Haribhaṭṭa.	Bik. 1123.
संगीतसारावली	......	Sangītasārāvali	......	
संगीतसेतु	गंगाराम	Sangītasētu	Gangārāma.	
संगीतशिरोमणी	......	Sangītaṣiromaṇī	......	Bik. 1124.
संगीतसुधा	......	Sangītasudhā	......	
संगीतसुधाकर	सिंहभूपाल	Sangītasudhākara	Simhabhūpāla.	
संगीतसुधाकर	हरिपाल	Sangītasudhākara	Haripāla.	
संगीतसुंदर	सदाशिव दीक्षित	Sangītasundara	Sadāṣivadikshita.	

Name of the Work.	Author.	Name of the Work.	Author.	Authority.
संगीतसुरामृत . . .	तुलाजीमहाराज भोंसले तंजावरचे राजेसाहेब	Sangītasurāmṛita .	Mahārāja Tuḷāji Bhoṇsalā, Raja of Tanjore.	Tan. p. 60, 4.
संगीत तारोदय चूडामणि	प्रताप मल्ल . . .	Sangīta-tarodaya chūḍāmani . . .	Pratāpa malla	Ben. p. 150.
संगीतउपनिषध . .	सुधाकलश . . .	Sangīta-upanishadha	Sudhākalaṣa.	Bik. 1126.
संगीतविनोद . . .	......	Sangītavinōda . .	......	Bik. 1125.
संगीतवृत्तरत्नाकर . .	विठ्ठल	Sangītavṛittaratnākara	Viṭṭhala.	Tan. p. 60, 8.
संकीर्णरागाध्याय . .	......	Sankīrṇarāgādhyāya	......	
सरागचंद्रोदय . . .	......	Sarāgachandrodaya	......	
सारसंहिता . . .	नारद	Sārasamhitā . .	Nārada.	
षट्रागचंद्रोदय . . .	पुंडरीक विठ्ठल . .	Shaḍrāgachandrodaya	Punḍarīkaviṭṭhala	Bik. 1128.
श्रुतिभास्कर . . .	भीमदेव . . .	Ṣrutibhāskara . .	Bhīmadēva.	
स्वरमंजरी	......	Svaramanjarī . .	......	
स्वरमेलकलानिधी . .	......	Svaramēlakalānidhī	Rāmamātya.	Bik. 1130.
तालाभिनयलक्षणं . .	नन्दिकेश्वर . . .	Tālābhinayalakshaṇam	Nandikēṣvara.	
तालदशप्राणदीपिका .	गोविन्द . . .	Tāladaṣaprāṇadīpikā	Govinda.	Tan. p. 61, 16.
काललक्षणं . . .	नन्दिकेश्वर . . .	Tālalakshaṇam . .	Nandikēṣvara.	Tan. p. 60, 14.
तालप्रस्तं	......	Tālaprastam . .	......	
तालप्रस्तार . . .	......	Tālaprastāra . .	......	Tan. p. 60, 13.
तालदीपिका . . .	टिप्पभूपाल . . .	Tāladīpikā . . .	Ṭippabhūpāla.	Tan. p. 60, 15.
वीणावाद्यलक्षणं . .	......	Vīṇāvādyalakshaṇam	......	
वीरपराक्रम . . .	वासुदेव . . .	Vīraparākrama . .	Vāsudēva.	

APPENDIX.

DESCRIPTION OF RÂJAH SIR S. M. TAGORE'S S'RUTI VINA.

[THE following minute account of the Râjah Sir S. M. Tagore's S'ruti Vina—intended to demonstrate the ancient system of 22—was kindly supplied by the late Mr. A. J. ELLIS, F.R.S.]

AS regards the construction of the instrument, I shall first quote the Râjah Sir S. M. Tagore's own words.[1] "We have hit upon another method to ascertain the nature and position of the s'rutis. The method is as follows:—Take a sitar or vina, measure the distance between Shaja (C) of the Madhya (middle) octave, and Shaja (D) of the next higher octave, in the C of the Tara octave. Divide the space between these two C's by putting a dot or line in the middle; put a dot or line on either extremity; place the note F over the dot or line in the middle, the note C on the other extremity of the first half portion of the divided space, and the note higher C on that of the second half portion; sub-divide the first half portion into *nine* equal and the second half portion into *thirteen* equal parts, and put a dot or line to mark off each sub-division. . . . Excluding the line marking higher C, there will be in all twenty-two lines. Each of these will represent a s'ruti."

This S'ruti Vina was, in fact, a long-necked sitar rather smaller than usual. It had two strings, one of brass and one of steel; the diameter of the brass wire was ·3 mm. (millimetres), and that of the steel wire was ·24 mm. The brass string proved useless, as the frets made the octave quite wrong with it. Hence it will be disregarded henceforth.

The string was nearly horizontal. At starting at the nut it was 12 mm. above the finger-board, and at the bridge 13 mm. above the belly, which had

[1] "The Twenty-two Musical S'rutis of the Hindus." S. M. Tagore. Calcutta, 1886.

curved upwards. But the first fret was 11½ mm. and the last fret only 2 mm. above the finger-board. The string was therefore pressed down only 1½ mm. for the first, but 12½ mm. for the last ; consequently, the tension greatly increased as we ascended the scale, so that if we had taken the octave at half the length of the string it would have been much too sharp.

There were twenty-three frets to give the s'rutis for one octave, numbered one to twenty-three on one side of the finger-board, with letters on the other, thus :—

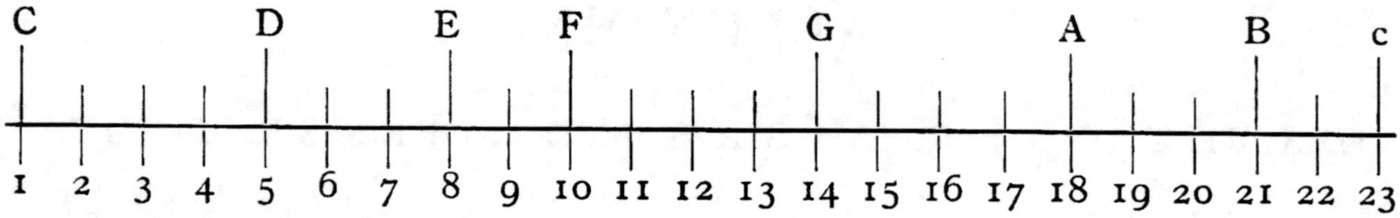

The frets for C D E F G A B c were of white metal, the others were yellow. The frets were flatly elliptical with hooked ends, round which a piece of gut was tied, and then brought about three times under the finger-board, catching the hooked ends each time and being firmly fixed. Each fret was therefore tightly fastened in its place, and could not be moved up and down the board without much force. But the fret itself could be deflected to the right or left, leaving the hooked ends fixed. This was not easy, but was possible.

Then again the distance by which the string had to be deflected to press it on to the fret varied, but not uniformly. The diameter of the frets was different, but I was unable to measure it, as I could not get my gauge in. However, I estimate the white frets at fully 2 mm. in diameter ; the others were narrower. The tops were rounded and it was difficult to appreciate the middle point, but I have endeavoured to measure the distance from the middle of one fret to the middle of the next.

The whole length of the string from nut to bridge was 906 mm. The bridge was thus shaped,

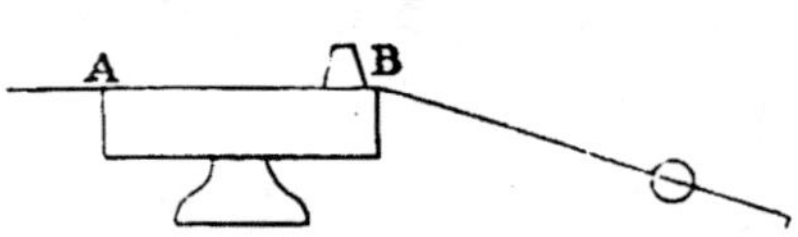

B being a ledge cut through for the strings, which lay on the flat part, A B, and the sounding length of the whole string was from the nut to A, but still the part A B was not firmly fixed and possibly influenced the pitch. The part of the string beyond B seemed to be damped by a perforated bead which ran on it.

The note from the first fret was marked C, but taking the pitch of the string as it was (for we did not venture to screw it up), it made 241·2 vib., which is not far from 244·23, the French pitch of B in the 4-ft. octave,

but I adopt the names of the notes as marked on the instrument. In this case the whole string gave F in the 4-ft. octave, a fifth below the first C and an octave below No. 10 fret, marked F, at any rate precisely enough. But the whole length of the string was 906 mm., and to the first fret 298 mm., so that the sounding length of C, or 608 mm., was only a little more than $\frac{2}{3}$ of 906=604 mm., the increased tension being here slight. The sounding length for **F** was 463 mm., considerably more than 453=$\frac{1}{2}$ of 906 mm., because the string was 7 mm. above the F fret, which caused an increase of tension that had to be allowed for. It is impossible to calculate the effect of these increments of tension which, however, served to alter the effect of the lengths considerably.

The principle followed seemed to be to find the position of the frets 1 and 23, giving the fifth of the open string and the octave of that fifth, *by ear only*, the shape and heights of the frets being assumed. The height of the first fret was, of course, as great as possible, and the last as low as possible to avoid jars. In this case the fifth is good, but the octave of it, or higher C, is too sharp by a trifle of 20 cents (one cent = the hundredth of an equal semitone, so that an octave has 1,200 cents and a comma 22 cents). The length of string for lower C was 608 mm., and that for higher c, 316·5 mm., which is much more than half the former or 304 mm., and yet the note is too sharp, so great is the distance of this string, 12$\frac{1}{2}$ mm., from the last fret.

The distance C c was divided into half at F, and the distance C to F into nine equal parts, and F to c into thirteen equal parts by frets; at least, that was the intention. Actually C to F contained 145 mm., of which $\frac{1}{9}$th = 16$\frac{1}{9}$, while the distances between frets really varied from 15$\frac{1}{2}$ to 16$\frac{1}{2}$. The distance F to C was 146$\frac{1}{2}$ mm., of which $\frac{1}{13}$th is 11·27 mm., while the distances between the frets varied from 9$\frac{1}{2}$ to 13$\frac{1}{2}$ mm. as well as I could measure. This gave very varying values to the s'ruti intervals. From C to F they varied from 45 to 73 cents, from F to c they varied from 37 to 84 cents. The intention, I presume, was to make them as nearly equal as possible or 54$\frac{6}{11}$ cents each.

The pitches of the notes produced were determined on May 21, 1886, by Mr. A. J. Hipkins, who tried to touch the frets as evenly as possible, while I furnished the forks from my tuning fork tonometer, the exact pitches of which had been accurately determined. By this means Mr. Hipkins was able to count the beats between the forks and the notes due to the frets for two or three seconds, and then to continue counting at the same rate to complete ten seconds. Each pitch was thus determined by two of my forks, one sharper and one flatter, and there was never so much as half a vibration difference in the determinations. When any difference existed a mean was taken. A scale was thus determined which satisfies modern Indian ears. As the s'rutis in it vary from all the circumstances named, and apparently on no conceivable plan, it is evident that if the mean of all were taken—that is, if a cycle of twenty-two were instituted, as I have effected by a series of forks—Indian ears would still be satisfied. I have endeavoured in the following table to bring out all these facts.

The width of the finger-board was 80 mm., and the steel wire was 40 mm. from each edge.

A set of forks was sent by the Râjah to the Inventions Exhibition at the same time as the S'ruti Vina, but as they had been tuned by means of sliding weights, without any appliance to fix them in position, these forks were quite useless, for the weights had shifted on the journey from India, and, in fact, shifted whenever the forks were struck.

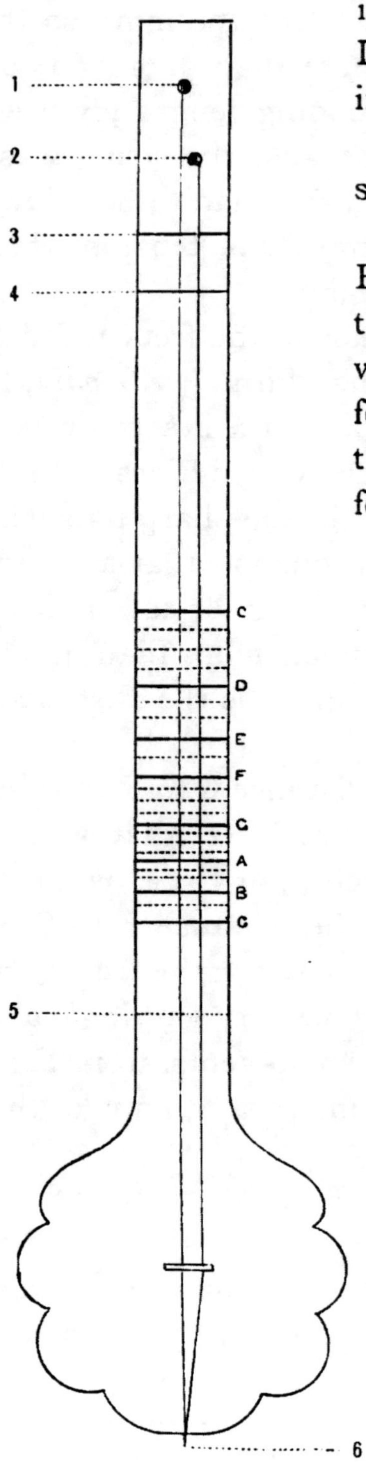

1.} 2.} Tuning pegs.
3.} 4.} Nut.
5. Carved ivory decoration.
6. Tail-pin.

REDUCED PLAN OF S'RUTI VINA.

TABLE OF THE PITCHES OF THE NOTES FURNISHED BY RÂJAH SIR S. M. TAGORE'S S'RUTI VINA, AS DETERMINED IN 1886 BY MESSRS. ELLIS AND HIPKINS.

Note, name, and number.	Observed number of vibrations.	Cents from note to note.	Cents from lowest note.	Cents from lowest in cycle of 22.	Vibrations in cycle of 22, with same C.	Sounding lengths of strings in millimetres.	Depression or height of string above fret in millimetres.
C 1	241·2	—	0	0	241·2	608	1½
2	247·6	45	45	55	248·9	592	3
3	257·2	66	111	109	256·9	576	4
4	266·0	58	169	163	265·1	559½	5
D 5	274·3	53	222	218	273·6	543½	5
6	281·5	45	267	273	282·4	527½	5
7	289·5	49	316	328	291·4	512	6
E 8	302·0	73	389	382	300·7	495½	6
9	310·3	47	436	436	310·3	479	7
F 10	323·0	69	505	491	320·3	463	7
11	330·3	39	544	545	330·5	451½	8
12	337·8	39	583	600	341·1	441	8
13	349·2	57	640	655	352·0	430	9
G 14	364·0	72	712	709	363·3	417½	10
15	371·8	37	749	764	374·9	408	10½
16	384·4	58	807	818	386·9	395½	10½
17	395·3	48	855	873	399·3	384½	10½
A 18	409·6	62	917	928	412·1	373	10½
19	418·5	37	954	982	425·3	363½	10½
20	432·9	59	1013	1036	438·9	351	10½
B 21	449·3	64	1077	1091	452·9	340	11
22	465·0	59	1136	1146	467·4	330	11½
C 23	488·0	84	1220	1200	482·4	316½	12½

NOVELLO, EWER AND CO., PRINTERS, LONDON.